THE INTERSTATE
BANKING
REVOLUTION

Recent Titles from Quorum Books

Real Interest Rates and Investment Borrowing Strategy
Peter S. Spiro

The Political Limits of Environmental Regulation: Tracking the Unicorn
Bruce Yandle

Summary Judgment and Other Preclusive Devices
Warren Freedman

Distinction Between Measurement and Interpretation in Accounting:
A Living Systems Theory Approach
G. A. Swanson and James Grier Miller

Strict Liability: Legal and Economic Analysis
Frank J. Vandall

Security Program Design and Management: A Guide for
Security-Conscious Managers
Donald B. Tweedy

The Improvement of Corporate Financial Performance: A Manager's Guide to
Evaluating Selected Opportunities
Sherman L. Lewis

The Director's and Officer's Guide to Advisory Boards
Robert K. Mueller

Present Value Applications for Accountants and Financial Planners
G. Eddy Birrer and Jean L. Carrica

Software, Copyright, and Competition: The "Look and Feel" of the Law
Anthony L. Clapes

Regulating Utilities with Management Incentives:
A Strategy for Improved Performance
Kurt A. Strasser and Mark F. Kohler

The Effort-Net Return Model of Employee Motivation:
Principles, Propositions, and Prescriptions
Philip C. Grant

THE INTERSTATE BANKING REVOLUTION

Benefits, Risks, and Tradeoffs for Bankers and Consumers

PETER S. ROSE

QUORUM BOOKS
New York · Westport, Connecticut · London

Library of Congress Cataloging-in-Publication Data

Rose, Peter S.
    The interstate banking revolution : benefits, risks, and tradeoffs
    for bankers and consumers / Peter S. Rose.
        p. cm.
        Bibliography: p.
        Includes index.
        ISBN 0-89930-438-9 (lib. bdg. : alk. paper)
        1. Interstate banking. I. Title.
    HG2491.R66 1989
    332.1′6 – dc20   89-10476

British Library Cataloguing in Publication Data is available.

Library of Congress Catalog Card Number: 89-10476
ISBN: 0-89930-438-9

First published in 1989 by Quorum Books

Greenwood Press, Inc.
88 Post Road West, Westport, Connecticut 06881

Printed in the United States of America

The paper used in this book complies with the
Permanent Paper Standard issued by the National
Information Standards Organization (Z39.48–1984).

10 9 8 7 6 5 4 3 2 1

To John R. Blocker
and, in memoriam,
to Jeanne Blocker —
a Couple Whose Generosity
Makes Much of My
Research and Writing
Possible

Contents

TABLES   ix

PREFACE   xi

1. The Scope and Thrust of American Interstate Banking   1

2. Causes of the Interstate Banking Movement   25

3. The History of Full-Service Interstate Banking in the United States   47

4. Research Evidence on the Benefits and Costs of Interstate Banking   77

5. Public Policy Issues Raised by the Expansion of Banking Across State Lines   101

6. Entering New Interstate Markets: How Do Bankers Decide Which States to Enter?   113

7. Methods for Analyzing and Selecting Banks for Interstate Acquisition: How Do Bankers Choose Their Target Firms?   133

8. Overcoming the Key Management Problems of Interstate Banking   145

9. Interstate Goals and Outcomes: What Bank CEOs See as Their Problems and Accomplishments from Interstate Expansion   161

10. Guideposts for Public Policy and the Management of Interstate Banking Firms   179

Appendix A: Important Interstate Banking Mergers and Acquisitions in Recent Years   196

Appendix B: Key State Banking Laws Applying to Branching, Holding-Company Activity, and Interstate Banking 209

BIBLIOGRAPHY 219

INDEX 227

Tables

1-1 Branch Banking Laws of the United States 6

1-2 Bank Holding-Company Laws of the United States 8

1-3 Types of Interstate Banking Laws Enacted in Recent Years 9

1-4 Number of Interstate Bank and Holding-Company Acquisitions by Year 10

2-1 Principal Economic Causes of the Spread of Full-Service Interstate Banking in the United States 26

2-2 Legal, Regulatory, and Technological Causes of the Spread of Full-Service Interstate Banking in the United States 27

3-1 Interstate Banking Laws for States in the New England Region 58

3-2 Interstate Banking Laws for States in the West North Central Region 61

3-3 Interstate Banking Laws for States in the South Atlantic Region 62

3-4 Interstate Banking Laws for States in the Middle Atlantic Region 65

3-5 Interstate Banking Laws for States in the West South Central Region 67

3-6 Interstate Banking Laws for States in the East North Central Region 70

3-7 Interstate Banking Laws for States in the East South Central Region 71

3-8 Interstate Banking Laws for States in the Rocky Mountain Region 72

3-9 Interstate Banking Laws for States in the Pacific Region 74

6-1 Population Size and Growth of the Principal Regions of the United States   122

6-2 Demographic Features of the Principal Regions of the United States   123

6-3 Age Distribution of the Population in Selected States   124

6-4 Population Growth, Density, and Projected Growth of Leading States in the United States   125

6-5 Growth and Volume of Personal Income in the Principal Regions of the United States   126

6-6 Leading States in the Growth and Size of Per-Capita Personal Income   127

6-7 Volume of Economic Activity by State, Measured by the Gross State Product (GSP)   128

6-8 Average Bank Profitability and Risk by State   129

7-1 Measures of Financial Strength in a Proposed Interstate Merger   139

9-1 Bankers' Evaluation of the Likely Public Interest Aspects of Interstate Banking   163

9-2 Characteristics of States and Local Market Areas that Influence Bankers' Acquisition Decisions   165

9-3 Characteristics of Target Banking Organizations that Most Influence Bankers' Acquisition Decisions   168

9-4 States Viewed as Most Promising for Future Entry by Interstate Acquiring Banks   170

9-5 The Most Important Advantages Interstate Banking Firms Have over Noninterstate Banks   173

9-6 Changes Made in Policies and Practices at Banks Acquired Across State Lines   174

9-7 Goals Achieved in Banking Acquisitions Across State Lines   176

Preface

This book focuses intently on an ongoing revolutionary movement in American banking — the rapid spread of banks and bank holding companies across state lines. Since its inception, the U.S. banking industry has been unique among the banking systems that girdle the globe. Unlike the majority of national banking systems abroad, American banking has been dominated for generations by thousands of small neighborhood and community banking firms. There are nearly 15,000 domestically chartered commercial banks serving national, regional, and local markets across the United States, operating an average of only three branch offices apiece. So dominant are small, locally owned banks in the American system that the five largest U.S. banks control less than 20 percent of the industry's resources.

In contrast, the United States' neighbor to the north, Canada, has only a dozen domestically chartered banking institutions, operating an average of about 700 branch offices apiece. Moreover, the five largest Canadian banks account for over half of their banking industry's total assets. Even the United States' troubled neighbor to the south, Mexico, is served by a handful of large branch banks that were concentrated even further when they were nationalized by presidential decree in 1982. The 31 private banks that were nationalized at that time controlled over 80 percent of all peso-denominated deposits in Mexico.

The unique small-bank dominated, localized, and fractured structure of U.S. banking grew out of a fierce American tradition that local problems are best dealt with by local institutions and also out of fear that concentrated financial power in the form of large, multi-state branch banks would soon overpower farmers, ranchers, small businessmen, and consumers. Not only did many states outlaw branch banking altogether, but as recently as 1980 a majority of states either prohibited or restricted the ability of banks to set up new branch offices, confining these branches within the narrow boundaries of counties, cities, and special districts.

In effect, these legal barriers to full-service banking prevented free entry into new and distant banking markets. With record-breaking speed, however, these traditional barriers to branch banking and multi-bank holding companies are falling in every region of the nation. By the end of the 1980s, legislation to allow banks and bank holding companies to cross state lines was enacted by 46 of the 50 states.

There is, however, growing concern in the regulatory community, among business researchers, and among some bankers and consumer groups that this new trend toward full-service interstate banking may exacerbate current problems of excessive risk exposure in the industry and threaten the viability of hundreds of small community banks. In addition, the interstate banking movement may lead to changes in financial-service availability and pricing that may not be in the public interest. One potentially damaging effect reported recently in smaller cities of the Southwest centers around the withdrawal of scarce funds from local areas in order to shore up troubled money-center banks. The result can be a "credit drought" that soon forces some local businesses to throttle back their own growth and cut their payrolls, leading to rising business bankruptcies and growing unemployment.

On the other hand, many economists and financial analysts believe that, in the long run, full-service interstate banking will bring badly needed new capital to struggling local economies and help stem the rising tide of bank and savings and loan failures across the nation. This book endeavors to evaluate these contending views and to point to the need for new federal and state policies that protect the public interest and bring greater stability to a vital industry that lies at the core of the financial system and serves as the repository for the savings of millions of individuals, businesses, and governments all over the world.

Among the many issues discussed in these pages are (1) how leading banking organizations assess states and local areas as to their desirability or lack of desirability for future entry, (2) how these same organizations select particular banking institutions as targets for acquisition, (3) what changes in services and service pricing are likely in the wake of an interstate bank acquisition, (4) what special challenges and problems the interstate banking movement appears to be creating for federal and state regulatory authorities, and (5) what new federal and state legislation and regulation may be needed to deal with these problems. It is the author's firm conviction that, just as American banks receive substantial support from agencies of government in competing for the public's funds — including support from government-sponsored deposit insurance and access to Federal Reserve credit — their responsibility to the public in providing reasonably priced financial services to *all* segments of the community is also very great.

The interstate banking movement must contribute to, rather than subtract from, a stable and efficient financial system that stimulates economic growth and raises the nation's standard of living. Otherwise, the new movement will lose its political base of support. After all, interstate banking is a creature of law as well as economics. And it is a movement on trial: its true benefits and costs for bankers and the public remain both uncertain and untested. The fundamental purposes of this book are to explore interstate banking's potential benefits and costs and to assess the movement's future in an increasingly globalized society and a volatile international economy.

Much of the information needed to evaluate the trend toward nationwide banking was gathered through personal interviews with bankers, economists, and federal regulators. Those interviewed included Dr. Richard Aspinwall, Senior Economist and Vice President at the Chase Manhattan Bank, New York City; John Borden, Vice President for Public Relations for Manufacturers Hanover Bank, New York City; Walter V. Shipley, Chairman of the Board of the Chemical Bank, New York City; Drs. Betsy White and George Budzeika, Vice Presidents in Research, Federal Reserve Bank of New York; Rob Clivens, Attorney for the Bank of Boston; Drs. Lynne Browne and Constance Dunham, Economist and Vice President, respectively, at the Federal Reserve Bank of Boston; Matthew Street, General Counsel for State Banking Laws for the American Bankers Association, Washington, D.C.; Drs. Stephen A. Rhoades and Donald Savage of the Banking Research Unit of the Federal Reserve Board, Washington, D.C.; Dr. William Watson, Research Director of the Federal Deposit Insurance Corporation, Washington, D.C.; Dr. Fred Cannon, Vice President and Senior Economist at the Bank of America World Headquarters, San Francisco; Dr. Harold Nathan, Vice President and Senior Financial Economist for Wells Fargo Bank, San Francisco; Dr. Gary Zimmerman, Vice President and Senior Economist at the Federal Reserve Bank of San Francisco; Zaccaria J. Barbieri, National Bank Examination Officer for the Comptroller of the Currency, Western District, San Francisco; Terry Perucca, Senior Vice President in Charge of Strategic Planning for Security Pacific National Bank, Los Angeles; and Jim Simmons, Chairman of the Board, Valley National Corp., Phoenix.

The information provided through these personal interviews has been supplemented by an extensive literature search. The author drew on data and research articles obtained through personal visits to the libraries and the economics and public information divisions of the Federal Reserve Bank of New York, Federal Reserve Bank of Boston, Bank of America, Security Pacific National Bank, Federal Reserve Bank of San Francisco, Federal Deposit Insurance Corporation, Federal Reserve Board, American Bankers Association, and Federal Home Loan Board during the fall of 1988. The author also wishes to express his deep gratitude for the receipt of an academic study leave from Texas A&M University, which made it possible to travel and gather data, analyses, and opinions and to write and rework the ideas in this book.

Finally, my family has had to endure, once again, the changing moods of an author deeply enmeshed in and unabashedly enthusiastic about his subject and, therefore, often oblivious to the needs of others. The author hopes fervently that they and others who read this book will find it worth the considerable cost it has exacted from those who contributed their precious time and patience to help this project reach its end.

THE INTERSTATE
BANKING
REVOLUTION

1

The Scope and Thrust of American Interstate Banking

Charles Dickens' epic novel of the French Revolution, *A Tale of Two Cities*, begins with this phrase: "It was the best of times, it was the worst of times." Those words could be applied equally well to American banking, which is today passing through a revolution of unprecedented proportions. American banking as an industry and the more than 15,000 individual banks across the nation currently face both the best of times and the worst of times.

The failure rate among U.S. banks of all sizes has soared to levels not seen since the Great Depression of the 1930s. Two hundred American banks failed in 1988, for example—not only a postwar record but by far the largest number of bank failures since the founding of the Federal Deposit Insurance Corporation in 1934. The decade of the 1980s as a whole averaged nearly 100 bank failures annually, dwarfing the average of 5 to 6 bank failures a year that characterized the 1950s and 1960s.

Staggering losses from international loans to troubled nations of the Third World eroded the capital positions of the nation's largest commercial banks. At the other end of the spectrum, hundreds of small community-oriented banks have been pushed to the threshold of failure because of an agricultural debt crisis. As world commodity prices weakened, American farm incomes and the value of farmland were driven sharply lower, wearing away much of the collateral that backed a mountain of farm debt held by commercial banks and the federal government's farm credit system. Moreover, American banks of all sizes found themselves enmeshed in a tangle of lawsuits and repossessions as world oil and gas prices plummeted—the combined result of substantially lower demand for energy and lack of agreement on oil production controls within the Organization of Petroleum Exporting Countries (OPEC). The loan-collateral value of oil-field property and equipment dropped sharply, creating a glut of commercial office space up and down the nation's mid-section. Of the 200 banks that closed their doors in 1988, for example, 70 percent were headquartered in just four states in the nation's heartland—Colorado, Louisiana, Oklahoma, and Texas.

American bankers caught in these immensely complicated problems could take small comfort from the fact that theirs was not the only industry mired in trouble. The critical savings and loan industry—the nation's premier supplier of home mortgage credit—was truly facing "the worst of times." In scarcely more than two decades an industry that had grown to more than 6,000 firms was reduced by failures and forced consolidations to less than 3,000 survivors. The collapse of so many savings and loan associations (S&Ls) after 150 years of successful operation was testimony to the combined destructive power of outmoded government regulations and narrow product specialization in an era that values diversity, flexibility, and free markets as ways to solve economic problems.

But there is another side to the unfolding story of structural revolution in American banking. It is the promise of better times, of a new era in which the best-managed banks survive and prosper and the poorly managed ones fail or face acquisition and consolidation. The foundation stone of this brighter future is *deregulation*—the lifting of federal and state rules that have restricted the operations of U.S. banks for generations. Until recently, every American bank, regardless of size or location, was regulated from birth to death by a potpourri of federal and state regulations administered by multiple government agencies: the Securities and Exchange Commission, the Department of Justice, the Federal Deposit Insurance Corporation, the Comptroller of the Currency, the Federal Reserve Board, and the banking commissions of each of the 50 states. No bank could be chartered, sell its services, establish new offices, close old ones, merge, or even go out of business without the approval of at least one of these government agencies.

These burdensome government restrictions, however, are slowly but surely being torn down. Banking regulations are falling because many of them are no longer relevant to a financial marketplace that today transcends state and national boundaries—a global market that transacts business 24 hours a day. It is a market dominated by the rapidly evolving technology of information; new channels of communication make it possible to deliver financial services to businesses and households situated next door or thousands of miles away.

For bankers who are prepared for this new era it could well be "the best of times." Their managerial skills and creative instincts can, for the first time, be fully unleashed. The potential rewards are nearly boundless, but so are the potential losses. Deregulation of an industry that has been closely regulated for decades exacts a stiff price for the gift of freedom. Banking markets today are intensely competitive precisely because they are no longer sheltered by regulation. Well-managed banks will succeed, and larger numbers of banking firms will surely fail because a free market, unlike a regulated one, does not forgive errors of management judgment, just as it often handsomely rewards sound business decision making.

Deregulation of banking and the financial-services industry has been well publicized in recent years. However, until now the focus of public attention has been largely on *product-line deregulation*—the lifting of restrictions against banks' paying competitive interest rates on their deposits and on offering new services, such as underwriting corporate bonds and underwriting stock. In 1980 Congress passed the Depository Institutions Deregulation and Monetary Control Act which began the process of lifting the half-century-old legal ceilings on the interest rates banks could offer their depositors. This new law also granted thrift institutions—such as credit unions, savings and loans, and savings banks—broader powers to offer new business and household financial services. Two years later Congress not only further broadened the service powers of thrift institutions through passage of the Garn–St Germain Depository Institutions Act, but also granted banks and other depository institutions authority to offer money-market accounts. These flexible-yield deposits are subject to withdrawal by writing checks and are also competitive with shares in money-market mutual funds offered by leading security brokers and dealers, such as Merrill Lynch and E. F. Hutton.

The reasoning behind these innovative laws was simple and straightforward: grant banks and thrift institutions the authority to offer new services, and this will improve their chances for long-run survival. It will also reduce their exposure to the risk of failure because declining revenue from the sale of old services may be offset by increasing revenue from the sale of new services. Congress was concerned (as were many U.S. bankers) that the nation's banks and thrifts could literally be regulated out of existence if these institutions were not free to find more creative ways to attract financial-service customers. As Walter Wriston (1981, 9), former Chairman of New York's Citibank, once noted: "Our commercial history is filled with examples of companies that failed to change with a changing world, and became tombstones in the corporate graveyard." The straightjacket of federal law and regulation that had driven the railroads to decline and ruin early in this century was now threatening the nation's depository institutions.

What Congress has consistently failed to recognize, however, is that risk-reducing diversification can be achieved in ways other than by simply developing and selling new services. Risk can also be reduced through *geographic diversification*—entry into new markets different from the markets that a bank now serves, such that declining service sales in old markets may be offset by rising sales in newly entered ones. Geographic diversification can stabilize a bank's operating revenues and net earnings, provided that bank is able to spread its marketing activities far enough across the landscape to enter states and regions with markets that perform differently from the markets it currently serves.

Indeed, it can be argued that the development of new services — known as *product-line diversification* — may not reduce risk at all if a bank is forced to sell those new services in the markets it already serves. The reason is that, if the local economy weakens, the demand for *all* bank services is likely to decline as well. One of the most tragic examples of this phenomenon occurred in the mid-1980s when several leading banks in the Southwest, seeing their energy loan business deteriorating rapidly, turned to invest more heavily in commercial and residential properties in the same cities and counties. However, when world oil prices plummeted, *both* energy and real estate markets were plunged into a deep recession because, clearly, these markets were all intertwined. Subsequently, dozens of banks, along with savings and loan associations, in Louisiana, Oklahoma, and Texas failed or were rescued by out-of-state acquirers.

The failure of Congress to recognize the pressing need for geographic diversification in banking and to tackle such a politically sensitive issue as interstate banking has allowed the states to re-emerge as leaders in American banking supervision and regulation. For nearly 50 years the federal government had dominated bank regulation, principally because of its legal authority over interstate commerce and because Congress had vested regulatory power over bank holding companies — the dominant organizational form in U.S. banking today — in the Federal Reserve Board. Literally, the decisions made by the Federal Reserve Board in slowing or accelerating holding-company growth reached into every state of the union and into thousands of local communities.

Today, however, it is the *states*, concerned about possible loss of jobs and economic growth, that have led the way toward full-service interstate banking. Interstate banking is a new form of state government deregulation which offers great opportunity to those bank managers and stockholders fully prepared for that opportunity. But interstate banking also promises new and more intense competition which could well bring failure to smaller banks unwilling to accept the challenge and to larger banks as well if they miscalculate and reach beyond their capacity to successfully manage and control a more complex and geographically diversified banking organization. Clearly, deregulation offers both the best of times and the worst of times for U.S. commercial bankers and for the consumers who rely heavily on this industry for credit, savings, and other essential financial services.

THE BACKGROUND OF INTERSTATE BANKING

Full-service banking across state lines has been the exception, rather than the rule, in American banking for most of the nation's history. Fear of the concentrated financial power that large banks might acquire and use to the detriment of farmers, ranchers, and other small business interests led state after state early in this century to restrict or outlaw the creation of full-service branch offices. Some states, such as Texas, were so set against the spread of branch banking that anti-branching statutes were made part of their state constitutions. Even drive-in windows were viewed as a form of branch banking in some states, and these, too, were strictly regulated, usually by requiring the drive-ins to be no more than a few hundred feet or a few miles from the main bank building and by severely restricting the services available through them. In states such as Texas the anti-branching law was so strict that even a bank's drive-in window had to be connected in some way to its head office, such as by a pneumatic tube.

The federal government added its own imprimatur to the actions of the states in 1927 and 1933. Both the McFadden-Pepper Act in 1927 and the Banking Act of 1933 affirmed the principle that the *states*, not the federal government, had the power to decide whether any bank could establish branch offices within their borders. Federally chartered banks were instructed to follow the same branching rules as banks chartered by the states. Moreover, no federally supervised bank could branch into the territory of another state without express permission to do so. If state law was silent on the branching issue, bank-branching activity was assumed to be prohibited.

These federal and state restrictions on the geographic expansion of American banks resulted in a crazy quilt of laws, spread with little rhyme or reason from coast to coast and border to border. For many decades until the 1980s most states either prohibited branch-office banking completely or severely limited the permissible territory over which a bank could operate branch offices. Until the 1980s about a third of the states permitted branching activity only in the home-office city, in the home-office county, or in surrounding counties or special districts. Roughly another third outlawed full-service branch offices, while the remaining third permitted statewide branching without significant restrictions. Even as late as 1989, although by that time many states had completely dismantled their legal restrictions against branching, there were still 15 states that either outlawed full-service branch offices or at least limited bank branching to designated areas within their borders (though two of these states are scheduled to permit statewide branching in the near future). (See Table 1-1.)

Although these anti-branching laws served to limit the growth in size of local banks, they also tended to limit competition by erecting effective barriers against selling key financial services—particularly checking accounts and loans—in many local communities. Many bank customers, especially household customers and small businesses, are averse to opening a checking account, renting a safety deposit box, or taking out a personal loan from a distant financial institution that may be unfamiliar with the local community and too far away to conveniently resolve disputes. Thus protected from the full force of competition, some banks were able to take advantage of the

Table 1-1
Branch Banking Laws of the United States

Type of Branching Law	Number of States Adopting Law	Names of States with Indicated Type of Branching Law
Statewide Branching Allowed (either through acquisition or by de novo branching)	34 States and Washington, D.C.	Alabama, Alaska, Arizona, California, Connecticut, Delaware, Florida, Georgia, Hawaii, Idaho, Indiana, Kansas, Maine, Maryland, Massachusetts, Michigan, Mississippi, Nebraska, Nevada, New Hampshire, New Jersey, New York, North Carolina, North Dakota, Ohio, Oklahoma, Oregon, Rhode Island, South Carolina, South Dakota, Utah, Vermont, Virginia, Washington, and Washington, D.C.
Limited Branching Allowed (in cities, counties, or other adjacent areas within a state)	12 States	Arkansas, Iowa, Kentucky, Louisiana, Minnesota, Missouri, New Mexico, Pennsylvania, Tennessee, Texas, West Virginia, and Wisconsin.
Unit Banking (no full-service branches, though limited service facilities usually are permitted)	4 States	Colorado, Illinois, Montana, and Wyoming.

Note: Indiana allows statewide branching by merger as do Florida, Georgia, Kansas, Mississippi, Nebraska, North Dakota, and Oklahoma. Arkansas is scheduled to convert to statewide branching in 1999, Mississippi to de novo branching in 1989, Pennsylvania in 1990, and West Virginia in 1991.
Sources: Board of Governors of the Federal Reserve System and Federal Deposit Insurance Corporation, selected annual reports.

situation by offering fewer services, reducing service quality, or levying higher prices for any services rendered.[1]

Nor were anti-branching laws the *only* vehicle for restricting competition. Several states saw fit to restrict the further spread of bank holding companies as well. These stock-investing corporations had emerged in the Midwest near the turn of the century in order to purchase bank stock and gain control of one or more banks. Fear began to emerge in the 1930s and again in the 1950s that a few powerful corporations, including out-of-state and foreign investors, could ultimately grab controlling interest in a state's banking industry to the detriment of local businesses and families. Some states, such as Louisiana and Oklahoma, simply outlawed bank holding companies, while others attempted to regulate their growth. As Table 1-2 shows, there are still nearly 20 states today with laws that limit either the share of statewide bank deposits or assets holding companies can control or the number and type of affiliated businesses a holding company can acquire.

The 1970s and 1980s, however, so changed the character and thrust of American banking that the exception — full-service interstate banking through both branching and holding-company activity — is, perhaps inevitably, becoming the rule. As Table 1-3 indicates, all but five states (Hawaii, Iowa, Kansas, Montana, and North Dakota) had enacted enabling legislation for banks from other states to enter their territory by the late 1980s. And of these five, Hawaii permits bank entry from selected other islands in the Pacific, while Iowa and North Dakota have granted special exemptions to grandfathered interstate banking firms that had entered their states in earlier years. Facing fewer legal hurdles, more than 200 banking companies made interstate bank acquisitions between 1980 and the first quarter of 1989. Moreover, as Table 1-4 suggests, these interstate mergers and acquisitions generally accelerated over time, reaching a record of about 50 mergers and acquisitions in 1988 before slowing significantly the following year. So powerful a force has the drive toward interstate banking become that in 1985 a national survey of leading U.S. bankers, all members of the Association of Reserve City Bankers, predicted a decline in the number of American banks by more than 20 percent in the 1990s and an increase of 70 percent in the number of large money-center banking companies holding more than $40 billion in assets apiece (Morrissey 1986, 15).

These new interstate ventures have *not* been equally distributed across the vast geography of the United States. Quite to the contrary, bankers have been highly selective in choosing new states to enter. For example, Illinois has accounted for a disproportionately large share of interstate banking activity thus far. Once that state's borders were opened, leading banking organizations from neighboring states fought aggressively to get a share of the greater Chicago market. Florida also has ranked high in interstate bank acquisitions due to its rapid growth in population and the presence of large numbers of senior citizens with ample pension incomes and the capital to invest in bank-managed trust funds. Arizona, California, Connecticut, Delaware, Georgia, Indiana, Maine, Massachusetts, New Hampshire, New Jersey, New York, Ohio, South Carolina, South Dakota, Texas, and Washington have been front-runners as well in the interstate movement due to a combination of factors: favorable legislation, a large population base, rapid growth in new business activity, strategic locations for future bank expansion, and large numbers of potential take-over targets that could be purchased cheaply, particularly if the targeted banks appeared to be mired in serious financial problems.

Table 1-2

Bank Holding-Company Laws of the United States

Type of Holding–Company Law	Number of States Adopting Law	Names of States with Indicated Type of Holding–Company Law
Holding–Company Acquisitions and Activity Permitted Essentially Without Restrictions	31 States and Washington, D.C.	Alabama, Alaska, Arizona, California, Colorado, Connecticut, Delaware, Florida, Hawaii, Idaho, Maine, Maryland, Massachusetts, Michigan, Minnesota, Montana, Nevada, New Mexico, North Carolina, North Dakota, Ohio, Oregon, South Carolina, South Dakota, Texas, Utah, Vermont, Virginia, Wisconsin, Wyoming, and Washington.
Acquisitions of Banks by Any One Holding Company Are Limited to a Specific Proportion of Statewide Deposits or Banking Assets[a]	12 States	Arkansas, Indiana, Iowa, Kansas, Kentucky, Missouri, Nebraska, New Hampshire, New Jersey, Oklahoma, Rhode Island, and West Virginia.
Number of Affiliates or Subsidiaries That a Holding Company May Acquire Is Limited or Prohibited.	2 States	Mississippi and Pennsylvania[b]
Miscellaneous Restrictions Imposed on Holding–Company Activity[c]	5 States	Georgia, Illinois, Louisiana, New York, and Tennessee.

Notes: a) Several states listed in this category also have other provisions of their holding–company law that would allow us to legitimately classify them in another category in this table. For example, Arkansas also limits holding–company acquisitions in that state to one subsidiary under specified conditions. Kentucky protects new banks from acquisition by a holding company for five years. Oklahoma also protects its new banks from acquisition for their first five years of existence. New Hampshire places a ceiling of 12 on the number of affiliates a bank holding company is allowed to acquire. b) Pennsylvania's restrictions on the number of banks a holding company may acquire are scheduled to end in 1991. c) Mississippi has no holding company law. In New York, holding–company acquisitions in smaller communities must be approved by state regulatory authorities. Georgia protects new banks from holding–company acquisition for their first five years. Tennessee restricts holding–company acquisitions based on the population size of the community involved and time of operation. Illinois allows holding–company acquisitions within designated regions.

Sources: Board of Governors of the Federal Reserve System and Federal Deposit Insurance Corporation, selected annual reports.

Table 1-3
Types of Interstate Banking Laws Enacted in Recent Years

Nature of State's Banking Law	Number of States Having Such A Law	Names of States With Indicated Type of Law
Nationwide Entry Allowed if Reciprocal Privileges Are Granted to the Home State's Banks	10 States	Kentucky, Louisiana, Michigan, Ohio, New York, New Jersey, Rhode Island, South Dakota, Washington, and West Virginia.
Nationwide Entry Allowed and Reciprocity Is Not Needed	9 States	Alaska, Arizona, Idaho, Maine, Oklahoma, Oregon, Texas, Utah, and Wyoming.
Regional Entry Allowed by Banks Headquartered in the Same Region of the Nation with Reciprocity Required	16 States and Washington, D.C.	Alabama, Arkansas, Connecticut, Florida, Georgia, Maryland, Massachusetts, Minnesota, Mississippi, Missouri, New Hampshire, North Carolina, South Carolina, Tennessee, Virginia, Wisconsin, and Washington, D.C.
Regional Entry Allowed, But a Switch to Nationwide Entry Is Scheduled by a Given Date	10 States	California (January 1991), Colorado (January 1991), Delaware (June 1990), Illinois (December 1990), Indiana (July 1992), Nebraska (January 1991), Nevada (January 1989), New Mexico (January 1990), Pennsylvania (March 1990), and Vermont (February 1990).
International Entry Permitted from Certain Other Territories (but not from other U.S. states), Provided Reciprocity Is Granted	1 State	Hawaii.
No Interstate Banking Law Yet Enacted	4 States	Iowa, Kansas, Montana, and North Dakota.

Sources: Board of Governors of the Federal Reserve System, Federal Deposit Insurance Corporation, and Legal Division of the American Bankers Association, Washington, D.C.

Table 1-4
Number of Interstate Bank and Holding-Company Acquisitions by Year

Year of Merger or Acquisition	Number of Interstate Bank Acquisitions and Mergers
1980	2
1981	5
1982	19
1983	11
1984	10
1985	3
1986	40
1987	53
1988	47
1989 (First Quarter Only)	11
Total for All Years	201

Source: Survey by the author of federal merger decisions and published merger announcements in The Wall Street Journal and American Banker, daily issues for the 1980–89 period, and in press releases of the Board of Governors of the Federal Reserve System.

In the latter half of the 1980s the high tide of interstate banking swept westward through the Midwest and then on to the Rocky Mountains and the West Coast. In these newer regions, state legislatures were slower to respond to the new trend but caught up quickly with sweeping banking legislation of their own. About two-thirds of all full-service interstate mergers have occurred from north to south along the nation's Midwest corridor, in Texas and the Southwest, astride the Rockies, and along the Pacific Coast. New England and the southeastern states have accounted for roughly one-third of all interstate bank combinations. As these relative proportions imply, the geographic center of interstate acquisitions has shifted recently from states along the Atlantic Coast into the Midwest and on to the Pacific Coast. That geographic shift could be traced to the need for major eastern banking organizations to consolidate their previously won positions and concentrate on planning to improve bank performance, while banking organizations west of the Mississippi aggressively moved toward full-service expansion into neighboring states to take advantage of strong economies and favorable bank stock prices (including takeovers of failed institutions). As we will see in later chapters, the states entered were not chosen at random, but reflected in most cases the careful calculation of financial benefits and costs as well as the long-range strategic goals of the nation's leading banking organizations.

THE PREDECESSORS OF FULL-SERVICE
INTERSTATE BANKING

The interstate banking movement unfolding across the American landscape today is not banking's first interstate wave. Bankers are no less intelligent than other corporate executives; where distant states offer economically strong markets and the potential for earning competitive returns on invested capital, bankers are likely to find legal routes around constraining regulations.[2] That route was found in the 1960s and 1970s through the bank holding company. A corporation holding bank stock could simply purchase controlling interest in any number of nonbank businesses which, because they were not banks, were not prohibited from producing and selling their services in any state of the union or in any foreign country.

The Acquisition of Nonbank Firms

The result in the late 1960s and 1970s was a prodigious number of interstate nonbank business acquisitions — especially acquisitions of finance companies, mortgage banks, leasing firms, data processing companies, travel agencies, credit card firms, credit life insurers, security brokers, management consultants, etc. — by U.S. and foreign holding companies. While full-service banking was not permitted, finance companies and other nonbank firms could offer "banklike" services — for example, installment credit, management of customer cash accounts, equipment leasing, and investment advice — anywhere their sales activities were not expressly prohibited by state law.

Unfortunately for American bankers, the nonbank business route was not the final solution to the barriers posed by geography and by federal and state law. None of the nonbank firms was allowed to offer a full slate of banking services, and, therefore, bankers could not offer the public in distant states one-stop banking convenience. Moreover, most customers did not trust nonbank businesses in the same way they trusted banks.

The movement of U.S.-based bank holding companies to acquire nonbank businesses across state lines faded in the late 1970s and was thrown into reverse in the 1980s. Many of the largest holding companies began to divest themselves of their nonbank business ventures. Lack of bank management experience with nonbank products and services often led to sub-par earnings and a severe drain on scarce capital. Moreover, bankers had reasoned that combining a wide range of services under the same corporate umbrella would enable them to cross-sell many different financial products more easily. Presumably, a customer coming in for a loan also could be tempted to purchase a new CD, a safety deposit box, an insurance policy, etc., etc. However, financial-service firms frequently found that the public preferred *not* to purchase financial services in clusters from the same company at the same time. Moreover, most financial-service customers showed little respect for the "halo effect," by which a bank's aura as a safe, prudently managed institution supposedly carried over to its nonbank business ventures as well.

Many banking organizations viewed nonbank businesses as vehicles for risk-reducing diversification. Expanding across state lines through the creation or acquisition of nonbank businesses allegedly would reduce risk exposure from two different directions. First, the entering of new markets across the nation would generate geographic diversification, with declining sales revenues and earnings in one state or region offset by rising revenues and earnings in another state or region. Second, product-line diversification, resulting from marriages between bank and nonbank service menus, also would lower the risk exposure of bank earnings because decreases in earnings from one service line could be offset by gains from the sales of other services.

Unfortunately, the second of these two forms of diversification—product-line diversification—turned out to be more apparent than real. Congress had declared in 1970 that only those nonbank businesses "closely related to banking" could be acquired or started by bank holding companies, leaving to the Federal Reserve Board the task of defining what product lines were sufficiently close to traditional banking products to satisfy the intent of Congress. Not unexpectedly, the Federal Reserve Board took the conservative approach—in most cases approving only those nonbank ventures and service lines already approved for federally chartered banks themselves. Subsequent research has confirmed that there were few real product-line diversification benefits from such ventures (Eisemann 1976; Eisenbeis, Harris, and Lakonishok 1984; and Stover 1982).

What remained, then, of potential risk-reducing diversification benefits from holding-company acquisitions had to center on geography. Acquiring nonbank businesses in distant markets not open to full-service banks created an opportunity, perhaps, to stabilize revenues and earnings through the creation of huge conglomerate banking firms, reducing their exposure to failure risk and lowering their cost of capital. Subsequent experience generally has revealed, however, that these potential geographic diversification benefits were largely offset (if not overpowered) by the lack of management experience and the high cost of either acquiring or starting de novo nonbank firms.

A good example of the stock market's adverse reaction to recent attempts at product-line diversification by financial-service firms occurred in August 1988 when Commercial Credit Group, Inc., announced its pending acquisition of Primerica Corp., linking a leading finance company with a major insurance and securities firm. Almost immediately Commercial Credit's common stock fell $7.50 per share on the New York Stock Exchange, while

Primerica's stock fell 50 cents a share (as noted by Swartz and Garcia [1988, 6]).

Nonbank Banks

Another possible avenue for interstate expansion was opened by Congress in 1984 in the form of *nonbank banks*. These hybrid institutions avoided commercial banking regulations by refusing either to make commercial loans *or* to accept checking accounts—two of the essential components of what constitutes a commercial bank under federal law. The result was the rapid expansion of largely unregulated banking competitors across state lines. One of the most frequently targeted states for nonbank-bank activity was Florida, where nonbank organizations, such as U.S. Trust Company of New York, set up branch offices. When the Federal Reserve Board announced in 1984 that it was accepting and would approve applications to establish nonbank banks, approximately 30 bank holding companies applied in a matter of days for 200 new nonbank-bank offices in 91 cities. Unfortunately, the nonbank-bank route to interstate expansion was closed by congressional moratorium in 1987, allegedly to give Congress more time to resolve the fundamental issue of what American banks should and should not be allowed to do. Both Congress and the bank regulatory agencies appeared to be concerned that the wall of existing regulation, designed to promote public safety and public confidence, now had so many holes punched in it there soon would be nothing left to protect if Congress delayed too long.

Nevertheless, the use of nonbank business subsidiaries and nonbank banks by the largest U.S. bank holding companies in the 1970s and 1980s established a solid beachhead for interstate banking. By year end 1988, according to King, Tschinkel, and Whitehead (1989), 14,600 interstate offices of banking organizations were in operation, of which 7,500 could offer a full line of banking services and about 7,100 could offer limited banking services. Moreover, the passage of regional reciprocal interstate banking laws by most states, which permit only banks from selected other states to enter, still provides an incentive to many bank holding companies to use nonbank business affiliates and grandfathered nonbank banks as weapons to pry open those states and regions of the nation still closed to them.

Acquiring Troubled Thrifts

A related vehicle for crossing state borders was the acquisition of troubled thrift institutions—savings banks and savings and loan associations—by bank holding companies, provided approval could be obtained from the

Federal Reserve Board. Examples included Citicorp's acquisition of both Biscayne Federal Savings and Loan in Florida and Fidelity Savings of San Francisco. But these takeovers of troubled thrifts had at least one serious disadvantage: they posed substantial and serious risks to the banks involved because few managers could foresee the problems or correctly forecast the costs of trying to turn around an all-but-bankrupt firm. In most instances public announcement of a holding-company acquisition of a troubled thrift caused the company's stock price to plummet.

Overall, the earlier holding-company and nonbank-bank forms of interstate banking proved to be only moderately successful surrogates for full-service banking. Pressure mounted in the banking industry for the real thing: full-service banking across state lines and, ultimately, from coast to coast. By turning their lobbying skills away from Washington, D.C., and toward the state legislatures, bankers in the 1980s struck fertile ground — a regulatory environment that would listen not only to the cries of bank lobbyists for new freedom, but also to the pleas of thousands of local communities across the United States. These communities saw in interstate banking a source of development capital and economic growth — particularly in the creation of employment opportunities for those who had lost their jobs when the nation's farms and ranches, construction firms, and energy industries tumbled into a deep recession. If there was to be an "economic miracle" at the local level, interstate banking *might* lead the way toward that miracle.

CRITICISM AND CONTROVERSY: PUBLIC REACTION TO INTERSTATE BANKING

As the decade of the 1980s drew to a close, approximately 200 U.S.-chartered banks and bank holding companies had made interstate banking acquisitions. No one state dominated the interstate movement, but certain regions of the nation clearly stood apart from the rest. The Southeast — principally the states of Florida, Georgia, and North Carolina — led the nation in the 1980s. The upper Midwest — particularly Illinois, Indiana, Michigan, and Ohio — along with the neighboring state of Pennsylvania, represented a second active banking region during the same period, followed by the six New England states. Toward the end of the 1980s the western and Rocky Mountain states — led by Alaska, Arizona, and Washington — opened their borders to interstate banking activity which soon accelerated, bringing about massive changes in the ownership and organizational structure of the banking industry within their borders.

These bank acquisitions across once-sacrosanct state boundaries have given rise to a scattering of praise and a storm of criticism and controversy. For example, corporate attorney and merger analyst Arthur Burck (1984, 659) recently testified before the U.S. House Banking Committee:

When the history of our times is written, the unrestrained mergers of recent decades may well replace the debacle of the stock market of the 1920s as the cataclysm most destructive to the nation's financial and economic foundations. . . . If there is any doubt about the above prophecy, there certainly won't be if the restrictions against interstate banking are fully removed. It will be only a question of time until the nation's banking industry will be concentrated in a handful of gargantuan big-city banks.

Burck finds no convincing evidence of significant gains in efficiency from allowing banks to grow by interstate acquisition, and, therefore, in his view society gains little or nothing from banking consolidation. Moreover, Burck contends that if the nation is to foster the rapid formation of new businesses (particularly in high technology), it will need small and moderate-size banks to fund them because the largest U.S. banks tend to bypass smaller firms.

Yet today's federal tax laws *encourage* the development of large bank holding companies, subsidizing corporate mergers with significant tax advantages. For example, a bank holding company can offset the profits earned by one of its subsidiary firms by taking losses from another of its affiliated firms, reducing its overall tax liability. In addition, the federal tax code still permits some types of tax-free stock exchanges and sanctions the tax deductibility of borrowing costs and the employment of retained profits to support merger activity.

Moreover, once interstate mergers are consummated, the largest interstate banking companies can expand their market shares by cross-subsidization of local banking affiliates, particularly by bidding away deposits from smaller independent banks and driving them from the scene. Jobs will be lost, and support for local communities will decline. Burck (1984, 659) contends: "The founders and executives of thriving companies—people with roots in the town—are eventually replaced by hirees of the acquirer. Local lawyers, bankers, and professionals are replaced by others in some distant headquarters."

Many of these arguments against interstate banking are shared by other authorities in the field. For example, the noted financial analyst Chris Welles (1975, 409) recently issued a stern warning concerning the dangers of holding-company banking:

The picture of bank power emerging from this analysis is not comforting. We can see banks becoming larger, more concentrated and more national and international in scope. . . . We can see them concentrating their rapidly growing trust holdings in the stocks of the nation's largest, best-established corporations. We can see them using their vast economic leverage to solidify their banking and nonbanking relationships with many of the same established corporations and to help those corporations resist challenges and maintain their dominant industry positions. We can see smaller companies hampered in their competitive efforts by the inaccessibility of bank money. We can even see the major banks and corporations gradually coalescing into a giant, mutually supportive, self-sufficient financial-industrial complex astride the economy, quietly frustrating change and suppressing innovation.

But there is another side to the interstate banking debate today—one that foresees substantial *benefits* to businesses, individuals, and the nation as a whole. In a speech to the Los Angeles Town Hall entitled "Who Cares About Interstate Banking? You Should!" Thomas G. Labrecque (1984), president of Chase Manhattan Bank, stated that allowing full-service banks from New York to enter the California market (and presumably other states as well) would promote lower prices for financial services, generate a broader menu of services, improve service quality, and create more jobs. He argued that U.S. laws restricting branch banking are "as repressive, antiquated, anti-competitive, and unjustifiable as those that govern any industry" (Labrecque 1984, 670). This comment is mindful of an opinion once penned by Justice Potter Stewart of the U.S. Supreme Court, who labeled U.S. banking laws as "a restraint of trade which would be a *per se* violation of other antitrust laws but for the fact that the restraint is governmental rather than privately imposed" (*Mercantile Bank* vs. *New York*, 121 U.S. 138, 156).

Labrecque argues that restrictive banking laws may have been understandable in the depressed economic environment of the 1920s and 1930s, but are simply indefensible today. They run counter to a current national effort to improve competition and leave U.S. banks virtually imprisoned within the boundaries of a single state when selling their services (especially the taking of deposits). Moreover, Labrecque finds little rationality in laws that prohibit New York and California banks from entry into other states, but permit nonbank financial conglomerates like Sears, American Express, and Merrill Lynch to set up shop anywhere they please. Rather, Labrecque and other advocates of interstate banking argue that the nation's financial markets should admit *all* bank and nonbank financial-service firms, creating an open market where *any* firm—regardless of its industrial and product origins—can enter, provided it offers financial services at competitive prices.

PERFORMANCE PROBLEMS ENCOUNTERED BY
INTERSTATE BANKING FIRMS

As we have seen in the foregoing pages, powerful forces have moved the United States for the first time in its history to the brink of full-service interstate banking. Economic recession and rising unemployment in several key states and regions, intense competition among sellers of financial services, rising operating costs, breakthroughs in the technology of information processing and transfer, and government deregulation of banking—all are playing critical roles in the gradual spread of interstate banking from coast to coast. But interstate bank expansion has not taken place without significant problems and pressures that today beset the industry and tomorrow are likely to continue to plague interstate firms. These major problem areas include (1) the poor financial condition of many of the banks and bank holding companies available for purchase across state lines; (2) management problems in coordinating and controlling effectively a larger and more diverse banking organization; (3) potential damage to customer and community good will in those local communities where an outside banking organization replaces the former owners; (4) the competing opportunities for bank expansion in international markets that will limit the financial capital and human resources U.S. banks will have available for geographic expansion inside the United States; and (5) a shortage of management talent among leading money-center banks that is reflected in serious problems with loan quality and soaring operating costs. We look briefly at each of these five key problem areas below and explore them more deeply in the chapters that follow.

The Poor Financial Condition of Many Interstate Acquired Firms

Many of the banking institutions acquired across state lines were on the brink of failure when they were purchased. In fact, several interstate acquisitions have required strong financial support from federal insurance agencies simply to complete the merger transaction. The most notable of these federally assisted takeovers occurred in July 1988 when the Federal Deposit Insurance Corporation pledged approximately $2 billion to facilitate North Carolina National Bank's (NCNB) takeover of First RepublicBank Corp., the largest banking company in Texas. Under the terms of this huge merger, the FDIC is not scheduled to recover all of its funds for several years, though NCNB, after several exceptional earnings reports, now appears ready to buy out the FDIC's interest earlier than expected.

On average, interstate acquired firms report significantly lower net earnings and greater risk exposure from loan losses than comparable banking firms not acquired by companies outside their home state. And there is no guarantee that all interstate acquirers will be successful in turning their acquired firms around. Sometimes the damage done by previous management or the weakness of the local economy is too severe to save a sinking company, no matter whom the acquirer is.

Moreover, the problems faced by acquired firms can be so severe that they have a substantial adverse impact on the overall performance of their acquirers. For example, in September 1988 First Interstate Bancorp of Los Angeles, one of the original interstate bank holding companies and one of the nation's most geographically diverse banking firms, reported pre-tax losses of $350 million, about $180 million of which reportedly were due to loan losses at its recent Texas acquisition, Allied Bancshares of Houston (as discussed by Hill [1988, 3]). First Interstate's stock fell sharply in price just shortly before the public announcement of that loss. The First Interstate

situation reflects another important dimension of the performance problems encountered by many interstate banking firms today: interstate activity
often adds to, rather than solves, the operating and financial problems
already present in many large banking firms. Interstate expansion is not
necessarily a panacea for all bank ills and is unlikely to be a quick fix for
most bankers' problems.

In First Interstate's case, two key problem areas surfaced following its
more recent mergers: (1) substantial net noninterest expenses (including
wages and salaries, cost of materials, and occupancy costs less noninterest
revenues) relative to total earning assets (predominantly loans and securities), compared to peer banking institutions in California; and (2) a few
underperforming subsidiary and affiliate firms (especially companies engaged in mortgage operations, foreign loans, and energy and real estate
loans from the Southwest and the Rocky Mountain region). Nevertheless,
First Interstate remains one of the better performers among U.S. interstate banking firms and has recently taken strong measures to deal with its
reported problems (such as laying off workers and selling low-performing
assets). These strategic choices are indicative of the kinds of management
decisions that many other interstate firms will be compelled to make if their
performance record is to substantially improve, thereby opening up the
capital markets for the additional fund raising their future expansion will
demand.

Management Coordination and Control Problems

Successful interstate expansion will also demand that acquiring companies
learn how to coordinate and control bank production and delivery over
wider geographic areas. This is not easily done in most cases, and local
competitors may gain a significant advantage due to delays in decision
making and the communications problems faced by the largest interstate
firms. As we will see in Chapter 4, analyses of the strengths and weaknesses
of those few interstate banking companies that existed before federal law
prohibited them indicate that affiliates of interstate firms do not necessarily
outperform neighboring local banks. Indeed, interstate firms may lag behind their competitors and lose their current share of many local financial-
service markets.

Damage to Customer and Community Good Will

Entry into new metropolitan areas and smaller cities and towns carries the
risk of alienating customers and the communities that surround them. One
of the biggest fears among borrowing customers is the loss of an established
credit relationship when new interstate owners and management teams take
over. Often these takeovers bring new standards and new procedures for

approving loans and added time delays in processing large loan requests because the home office now may be included in the decision loop.

A related problem surfaced in economically depressed Texas where troubled money-center banks tapped heavily into the capital resources of their smaller satellite banks to offset heavy deposit runoffs. Many of the money-center banks' largest corporate depositors feared loss of their funds if the leading banks in the Southwest collapsed. The result was a diminished supply of credit in dozens of smaller communities throughout the region. With less credit available, many small businesses failed and unemployment in satellite communities, as well as in the central cities, increased significantly. There is no one best solution to the customer and community acceptance problem, but interstate banking organizations, perhaps more than any other type of business, can ill afford to ignore it.

Competing Opportunities for Bank Expansion in International Markets

The spread of interstate banking has been much *slower* than many analysts had expected. One key reason is the appearance of significant opportunities for bank expansion abroad due to deregulation in Canada and around the Pacific Basin and to the developing Common Market in Europe where trade restrictions are scheduled to be phased out by 1992. Several U.S. banks have moved aggressively to take advantage of these opening doors. For example, Republic New York Corp. announced in September 1988 that it was restructuring its banking programs in order to expand its private banking business in western Europe (as reported by Forman [1988, 4]). A new subsidiary, Safra Republic Holdings, S.A., announced plans for a large stock offering in the Eurocapital markets in order to prepare for planned deregulation in the European Economic Community (EEC). The EEC has a population of approximately 320 million – a larger retail banking market than the United States. The private banking market in Europe has already attracted the entry of such formidable bank competitors as American Express, Citicorp, and Merrill Lynch.

In Asia, too, a strong economic expansion, led by a rapid increase in consumer spending and an upward surge in manufactured exports, has been underway in recent years, fueling the interest of American banks in that huge geographic region. A recent Bank of America forecast suggests that Asia will be the fastest-growing region of the globe over the next five years, averaging a 4.3 percent annual gain in real gross domestic output. Among the fastest growing and economically most promising countries in the Pacific region are Japan, South Korea, Malaysia, Taiwan, and Singapore. While inflation has increased significantly in Asia, particularly in China, most of the recent growth has been in real production and real income adjusted for inflation. The demand for Asia's most important commodities and manufactured goods—especially tin, copper, textiles, palm oil, coconuts, rubber, wood, and personal computers—is growing. In addition, the two principal buyers of Asian commodities—the United States and Japan—are experiencing the longest peacetime economic expansions in their history. There is some concern among economists, however, that labor shortages coupled with high employee-turnover rates, especially in Hong Kong, Japan, Singapore, and Taiwan, will limit Asia's future growth (as noted by Jones [1988, A26]). With investments by U.S. corporations increasing rapidly, American banks generally view the Pacific Basin as a prime area for future expansion—one where banking competition is not yet as intense as it is in many markets inside the United States.

Capital Shortages Among Leading Interstate Firms

Many of the largest interstate banking firms have suffered severe drains against their capital base due to heavy loan losses related to international lending and to troubled domestic farm, real estate, and energy loans. These losses have sapped earnings that would have increased bank capital and provided a base for rapid interstate expansion. Moreover, there is evidence that the largest U.S. banking conglomerates, especially the nation's top ten banks, are unlikely to be able to significantly expand their organizations in the near term due simply to their current financial limitations. For example, two Federal Reserve economists, Korobow and Budzeika (1985), estimated that if the largest U.S. banking companies tried to expand their size by more than, say, 5 percent, they would run into serious financial constraints, such as a substantial dilution of ownership for their current stockholders, increased risk exposure due to high levels of debt relative to their required interest and dividend payments, higher capital costs with depressing effects on their stock prices, and the necessity of increasing their equity capital levels to the high levels called for by regulation.

Until recently, the most troubled banks in the nation appeared to be the largest money-center banks in New York, Chicago, San Francisco, and Los Angeles, on the one hand, because of their problems with international loans, and banking firms in the Southwest and Midwest, on the other hand, that were confronted with staggering losses on agricultural, energy, and real estate loans. However, more recently several of the "super-regional" banks in Atlanta, Boston, Charlotte, Columbus, Denver, and similar-size cities, long thought to be relatively isolated from serious economic problems, have watched their losses mount and their previously favorable stock price-to-earnings (P–E) ratios decline significantly.

Thus far, these regional banking problems have centered on commercial and residential real estate markets. For example, such regional leaders as the Bank of New England, Bank of Boston Corp., First Fidelity Bancorp, and Shawmut National Corp. reportedly have experienced a substantial number of problem credits, mainly in their real estate loan portfolios. However, some of the regionals' loan problems have also come from abroad where they rushed into global corporate and government loan markets after the leading New York and West Coast banks had pulled back from international lending to cut their own losses.

Some financial analysts think these recent problems reflect a flaw in the foundations of many of the largest super-regional U.S. banks, which, thus far, have been the driving force in the American interstate banking movement. Many of these rapidly growing regional giants appear to have "pasted together" loose banking confederations, which have imposed multiple constraints on their performance and future ability to grow. For example, the price of acquiring a bank in Florida, Illinois, Texas, or some other large state that has strong growth potential may also include a pledge by the acquirer to leave existing management alone, even though the old management team is weak and faltering. Moreover, some of these leading regional banking firms may have overextended themselves into markets and products of which management has insufficient knowledge and over which it has little control.

Shortage of Management Talent Among Leading Interstate Firms

Finally, interstate expansion may spread senior management and staff too thin to do an exceptional job of maintaining or improving the performance of both the acquiring and the acquired banking organizations. One recent interstate merger that, at first, had financial analysts concerned about this potential problem was the acquisition of First RepublicBank of Dallas by NCNB Corp. According to Christie and Helyan (1988, A8), about half of NCNB's senior managers were sent to Texas to complete that acquisition which *may* have left less-experienced managers in charge of the company's existing units. However, recently both NCNB Corp. and NCNB–Texas have reported very promising net earnings.

Many financial analysts believe that, sooner or later, a substantial portion of interstate banking companies will encounter great difficulty in balancing the demands made on their management and staff by their newest and, often, most troubled affiliates. Moreover, banking competition is not diminishing; rather, it is intensifying nationwide. The growing competitive struggle around the globe and in thousands of local markets across the United States could exacerbate the problems confronting a struggling interstate banking institution.

PROLOGUE

In this opening chapter we have traced the background and the scope of the dominant structural movement in American banking today—the interstate expansion of leading U.S. banks. Many of the walls erected by federal and state legislation and regulation—the rules for bank conduct—that took more than a century to erect have come tumbling down in less than a decade. By the late 1980s all but *four* states had voted to admit outside full-service banking firms within their territory, subject to a few restrictions designed in most cases to soften the competitive impact on their indigenous banking industry. Not surprisingly, a movement of such magnitude, and occurring with such speed, has unleashed a storm of controversy and criticism. In legislative testimony, public speeches, and editorials the fears and concerns of bankers, consumer groups, bank regulators, and the general public have come to the surface sufficiently now for us to render at least a preliminary verdict on the likely benefits and costs of interstate bank expansion.

The most important costs that *may* be left behind as a legacy of this newest banking revolution include destructive competition that may drive smaller independent banks from the market, decreased service to and concern for important groups of bank customers (such as small businesses and households), and the possible draining of funds out of smaller communities toward domestic money centers and abroad. Moreover, as we will see later in this book, recent research suggests the possibility that interstate banking may *not* live up to its promise of accelerated economic development for those states that have recently opened their borders. Even more ominous, however, is the clear and present danger that the movement will leave each state with a highly concentrated banking industry that stifles competition. There is also the risk that thinly spread management and depleted capital resources among leading interstate banks will render them incapable of strengthening their troubled affiliated firms, resulting in still more bank failures that weaken public confidence in America's banking system. It is to these important issues for public policymakers, for bankers, and for the public they serve that we turn now in the ensuing chapters of this book.

NOTES

1. The author recalls attending a meeting of community bankers in the Southwest when the discussion turned to bank profits: which banks were the most profitable and why? The speaker asked his audience how many bankers in attendance came from banks with a rate of return on total assets that was at least 1 percent (then about the average for U.S. banks as a whole). Hands went up in every corner of the room. Then the speaker asked how many bankers present earned a 2 percent return on their institution's assets. Many fewer hands went up, but still a surprising number. At this point the speaker began to raise the stakes of the game. How many earned a 3 percent return? A 4 percent return? How about 5 percent? As expected, few hands were left when 3 percent was reached, and by 5 percent, there was only one hand still in the air. Stunned, the speaker approached the elderly gentleman in the rear of the room whose hand had remained aloft. "What rate of return does your bank earn, sir?" "Seven percent of total assets," replied the man. "But how is that possible?"

asked the speaker. The banker replied, "It's simple. We are the *only* bank in town; branching is outlawed, and the nearest town is 70 miles away. We accept checking accounts, but no interest-bearing deposits."

The absence of entry privileges to set up new branch offices often works in favor of local banks and can wreak havoc with the public interest unless the industry's regulators are vigilant.

2. The author at one time worked as a research economist in the Federal Reserve System. One of his occasional duties was to sit in on the conference call that occurs every morning, linking economists and policymakers at the Federal Reserve Board in Washington, D.C., with the manager of the Fed's Trading Desk housed at the Federal Reserve Bank of New York and the president of 1 of the other 11 Federal Reserve banks. The purpose of these calls is to make a final decision about what the Federal Reserve should do that day in the financial marketplace, buying or selling government securities to influence interest rates, to encourage the growth of money and credit in the United States, and, hopefully at least, to avoid inflation and unemployment. The author recalls one conversation in which the Trading Desk manager noted that leading banks around the nation had recently developed several clever ways to get around new Federal Reserve rules limiting the interest rates banks could pay on their deposits. Several of the nation's leading banks had begun to sell commercial paper through their holding companies (which were not regulated effectively at that time) and then to channel the proceeds to the bank or banks in the same holding company.

The Reserve bank president participating in this particular conference call asked, "Is there any way we can stop that?" The Trading Desk manager replied, "I don't think so. We figure that for every person in the regulatory agencies thinking up new rules, there are at least a thousand people in the banking industry looking for ways around each new rule." The problem with burdensome regulation is that it often wastes managers' creative energies on finding devious ways to bend the rules. That time probably could be better spent on improving the quality and convenience of services sold to the public.

2

Causes of the Interstate Banking Movement

Full-service interstate banking is, by any measure, the most important structural change in American banking in the final quarter of the twentieth century. A movement of this magnitude typically has not one, but multiple causes — economic, legal, regulatory, and technological forces that have combined to restructure one of the nation's most critical industries. Moreover, some of these causal factors are regionally specific, while others arise from pressures affecting the global economy and American society as a whole.

In this chapter we examine more fully the most important factors that have shaped the current nationwide movement toward interstate banking, examining, in turn, state and local pressures to increase the availability of jobs and economic growth, to rescue troubled banks and promote regulatory equity, to make fuller use of new technologies and increase the value of bank stock, to access both distant labor markets and new customer segments, to escape the burdens of domestic and foreign regulation and take advantage of more liberal anti-trust policies, and to expand bank production volume in order to lower unit operating costs. (A summary of the economic, legal, regulatory, and technological causes of interstate banking is presented in Tables 2–1 and 2–2.) All have played major roles in the unfolding story of American banking today — an industry in transition from a local focus to a nationwide presence.

THE NEED TO BRING IN NEW CAPITAL AND STIMULATE LOCAL ECONOMIES

Pressure has been growing in many different regions of the nation to attract scarce capital funds in the hope of expanding business activity, increasing the availability of jobs, and adding to tax revenues in order to improve the

Table 2-1

Principal Economic Causes of the Spread of Full-Service Interstate Banking in the United States

* Rising Unemployment and Business Failures in Selected States and Regions, along with a Trend Toward Greater Economic Inequality Among the States, Resulted in New Interstate Banking Legislation in an Effort to Strengthen Local Banks and Bring in New Capital.	* The Need for Qualified Management and Skilled Professionals Has Required Banks to Enter Broader Regional, National, and International Labor Markets, Which an Interstate Banking Organization Can Do More Effectively Than Smaller Banking Organizations.
* A Search for the Risk—Reducing Benefits of Geographic Diversification — Spreading Service Offerings Across Many Different Markets — Led Larger Banks to Seek New Authority to Cross State Lines.	* The Desire to Expand Domestic Operations That Are Considered Less Risky and Require Less "Tooling Up" Than Venturing into Foreign—Based Assets (especially international loans) Encouraged Many Large Banks to Enter Neighboring States.
* Competitive Responses of the States to the Legislative Initiatives of Neighboring States Trying to Attract Their Banks Away Led to New Interstate Banking Legislation, Even in States Such As Texas and Oklahoma Where Branch Banking Had Been Prohibited for Many Years.	* The Departure of Many Large Business Customers Who Choose to Raise Their Funds in the Open Market Through Sales of Securities Rather Than Through Bank Loans, Pressured Banks to Seek Out New Customers in Distant Markets.
* Improved Stock Values for Banks and Bank Holding Companies That Had Become Targets for Interstate Mergers and Acquisitions Encouraged the Stockholders of Banks Targeted for Acquisition to Sell to the Highest Bidder.	* The Rise of Franchising of Financial Services Produced by One Banking Firm and Sold Through Other Firms Has Helped to Spread the Cost and the Risk of Developing and Marketing New Services.

quality of local government services. Indeed, it was this same reasoning in the nineteenth and early twentieth centuries that led many of the states bordering the West Coast and the Rockies to adopt statewide branch banking. If funds gathered by bank branch offices from many local communities could be pooled together, the capital needed by local and regional industries could be raised in sufficient amounts to sustain a high level of production

Table 2-2

Legal, Regulatory, and Technological Causes of the Spread of Full-Service Interstate Banking in the United States

*Changes in Federal Legislation During the Early and Mid-1980s Gave the FDIC and Other Federal Supervisory Authorities Greater Latitude in Dealing with Failing Depository Institutions and Arranging Mergers with Healthy Out-Of-State Banking Firms.

*Revisions in State Statutes Affecting Branching and Holding -Company Activity in Order to Promote Regulatory Equity Between Banks and Nonbank Financial-Service Firms Stimulated Greater Interest in Geographic Expansion.

*Deregulation of Deposit Interest Rates (lifting the federal government's limits on permissible deposit rates) Resulted in a Rise in the Average Cost of Bank Funds and Encouraged Bankers to Search for Lower Cost Funds and New Sources of Revenue.

*Further Development of Electronic Delivery Systems for Banking Services (including automated teller machines, fiber optic cable systems, facsimile machines, laser printers, integrated computer networks, and improved microchip technology) Has Made Possible Lower Costs for Producing and Selling High-Volume Services and Has Encouraged Banks to Expand Their Market Areas to Promote the Higher Volume of Sales Needed to Employ Up-to-Date Production and Delivery Equipment.

*The Failure of Congress and Many of the States to Liberalize the Service Powers of Banks (particularly in the real estate, consumer credit, and insurance areas) Has Forced U.S. Banking Firms to Search Harder for New Expansion Opportunities and for New Markets Within Traditional Legal and Regulatory Boundaries.

*The Barriers to Geographic Expansion into Foreign Markets Posed by Regulations and Cultural Barriers in Otherwise Economically Attractive Foreign Markets Have Caused Many Large Banks to Look Inward Toward Other States.

*A More Liberal Federal Anti-trust Policy That Has Approved More Mergers and the Possibility of a Return to More Restrictive Anti-trust Policies Under Future Presidential Administrations Has Acclerated Interstate Mergers.

*Economies of Scale for the Largest Banking Firms in Developing and Marketing New Services and in the Delivery of Some Traditional Services Have Motivated Bankers to Seek Out New Markets and New Service Offerings to Increase Their Sales Volume and Drive Down Their Operating Costs.

*Economies of Scope Have Created Opportunities for Banks to Save on Scarce Resources and Operating Costs If They Can Produce and Sell Multiple Services Using the Same Management Team and Physical Facilities.

and employment, effectively raising living standards. Farther east, such states as Delaware, Maine, and South Dakota, which had long struggled to increase their growth and expand their local economies, saw full-service interstate banking as an important first step toward their longer-range economic objectives.

However, perhaps nowhere in the United States was the need for an infusion of new capital to restore economic growth greater in the 1980s than in the Southwest—in particular, in the states of Louisiana, New Mexico, Oklahoma, and Texas. Texas is the third most populous state in the United States and, until the cataclysmic decline in oil prices in the mid-1980s, was a veritable engine of prosperity and new jobs. Between 1981 and 1987, however, Texas lost just over a quarter of a million jobs, brought on by plunging oil prices that sharply reduced both private royalty incomes and state tax revenues. The entire southwestern region also was severely impacted by declining prices for agricultural commodities, especially beef and cotton.

Moreover, as oil and agricultural prices spiraled downward, commercial and residential real estate markets, particularly those connected to key cities in the South and Southwest, such as Albuquerque, Dallas, Houston, New Orleans, Oklahoma City, and Tulsa, suddenly became glutted with vacant properties. Office buildings, apartment complexes, and homes sold at auction for a fraction of their former value, sometimes for even less than their construction cost. Adding to the swelling economic problems of this region was the deteriorating Mexican economy, severely wounded by declining oil prices and falling farm values. As the Mexican peso plummeted against the U.S. dollar in international markets, cross-border trade declined sharply due to increases in the relative prices of American goods. The results of all these economic pressures were increasing numbers of business bankruptcies and loan defaults, leading to the collapse of dozens of commercial banks and thrift institutions in the region. In Oklahoma and Texas—the most severely impacted of the southwestern states—the possibility that bank entry from outside this troubled region could rescue their banks and savings and loan associations and restore prosperity and jobs was an irresistible lure to these state governments to pass liberal interstate banking legislation.

Without question, the desire to improve local economies and to stimulate local and regional economic development stands at the top of the list of causal factors behind interstate banking. Yet, remarkably, it must also rank as one of the most questionable reasons for allowing full-service banks to cross state lines. Several research studies dating from the 1960s (which we will examine in Chapter 4) find little correlation between the type of banking structure a state has and its economic growth or the standard of living enjoyed by its citizens. Rather, other powerful forces—a state's natural resources, its strategic location vis-à-vis markets for manufactured goods and farm commodities, and the propensity of its citizens to save—appear to be far more important in shaping the character of a state's economy, the availability of jobs, and the speed with which economic development occurs.

Moreover, it should be obvious to state and local economic planners that a policy that encourages new industry to leave other states and move to a new locale can only be successful if those other states are willing to stand idly by and let their firms leave. A fundamental lesson of American history is that the 50 states are competitive with each other and will quickly mimic successful economic programs that other states have developed. Typically, the first states to gamble with a new economic-development plan, such as attracting firms from other states, are most likely to reap significant economic advantages. Those states that act later, however, are far less likely to achieve the economic benefits they seek.

THE NEED TO RESCUE FAILING BANKS AND THRIFT INSTITUTIONS AND THEIR DEPOSITORS

Related to the desire to foster economic growth and development is public concern for the fate of failing banks and thrifts, and especially for their depositors. Colorado is an excellent case in point.

In 1987 and 1988 Colorado lawmakers were confronted with serious financial problems undermining the soundness of the state's industrial banks. Similar to consumer-finance companies that attract savings deposits from individuals and families and make personal loans, the industrial banks of Colorado had fallen on hard times due to deregulation of financial services and a troubled regional economy caught in the worldwide oil glut. The Colorado legislature subsequently ordered all industrial banks within the state to apply for FDIC deposit insurance. However, shortly thereafter, 14 of the state's industrial banks were declared insolvent. A payoff of depositors from Colorado's deposit insurance fund was not possible because that fund held only about $2 million in reserves—a small fraction of the amount of deposits held by its insolvent industrial banks. The endangered depositors formed a vocal lobby group and picketed the state capital, leading the legislature to grant an exception to the scheduled gradual phase-in of interstate bank entry into Colorado.

A special 90-day period was set aside in the spring and summer of 1988 during which out-of-state banking companies could enter Colorado, either to buy out the interest of an existing out-of-state investor in the state's banks (e.g., First Interstate Banks of California or Ameritrust of Ohio) or to make a new Colorado acquisition, provided the acquirer also agreed to make a substantial contribution to the industrial banks' insurance fund. On June 15, 1988, Ameritrust Company sold its interest in Central Banks of Colorado to First Banks of Minneapolis, Minnesota, which turned out to be the only bidder. Presumably, other out-of-state banking organizations could see little benefit from early entry into Colorado because they would have to bail out the industrial banks' insurance fund and because significant uncertainties surrounded the condition of the Colorado economy in the wake of the oil boom's collapse.

Similarly, in Texas and Oklahoma, the worldwide oil-price collapse in the mid-1980s generated bank failures at a rate not seen since the Great Depression of the 1930s. In 1986 Texas accounted for about one-quarter of all bank failures in the United States, and that state continued to experience record bank and savings and loan failures in 1987, 1988, and 1989. Texas' holding companies had grown very fast when the region's economy was booming and soon held more than three-quarters of the state's total bank assets and deposits. When several of these industry leaders were on the brink of toppling, state lawmakers feared dire consequences for hundreds of smaller banks with whom they had close ties, as well as the possible loss of millions of dollars in tax revenues and thousands of jobs. The result was that Texas, which had written a prohibition against branch banking into its state constitution in the nineteenth century, quickly passed enabling legislation to allow interstate entry, effective on January 1, 1987, just four months after that law was passed. Moreover, Texas enacted one of the most liberal interstate banking laws at the time – a nonreciprocity statute allowing outside banking firms to enter even if other states blocked Texas banks from entering their territory. While four other states then had similar laws on their books, Texas was by far the largest nonreciprocity state to enact interstate banking legislation during the mid-1980s.

THE NEED TO PROMOTE REGULATORY EQUITY

Many state governments have experienced strong pressure from their banking lobbies over the years to "level the playing field" for their bankers vis-à-vis major nonbank competitors. Insurance companies such as Prudential-Bache, security dealers such as Merrill Lynch, and credit-card firms such as Shearson–American Express have increased their offerings of banklike services across the United States, unimpeded by restrictive federal or state branching laws. Many bankers, particularly those representing the largest money-center banks and bank holding companies, pleaded for parallel privileges that would allow them to grow at least as rapidly as their principal financial-service competitors and as fast as their largest corporate customers.

A survey conducted among Texas bankers by the Federal Reserve Bank of Dallas (1971) found many bankers lamenting the fact that several of their largest business customers had outgrown their banks' ability to provide credit. Both federal and state law prevented banks from lending unsecured more than a small percentage of the bank's capital and surplus.[1] Many bankers saw nothing less at stake than the future of banking itself. Traditional banks were in danger of being bypassed and made irrelevant because of their inability to overcome the burden of anachronistic federal and state regulations. True enough, bankers interested in penetrating interstate markets had found ways to do so (as we saw in Chapter 1) through nonbank business units, including Edge Act and Agreement corporations,[2] 4(c)(8) affiliated firms,[3] subsidiary service firms, and LPOs.[4] But these businesses were, for the most part, poor substitutes for full-service interstate banking. In fact, major bank holding companies divested themselves of some of their nonbank businesses during the 1980s due to lagging earnings, management control problems, and the appearance of more profitable opportunities elsewhere in both domestic and foreign markets.

IMPROVEMENTS IN TRANSPORTATION AND IN THE COMMUNICATION OF INFORMATION

Both the nation and the world have grown functionally smaller in recent years due to improvements in transportation and advances in communications equipment. Fiber optics, satellite transmission of radio and television signals, facsimile machines, computer networks, and laser technology have come to play key roles in the processing and transfer of information, including the information required to supply banking services to business and household customers.

These technological advances improve efficiency and reduce operating costs, provided a sufficient volume of sales is reached. Unfortunately for bankers, recent improvements in electronic transfers of information and financial transactions have also opened the door to nonbank suppliers of financial services that have reached into traditional banking markets and have stolen customers away. In brief, electronic transfers and other technological innovations have rendered state boundaries virtually meaningless to the production and delivery of banking services, especially the taking of deposits and the making of payments (as noted by Frodin [1982]).

Moreover, U.S. bankers have learned through hard-won experience in global markets that, unless they are willing to follow their customers into distant states and serve them irrespective of the distances involved, those same customers will be attracted away by other banks. Interstate expansion also gives banking firms access to more financial and human capital (managerial skills) — necessary ingredients for those banking organizations that choose to compete in global markets as well for the largest commercial and governmental clientele.

While improvements in transportation and communications technology have made full-service interstate banking more feasible now than at any other time in U.S. history, these technological changes have also presented bank managers with a serious dilemma. Acquiring brick-and-mortar banking facilities in distant states may no longer be as necessary as it was in the past because each bank's largest customers increasingly can be served electronically via telephone and satellite, through ATM networks, or through direct linkage of bank, home, and office computers. Yet banking firms with a strong *local* presence can build customer good will that promotes loyalty to the bank, even when other banks offer better terms on loans, deposits, and other services.

Banks with a local presence in the neighborhoods of large cities and in smaller outlying communities can be potent competitors in attracting retail (household) customers. This fact was demonstrated graphically in the 1970s when NOW accounts (interest-bearing checking accounts) were first developed in New England by mutual savings banks — state-chartered competitors with commercial banks. While commercial banks were late comers to New England's NOW market, they soon wrested away the leading market share of this new service from all other competitors in hundreds of local communities across New England. Why? Commercial banks had extensive branch office systems, which gave them a *local* presence in all of their target markets, while most of their competitors did not. Many household customers value having a local branch office to visit in order to resolve any problems that occur — for example, with checking account disputes that often arise concerning account balances, overdrafts, and service charges.

The dilemma for interstate banking organizations today, then, is a clash between their operating efficiency and the stability of their customer relationships, between greater cost effectiveness through adopting technological changes and greater service effectiveness through establishing full-service branches and making acquisitions in those local cities and towns with acceptable profit potential. Electronic advances have made it possible to serve distant customers, but, at the same time, have eroded customer loyalty to any particular bank and reduced personal contacts between bankers and their customers — a personal feature that many business and household customers value highly.

IMPROVED STOCK PRICES FOR BANKS
TARGETED FOR ACQUISITION

While many bankers fear takeovers — especially takeovers of family-held banking corporations — others have sought out potential acquirers in the hope of making substantial financial gains from rising stock prices. Indeed, even if banks are only courted as potential acquisitions but are not actually acquired, there is substantial research evidence now that mere *announcements* of planned acquisitions can result in short-term windfall gains to the shareholders of banks targeted for takeover. Thus, a substantial wealth incentive exists for small and moderate-size banks to position themselves for possible interstate mergers. This positioning strategy usually includes efforts to improve profitability, strengthen equity capital, maintain close control over operating expenses, rid loan portfolios of questionable assets, buy out dissident shareholders, and acquire desirable future office locations.

However, as we shall see more clearly later on, often the stockholders of acquiring interstate firms receive much smaller gains or no gains at all in the wake of announcements of interstate mergers. Consistent with the results observed for thousands of industrial mergers over the years, most of the financial benefits accruing to corporate stockholders appear to flow to shareholders of the acquired banks, rather than to those of the acquiring banking firms, as reported most recently in comprehensive studies by Fortier (1989) and Dennis and McConnell (1986). Indeed, shareholders of many acquiring firms may suffer a significant loss in the wake of interstate takeovers.

A dramatic example of this phenomenon occurred in July 1988 when NCNB Corp. of Charlotte, North Carolina, successfully bid to the FDIC to acquire troubled First RepublicBank Corp. While NCNB had a strong reputation for successful management, news of its bid for embattled First Republic sent the former's stock price sharply downward within minutes of the takeover announcement, though it recovered subsequently. Capital-market investors apparently feared that NCNB's capital and management skills would be strained to the breaking point in attempting to salvage First Republic's assets and customer relationships.

Interestingly enough, in those cases where a company's market value *increases* after a merger, there is evidence from studies by Lewellen (1971), Mason and Goudzaard (1976), and Levy and Sarnat (1970) that most of the gain is due to lower exposure to risk for the combined firm. Specifically, the debt capacity of the merged company appears to rise above the sum of the debt capacities of the individual firms involved. This *financial synergy* from a merger has far more research evidence to back it up than does the appearance of increased profitability—what many authorities call *operating synergy*—from a merger. In fact, not only is there little supporting evidence that mergers increase profits, but also some research studies find that businesses in the same industry that do *not* merge often outperform those that do. However, the existence of financial synergy in many mergers can bring major long-run benefits to the companies involved, including lower costs from raising financial capital, reduced bankruptcy costs, and increased investor interest in the resulting combined firm. At least some of these gains appear to arise from a wealth transfer from the creditors of premerger firms to the stockholders of postmerger companies. Thus, while profitability may be the principal goal pursued by the shareholders of *acquired* banking firms, more plausible goals for *acquiring* banks appear to be risk reduction, lower capital costs, and expanded borrowing capacity to support the future expansion of the consolidated banking company.

THE NEED FOR QUALIFIED PROFESSIONAL TALENT

The changing technology of bank service production and delivery, increases in the span of management control associated with the growth of bank size, and asset-quality problems have all necessitated an upgrading of the skills required of bank managers today. Many banking firms have found that their local labor markets, including the universities and business schools they have traditionally relied on for new professional and managerial talent, can no longer fill all their staffing needs. Contacts with broader professional labor markets are required, and that need has stimulated many banks to cross state lines simply to find professional talent, especially in the fields of management information systems, auditing, legal affairs, and computer software.

This personnel factor has motivated both interstate acquirers and the institutions they purchase to become more conscious of the quality of personnel they attract and also more aware of the need for excellent bank management training programs. Historically, in American banking the largest money-center banks and bank holding companies have established the most elaborate management training programs; many of these last from several months to as long as two years during which time the new employee learns about the objectives, accounting procedures, marketing programs, and credit procedures followed by his or her institution. Often, the new employee is moved around every few weeks so the bank can discover where that person would best "fit" within the bank's organizational structure.

Smaller banks, which typically cannot afford such elaborate and expensive training procedures, will often attract away employees emerging from these training programs, particularly if the new manager has been able to add a few years of banking experience after graduating from a strong bank training program. Unfortunately for the smallest banks across the nation, deregulation and intense competition from other financial-service providers have forced many of these smaller banking firms to give up any pretense of a sound and thorough employee training program. In some cases the only choice possible in order to attract and hold quality management has been to sell out to an interstate banking company.

EXPANSION INTO DOMESTIC FIELDS
CONSIDERED LESS RISKY

Many regional money-center banks and bank holding companies have seized the opportunity created by interstate banking legislation to invade new markets with old services. Selling traditional banking services in new domestic markets is a form of bank growth and expansion that most bankers know how to deal with. Advertising slogans, marketing initiatives, and the pricing of traditional banking services represent challenges that most bankers feel comfortable in handling. Domestic expansion, therefore, is usually viewed as a less risky investment than venturing abroad into markets that are both economically and culturally unfamiliar.

An excellent example of how to be successful with an overwhelmingly domestically oriented growth strategy that emphasizes intensive "mining" of its well-understood geographic base is Barnett Banks of Florida. Barnett has managed to maintain adequate profitability and shareholder returns with an aggressive branch-office expansion program and numerous service innovations (such as discount security brokerage and free customer access to copy machines). Moreover, each service innovation appears to be tailored to the unique characteristics of the local communities Barnett serves. Barnett has successfully directed many of its service innovations and advertising campaigns at Florida's retired citizens, resulting in the rapid growth of high-balance deposit accounts and a doubling of its Florida deposit share over the past decade to more than 20 percent of the Florida market.

Barnett has rapidly expanded its branch-office network and, at the same time, promoted locally oriented, decentralized management. The local Barnett branch manager appears to have more responsibility than is true of most bank branch systems in the United States and can make several key decisions on site without consulting the home office. This decentralized management style allows the bank to respond more quickly to the challenges of a deregulated marketplace that has attracted many new competitors in recent years.[5] Moreover, Barnett's successful branch system emphasizes comprehensive planning at all levels, including detailed comparative monthly performance reports that relate current individual-unit performance to the historical performance of each member bank and to the latest company plan. The recent exceptional performance of Barnett Banks is evidence that decentralization and comprehensive planning are keys to the successful management of large interstate banking systems today.

THE DEPARTURE OF MANY LARGE BUSINESS
CREDIT CUSTOMERS FOR OTHER MARKETS

Beginning in the 1950s and 1960s large numbers of corporations that formerly relied on U.S. banks for most of their short-term and medium-term funding began to bypass their banks. Most of these firms entered the domestic commercial paper market where large amounts of funds could be raised on short notice by those businesses with impeccable credit ratings. While initially the paper market met the needs of only the largest and best-known U.S. corporations—the roughly 700 to 800 U.S. companies with unquestioned credit quality—this market rapidly expanded in the 1970s and 1980s to bring in hundreds of new, smaller domestic firms, as well as large foreign industrial and financial-service firms. These new entrants were able to break into the high-quality paper market by getting selected banks to guarantee their credit, thus substituting a bank's superior credit rating for the lower credit rating of its customers. Later, as the Eurodollar market rose to a position of global dominance in the 1970s, U.S. banks found themselves losing more of their best borrowers to foreign banks (especially the British, Canadian, French, Japanese, and West German merchant banks) which could accommodate the loan requests of American firms by selling dollar-denominated certificates of deposit in London, Singapore, and other world financial centers.

Still another new competitor with American banks for the credit accounts of the largest U.S. corporations—the Eurocapital markets—emerged in the late 1970s and 1980s. Major corporations from all over the globe discovered the phenomenon of *spread compression* in the financial markets of Western Europe. While the largest U.S. firms often found that prime-rated borrowings in European markets were as costly or even more costly than those in the United States, the cost spread between top-quality and lower-quality borrowings frequently was much narrower (e.g., less than a percentage point in Europe compared to as much as two percentage points in U.S. financial markets). These lower credit-risk premiums in Europe, as Beidleman (1985) observes, have lured many American companies to overseas markets to find the capital they need.

As more and more U.S. companies left their home banks in favor of foreign markets, leading American money-center and regional banks began to look inward for other business customers. Their particular interest soon came to rest on domestic businesses that were too small in size, too constrained by their lower credit ratings, or too specialized in their funding needs to be able to tap the open market for funds. This so-called "middle market" of smaller and medium-size firms represents a potentially high-profit market with a unique combination of financial-service needs, such as management consulting services, financial planning, property management services, cash management assistance, and both short- and long-term financing to purchase inventories and capital equipment. Today it is this middle market of business-oriented financial services that has become the principal battleground on which contending interstate banking firms struggle for industry leadership in the United States.

THE RISE OF FRANCHISING IN RETAIL BANKING

As important as this middle market is to most interstate banks today, it is not the *sole* battlefield on which these firms fight for market share. Interstate banking organizations also have targeted a second market at least as important and potentially much larger than middle-size business firms—the high-volume household financial-services market. This market, with its great potential for growth and profitability, has resulted in the spread of franchised financial services.

Indeed, the concept of franchised banking services appeared at roughly the same time that interstate banking began to grow. Three major franchise networks emerged in the early 1980s to sell primarily retail banking services—First Interstate Bancorporation, First Nationwide Network, and Norwest Corporation. The basic idea was to give subscribing smaller banks across the nation access to service production and delivery capacity normally available only to the largest money-center institutions and to make bank service offerings fully competitive with the retail financial services sold by the largest nonbank institutions, such as Merrill Lynch, Prudential-Bache, Sears, and Shearson–American Express. Banks signing onto these networks could remain independently owned, but still capture the advantages of professional expertise in marketing and customer service and gain access to the latest technology. The principal banking services sold through franchise networks today include credit cards, debit cards, check cashing and automated teller networks, discount brokerage, insurance protection, financial planning and counseling, mortgage banking, and customer account relocations. Many franchises also provide aid related to internal operations, assisting these smaller institutions with advertising, management consulting, employee training, and asset-liability management.

Signees to current franchise networks are predominantly banks already armed with a full range of services, but without the capability of successful service innovation. Most franchise systems require their subscribers to adopt the name of the franchise network, pay a sign-up fee, and assess royalties connected to the volume of sales, volume of earnings, or asset size of the subscribing organization. In general, franchise-purchasing banks have been successful at increasing their market share of local deposits and loans, and some have been able to lower their interest costs, as well as gain a small edge over competitors in sales promotion.

Franchised banking services, including the major bank credit-card systems—Visa and Master-Charge—have made a significant contribution to the spread of interstate banking in promoting nationwide bank name identification. For decades, bankers have sought to achieve the name recognition for quality services held by motel chains (e.g., Ramada Inn and Holiday Inn), oil companies (e.g., Texaco and Shell), and realtors (e.g., Gallery of Homes and Century 21). Leading American banks—BankAmerica, Chase Manhattan, and Citicorp—have become recognizable names to millions of household and business customers through their franchised credit-card programs, building trust with both existing and potential customers throughout the nation. In the future, bank credit cards will also give most of these customers access to other banking services, such as savings accounts, funds transfer, balance inquiries, and check verification. In effect, through franchising many money-center banks have moved in "next door" to serve customers located anywhere. Franchised financial services have literally opened the door to nationwide banking in the United States.

THE FAILURE OF CONGRESS AND THE STATES TO LIBERALIZE BANK SERVICE POWERS

The U.S. Congress and many of the states have continued to follow a conservative, "go slow" attitude toward the expansion of service powers for banks. Moreover, pressure from competing nonbank industries, especially security dealers and insurance carriers, has frequently brought forth legislative proposals to strengthen existing roadblocks against new services for banks. For example, in 1987 Congress passed the Competitive Equality Banking Act which placed a moratorium on any federal legalization of new banking services. Again in September 1988 the Energy and Commerce Committee of the U.S. House of Representatives proposed legislation to block any new laws that would grant banks broad security underwriting and insurance powers. As noted by Taylor (1988), the Energy and Commerce Committee proposed to prevent banks from underwriting corporate debt obligations, from selling investments in mutual funds, and from marketing additional insurance products. However, smaller banks holding total assets of less than $500 million would be permitted to sell shares in mutual funds to their customers and to engage in municipal revenue bond underwriting.

This version of the newest proposed banking bill appears to increase the chances for congressional deadlock over how much freedom U.S.-chartered banks and bank holding companies should have, at least within their domestic markets. Similar policy deadlocks at both federal and state levels in recent years have led many larger banking companies to, first, seek out those few states that have enacted broader service powers for banks (e.g., South Dakota which permits bank sale of some insurance policies). Moreover, Congress' failure to broaden bank service capabilities has led the largest banks to substitute greater geographic diversification (through acquisitions and mergers) for product-line diversification (e.g., offering new services).

However, at least some of these federal barriers to bank entry into new service lines, especially in underwriting and dealing in corporate securities, are eroding, thanks to the bank regulatory agencies. When Congress failed to pass new legislation expanding the list of permissible services for banks in 1988, for example, the Federal Reserve Board announced early in 1989 that it would look favorably on bank holding-company applications for greater securities underwriting powers to buy and resell their customers' security offerings. By October of that year both Bankers Trust Company and J. P. Morgan of New York had filed applications to deal in and underwrite corporate notes and bonds, preferred stock, and common stock. Almost simultaneously, Citicorp asked for the Federal Reserve's permission to launch an underwriting service for its customers' corporate bonds, while Chase Manhattan Corp. indicated its intention to apply for authority to underwrite and deal in preferred stock, as well as in corporate notes and bonds.

Obviously, if federal banking rules in the potentially high-profit securities field are further liberalized, this step will have profound implications for the future of interstate banking. For one thing, such a policy decision would be likely to shift the attention of leading U.S. money-center banks in New York, Illinois, and California from an intense focus on interstate banking toward the new opportunities available in security underwriting. This would leave leading regional banks in Atlanta, Charlotte, Dallas, Denver, Houston, Kansas City, Miami, Minneapolis, Phoenix, Portland, and St. Louis a more wide open field in which to pursue their strategies for interstate expansion in order to capture a larger share of the nation's small business and household service markets.

Interestingly enough, whenever Congress has reached a stalemate over new bank service powers or the possible geographic deregulation of U.S. banking, these issues have tended to gravitate toward the state legislatures and the federal regulatory agencies, which can use their authority to interpret the law in order to grant banks more opportunities to develop new markets. And, for the most part, state and federal banking agencies have responded positively, providing at least some of the freedoms sought by U.S. bankers. As we saw above, authority to engage in the underwriting of corporate securities has now come from the Federal Reserve Board. In contrast, the issue of banks gaining access to real estate and insurance services now seems to reside largely at the state level. For example, by the end of 1988, 22 states had passed legislation giving the banks they charter authority to offer various kinds of insurance services. These state legislative initiatives, too, could have a powerful impact on the scope and direction of future interstate bank expansion.

Banks headquartered in states that grant their banking institutions new service powers may have less need to expand across state lines because they can substitute product-line diversification for geographic diversification in order to reduce risk and open up fresh sources of revenue. Moreover, states that have not enacted such enabling legislation will be under pressure to extend greater service powers to their own banking institutions. And, judging by the speed with which the states have responded to each other's earlier legislative initiatives in the banking field, the future liberalization of banking service powers in a majority of state capitals now appears highly probable. If so, this movement at the state government level will *slow* the pace of full-service interstate banking significantly in the years ahead.

DEREGULATION OF DEPOSIT INTEREST RATES HAS RAISED BANK COSTS

Two landmark pieces of federal legislation—the Depository Institutions Deregulation and Monetary Control Act of 1980 and the Garn–St Germain Depository Institutions Act of 1982—set in motion sweeping changes in the rules binding banks and thrift institutions, such as savings and loan associations. Probably the most important change for banks was the gradual lifting of federal interest-rate ceilings on deposits. These maximum legal deposit rates were originally set in place during the 1930s in the mistaken belief that excessive rate bidding for deposits had gotten many banks into serious trouble, contributing to record numbers of bank failures during the Great Depression. The Depository Institutions Deregulation Committee, composed of the chairmen of the Federal Reserve Board, the Federal Deposit Insurance Corporation, and the Federal Home Loan Bank Board, as well as the Comptroller of the Currency and the Secretary of the Treasury, began dismantling these deposit-rate ceilings in 1981. By the spring of 1986 all deposit-rate ceilings except those applying to conventional checking accounts had been removed.

The lifting of these deposit interest-rate limits had at least two major effects on American banks—one favorable and the other potentially unfavorable, especially for smaller banking institutions. Without these legally imposed rate ceilings, banks could more easily retain their customers' deposits, rather than losing these deposits to competitors, as long as each bank was willing to pay the going market interest rate for use of its customers' money. However, the *average cost* of bank funds rose significantly because American banks were now compelled to pay *market* interest rates on most of their deposits, rather than being able to attract and hold deposits with submarket interest rates.[6] Compounding this rate effect was the rational response of tens of thousands of bank customers who shifted both their checking account balances and the funds originally placed in low-yield savings deposits into higher-return money-market accounts that carried flexible interest rates and checking account privileges as well.

This sudden upward surge in deposit costs forced the management of thousands of American banks to search for new ways to reduce operating costs—such as making greater use of automation and reducing their staffing in order to lower labor costs—and to increase operating revenues—such as developing new services and entering new markets. The spreading legalization of interstate banking has made *both* bank responses—cost reduction and revenue enhancement—more possible. Entering new markets via interstate acquisition and merger has increased sales volume for those U.S. banking organizations active in the interstate market which can help lower their production cost per unit of service provided. Interstate banking has also allowed the tapping of new sources of revenue from new markets, helping to offset the higher deposit costs created by federal government deregulation of the industry.

BARRIERS TO FOREIGN EXPANSION ENCOURAGE BANKS TO EXPAND MARKETS AT HOME

Until recently, many otherwise attractive foreign markets were simply closed to United States banks due to government regulations which, in some cases, were reinforced by cultural and language barriers. For example, while liberalized significantly in 1982, Japanese regulations still tightly control the entry of United States and other foreign banks into Japan's home markets. Once admitted, U.S. banks operating in Japan also face restrictions on selling certificates of deposit and on currency trading. Foreign investments in Japan carry the prior regulatory requirement that the home government must be formally notified of the intended investment, and any such investment plan can be rejected for national security or competitive reasons. Switzerland requires approval from local governments for some real estate transactions involving foreign investors. Foreign banks lending in Canada face the imposition of official lending limits and possible governmental influence on the composition of their loan portfolios. France restricts the ability of foreign-based firms to underwrite securities in the domestic market, while the United Kingdom imposes limitations on the ability of foreign firms to acquire domestic financial institutions.[7]

When the states began to open their borders to outside entry, many of the largest U.S. banks simply took the path of least resistance and chose to expand across state boundaries rather than stepping up their operations overseas. The international debt crisis of the 1980s, precipitated when many nations of the Third World were simply unable to pay off their bank loans, added to this tendency for larger U.S. banks to stay at home and look for promising sales opportunities inside U.S. markets, either in their traditional markets or across the nation.

THE SEARCH FOR PRODUCTION ECONOMIES TO KEEP OPERATING COSTS DOWN

Commercial banks, like many other firms operating in the volatile era of the 1970s and 1980s, faced the specter of rapidly rising operating costs. While the negative impact of soaring energy costs was well publicized, increases in bank labor costs — particularly the cost of hiring new personnel — outpaced all bank operating costs in the long run. A developing shortage of entry-level workers caused by the shifting age distribution of the U.S. population forced banks to compete against each other, and against nonbank firms as well, to secure their fair share of each year's crop of college graduates. The obvious solution to this long-run problem seemed to be for aggressive banks to grow in size, striving to reach that optimal volume of service output at which production cost per unit is the lowest.

In actuality there are two kinds of production economies that each banking firm may be able to enjoy if its output of services grows large enough as it penetrates new markets. The first is economies of scale — cost savings related to the growth in output of one or more banking services. Any bank or bank holding company may be able to reach a range of service output in which production costs increase more slowly than output. The result is a decline in average production cost per unit as a bank's output of services expands. In contrast, economies of scope exist where the bank can *jointly* produce two or more services at a lower cost per unit than if each of these services were produced by a single-product firm. In theory, a bank producing and selling several different services has a cost advantage over a firm producing only one banking service because the former can make more intensive use of both management and capital than the latter.

Economists argue that any industry possessing substantial economies of scale and economies of scope will, in the long run, come to be dominated by relatively large, highly diversified firms. This is because the largest companies, over time, will use their lower production costs to price services lower than their competitors and drive out smaller firms. For those industries with *some* output-related cost savings, but not great size-related cost differences, a mixture of both small and large firms in the industry is more likely.

As we will note again in Chapter 4, however, there is little convincing evidence that banks experience significant cost savings as they grow. The optimal bank size, costwise, appears to be around $100 million in deposits or perhaps $150 million in total assets. Beyond that size limit, bank operating costs per unit begin to grow again. To be sure, U.S. bankers may still perceive cost savings from growth and market expansion and use that perception as a guiding star for their interstate ventures. However, recent research on the behavior of bank production costs suggests that cost savings due to growth in the production of most financial services are largely illusory. If production cost savings are a key motivating factor for interstate banking, either U.S. bankers who elect to expand across state lines in pursuit of those savings are going to be sadly disappointed, or there must be significant bank cost–bank size relationships that recent research has yet to find.

EFFECTS OF A MORE LIBERAL FEDERAL ANTI-TRUST POLICY

The wave of bank and nonbank mergers of the 1980s, including interstate banking acquisitions, has been ascribed by many observers to the more liberal anti-trust policies of the administration of President Ronald Reagan, as opposed to the anti-trust rules followed by earlier federal administrations. For example, the Justice Department under President Reagan challenged less than a third the number of mergers that were challenged by federal government lawyers during the Carter administration. Of the 20 largest business mergers in U.S. history, nearly all have occurred since 1980, after the Reagan administration took office.

Recent American anti-trust policy has its roots in the widely debated efficient markets theory. This conceptual model posits that the financial markets are so efficient that all firms are appropriately valued, so there are no substantial bargains obtainable through merger. Moreover, if one firm acquires another and thereby diminishes competition in the relevant market area, the private marketplace will soon respond to such an adverse structural change. If a market becomes significantly more concentrated as the result of a merger, the surviving firms will reap increased profits, and those incremental returns will attract *new* competitors. As new firms do enter and begin to produce and sell goods and services, prices charged the customer will tend to fall, and the excess profits soon will be eliminated.

When a change in presidential administrations (and in regulatory philosophy) became imminent in the late 1980s, the pace of interstate bank mergers accelerated because of uncertainty over what the new administration's anti-trust policy would be. There were, for example, investor fears that a new administration in Washington would revert to the more traditional approach to anti-trust law, challenging all those those acquisitions and mergers that threatened to bring about significant increases in market concentration and reductions in competition. Thus, many interstate bank acquisitions were rushed forward in the late 1980s before the wide-open gate of federal anti-trust policy was slammed shut or, at least, appreciably narrowed by the next presidential administration.

INTERSTATE BANKING FROM A BROADER PERSPECTIVE

In this chapter we have examined the most important causes of the full-service interstate banking movement — the dominant structural trend in U.S. banking as the twentieth century draws to a close. As we have seen, these causes have their roots in fundamental economic, demographic, technological, and regulatory changes that are reshaping American business and society and redefining the role of banks within that society. For most of its history, U.S. banking has been predominantly a locally oriented business, operating within narrowly defined boundaries of geography and service lines. Today, however, American banks increasingly find themselves immersed in the broad social, political, and economic issues of their states and regions as the industry becomes increasingly dominated by the largest banking organizations.

Whatever its causes, then, the specter of unprecedented interstate (and, ultimately, nationwide) full-service banking makes bankers and their institutions ever more visible to the public eye. As a result, American bankers are expected to do more and to contribute more to their local and regional communities and to the statewide markets they serve. Indeed, as we have seen, the potential of interstate banking to bring in new capital and create new jobs has been a key motivation for the passage of most new interstate banking laws. Whether the interstate banking movement can deliver those hoped-for economic benefits will depend not only on the skill of the management and staff of these institutions, but also on the willingness of federal and state governments to further deregulate the industry and provide it with new service powers that fully accommodate changing public service needs.

Much has already been accomplished in the movement toward nationwide full-service banking. However, deregulation of an industry is not a halfway journey. If a deregulated marketplace for financial services is to serve the common good to the fullest extent possible, it must be pursued to its logical conclusion: freedom for private decision makers on both the demand side and the supply side of the financial marketplace. Only then can we step back from the competitive cauldron of daily activity and see if the journey toward complete deregulation has been worth the price we have paid along the way. Today we find ourselves only partway there; nevertheless, we cannot fairly disparage what has been accomplished to date because it offers us the prospect of a still brighter future. We would do well to remember an old Chinese proverb: "Even the journey of a thousand miles begins with a single step." The passage of enabling legislation to open the doors to interstate banking by a majority of the states *is* that first important step in the long and controversial journey toward full-service nationwide banking.

NOTES

1. Since passage of the Garn–St Germain Depository Institutions Act of 1982, national banks have been permitted to lend unsecured to a single customer only up to 15 percent of their capital and surplus. Most states have allowed somewhat more liberal lending policies. Texas, for example, has permitted unsecured loans up to 25 percent of a state-chartered bank's capital and surplus.

2. Edge Act corporations are special subsidiaries of national banks, created by application to the Federal Reserve Board and required to devote a majority of their resources to international transactions. Agreement corporations are international subsidiaries of state-chartered banks with powers similar to Edge Act corporations.

3. An affiliated business firm that offers services closely related to banking (e.g., offering credit life insurance or dealing in mortgage loans) and has been approved by the Federal Reserve Board for acquisition by banking companies under the terms of Section 4(c)(8) of the Bank Holding Company Act is referred to as a 4(c)(8) firm.

4. LPOs are loan production offices which seek out new accounts for the bank's home office, but do not take deposits.

5. For example, as noted recently by Ricks (1987), the presidents of individual banks within the Barnett system have the option to turn down loan participations with other Barnett banks and make local decisions on the terms of large business loans that most branch and holding-company systems normally decide on only at the headquarters level.

6. It has been argued, however, that federal deposit-rate ceilings did not really give American banks a free ride at the depositors' expense. In order to retain each customer's deposit, banks in a competitive financial marketplace must offer equivalent value to at least match the customer's next best alternative use of funds. This means that the rational depositor must be offered an explicit rate of return up to the legal ceiling rate allowed plus an implicit rate of return (such as free postage to send in deposits or make withdrawals and a convenient branch office in the depositor's neighborhood to reduce transaction cost and inconvenience) at least equal to market

rates of return on investments of comparable risk. The elements that make up the implicit return to the depositor are expensive items for a bank, especially the building of new neighborhood-convenient branch offices. In all probability the more than 40,000 bank branch offices in the United States today represent overbuilding on a grand scale — something that would not have been necessary had American banks been able to offer explicit deposit rates competitive with going market interest rates instead of below-market regulated interest rates.

7. For a good summary of the regulations placed on banks and nonbank investors in industrialized countries, see Federal Reserve Bank of New York, *International Integration of Financial Markets and U.S. Monetary Policy*. (New York: Federal Reserve Bank of New York, December 1987), especially pp. 57–59.

troller of the Currency) held, in a series of rulings between 1865 and 1920, that national banks could offer their services from only *one* location. This regulatory decision to outlaw branch offices was based on language contained in the National Bank Act of 1863, which had created a new system of federally chartered (national) banks. That Civil War statute stipulated that the charter application of any proposed new national bank must contain a description of "'the place where its operations . . . were to be carried on, designating the state . . . and also the particular county and city'" (Trescott 1963, 87).

Congress had planned on many state-chartered banks' leaving their state banking systems and joining the new national banking system after the Civil War. The national banking system was generally thought to be stronger than any state banking system, thereby promoting industry safety and public confidence in American banks. In addition, Congress expected a significant increase in federal government revenues as the hundreds of what were formerly state-chartered banks paid their membership fees and became part of the national banking system. Even more important, during the Civil War itself the National Bank Act required new national banks and any state-chartered banks joining the national system to purchase federal government bonds before they made any loans.[1] This would aid the government in financing the Civil War through borrowing, rather than taxation, and thus avoid further public outcry against continuing an unpopular and costly war. Unfortunately for congressional planners, large numbers of state-chartered banks refused at first to join the national banking system due to its restrictions prohibiting branch banking. The state banks that had branch offices simply did not want to give up those offices. Congress then amended the National Bank Act in 1865, allowing those state-chartered banks that elected to join the federal system to retain the branch offices they already owned and operated.

THE RISE OF BRANCH BANKING

Late in the nineteenth century, concern that many smaller communities were not receiving adequate banking services led to proposals that branching by both federal and state banks be allowed. The onset of deep economic recessions in the 1870s and 1880s and periodic panics on Wall Street created financial problems for smaller banks in outlying areas. Most of these institutions had placed their cash surpluses with large money-center institutions which, in turn, loaned out those funds to large corporate borrowers and security investors. When bond and stock prices fell, many of those loans were defaulted, and smaller banks in outlying areas were frequently unable to recover their funds.

The damage wrought by economic recessions and financial panics on Wall Street freshened the historic debate over the territorial powers of American banks. Branching seemed to promise greater protection against the risk of economic downturns that might weaken a particular local market and threaten any bank that was selling its services exclusively in that market. An important parallel with the Canadian banking system was drawn by branching's advocates. During the Great Depression of the 1930s, for example, the United States lost thousands of banks due to massive business bankruptcies and unemployment, but in Canada, where only a handful of banks operated hundreds of branch offices, there was not a single bank failure.

Interestingly enough, it was not economic downturns, but changing technology that provided the foundation for the growth of branch banking in the United States. The advancing technologies of communication, transportation, and agricultural production began to have a profound effect on the territorial spread of U.S. banking early in the twentieth century. The mechanization of agriculture sharply reduced the demand for labor on the nation's farms. At the same time the development of the automobile and continued expansion of the nation's rail system made possible the movement of both people and produce from farms and smaller rural communities into the cities. In turn, the development of large-scale industry and assembly-line production created a demand for the labor power being released by the nation's farms. Within the cities themselves an urban fringe of homes and businesses soon developed, linked to the central city by auto and rail and by radio and newspaper advertising. More profit-motivated and less risk-averse bankers moved to take advantage of these developments, requesting permission to establish remote branch offices in order to follow their customers and to attract new loan and deposit business. Then, too, the greater ease of communications and more fluid movement of people made it easier for bankers to manage and supervise more complex and geographically diverse banking organizations.

Curiously, it was principally the banks chartered by the states that benefitted initially from these economic and technological changes. A few states hastened to grant their own banks express permission to establish branch offices or, at least, posed no opposition to branching activity, provided it was prudently managed and confined largely to further expansion within those communities already served. Federally chartered banks, on the other hand, were still barred by the anti-branching regulations enforced by the Comptroller of the Currency.

THE EMERGENCE OF BANK HOLDING COMPANIES

For many national banks, as well as smaller state-chartered banks, however, a new organizational form—the bank holding company—was soon developed to avoid regulatory restrictions against branching and to provide other advantages as well, such as savings on taxes. A bank holding company could be a corporation, partnership, or proprietorship that held a substantial ownership interest in one or more banks. In some instances the holding company simply held bank stock as a security investment, content to receive the interest or dividends generated by the stock of the banks it had acquired, but not interested in managing those banks. In other cases the holding company would treat its affiliated banks as though they were branch offices, with all the key decisions about personnel, fund raising, and funds management made at the holding-company level.

In the great majority of instances, however, bank holding companies tended to be less centralized and less closely controlled than branch banking organizations. This has frequently been true because their affiliated banks may not be completely owned by the company. Even where an affiliate is 100 percent owned by the holding company, however, concessions granted to shareholders or management of the bank when it was first purchased may have left the acquired institution with considerable autonomy to make its own decisions. In this instance the holding-company form becomes more a loose confederation of banking firms than a centralized organization closely controlling a network of satellite offices.

Early in the history of the holding-company movement, holding-company acquisitions of banks were disproportionately heavy in the Midwest and the South—for example, in the states of Florida, Minnesota, Missouri, Texas, and Wisconsin. These states prohibited or severely restricted the creation of branch offices by their banks, which were struggling to keep up with a changing and more mobile customer base. The most pressing needs in these particular states were for larger business loans to speed the development of the industrial sector and for consumer credit to meet the growing financial needs of individuals and families. The key advantage of the holding-company form of organization in bringing smaller banks together to make more credit available was the absence of federal restrictions. There would be no effective federal law limiting bank holding-company activity until after World War II and very few serious state restrictions against holding-company operations at any time in American history.

Unfortunately for the advocates of branch banking and holding companies, better organized and more vocal opposition emerged early in this century and, for a time, dominated the public pronouncements of bank regulators and trade organizations, especially the American Bankers Association (ABA). While World War I was raging in Europe, the ABA at its annual convention in 1916 voted against branch banking, opposing its adoption "in any form" by either the federal government or the states. The Federal Reserve Board and the Office of the Comptroller of the Currency, on the other hand, argued that federally chartered banks should be allowed to open and operate branch offices in those metropolitan areas and counties where their home office was situated.

A key reason for this reversal of long-time federal policy against branch banking was the emerging opinion in Washington, D.C., that serious prob-

lems with competitive inequality were emerging within the American banking system. Federally chartered institutions were limited to a single office,
while banks chartered by the states and often serving the very same communities were able to hold onto their more mobile customers by establishing
neighborhood-convenient branch offices. Nevertheless, vocal opposition to
branching from the industry's principal trade groups continued to grow and
surfaced repeatedly in national and regional bankers' meetings for another
decade before action was taken by the Congress in 1927.

The philosophy of outlawing branch offices to avoid concentrated banking power was jolted and then severely weakened by a series of economic
cataclysms in the 1920s and 1930s. The agricultural depression of the 1920s
brought on the failure of hundreds of small community banks, particularly
those serving farming communities and smaller trade centers. At the same
time heavy industry in the northeastern and upper-midwestern states, which
had adopted mass production methods, needed large doses of financial
capital that only the largest domestic and foreign banking institutions could
supply. Fearful of losing more of their biggest business customers to foreign
banks, federally chartered banks in the nation's financial centers began to
pressure Congress for new branching powers.

PASSAGE OF THE McFADDEN–PEPPER AND
GLASS–STEAGALL ACTS

Some national banks doubted the will of Congress to ultimately grant
branching privileges and simply switched their allegiance from the federal
system to their home-state bank-chartering authority. Facing lobbying pressure from both sides of the issue and the threat of large-scale withdrawals of
banks from the national banking system, Congress finally responded in
1927 with passage of the McFadden-Pepper Act. This new law allowed
national banks to branch within their home-office cities, provided state-
chartered banks had been extended the same privilege.

Many national banks still operated at a competitive disadvantage vis-à-vis
state-chartered banks, however, because the latter were allowed, in some
cases, to branch outside the city where their headquarters was located. Even
more liberal branching powers were wrested away by the money-center institutions in 1933 when the Glass-Steagall Act was passed. This federal law
allowed national banks to branch within a state, even outside their headquarters city, unless expressly denied that privilege by state law. With the
enactment of Glass-Steagall, national banks now possessed the same
branching powers that state-chartered banks did in their respective home
states. More important, the 1933 law affirmed the principle that was to last
for the next half century: the borders of each state should represent the outer
boundary for bank-branching activity and each state has the power to estab-

lish branch banking rules for all banks — state-chartered and federally chartered — within its own territory.

Much of the rationale for these broader branching powers was economic — to allow banks to grow large enough to be efficient and to survive in difficult economic times. This concession was won only at a substantial price, however, because the nation's largest money-center banks were compelled at the same time to give up the most profitable of their investment banking powers — the privilege to underwrite new issues of corporate stocks and bonds — from which they had garnered high profits in the past. Moreover, both the McFadden-Pepper Act and the Glass-Steagall Act goaded several states into action in order to take full advantage of the window of authority over branch banking granted them by Congress. For example, shortly after the McFadden-Pepper Act was passed, six states scattered across the nation voted to simply outlaw branch banking within their borders.

THE BANK HOLDING COMPANY ACT BECOMES LAW

The formula used by Congress to tackle the branch banking issue in the 1920s and 1930s was seized on again by the U.S. House and Senate in the 1950s to slow the nationwide spread of bank holding companies. Holding companies had become a significant force in banking early in this century, particularly in the nation's midsection. The Glass-Steagall Act of 1933 had granted regulatory powers over holding companies to the Federal Reserve Board, but the holding-company provisions of this law were so weak as to be ineffective.

Congress passed a stronger bill — the Bank Holding Company Act — in 1956, however. This new law granted supervisory powers to the Federal Reserve Board which was empowered to oversee holding-company acquisitions of banks (except where a holding company controlled only one bank) and the creation of *new* holding companies. Future acquisitions of banks were to be judged and evaluated by common standards, including the avoidance of significant damage to banking competition and the promotion of more prudent bank management policies that would strengthen, rather than weaken, any banks acquired.

Actually, the original Bank Holding Company Act as first passed by Congress did not forbid interstate expansion by banking companies or, for that matter, even mention the subject. However, several states, especially those in the upper Midwest, were fearful of the changes holding-company activity might bring to the banking industry within their borders. Senator Paul Douglas of Illinois subsequently introduced an amendment to the Bank Holding Company Act that became law in 1957. The Douglas Amendment [Section 3(d) of the Bank Holding Company Act] prohibited holding companies from acquiring banks in more than one state unless the new state to be entered expressly approved of entry from outside its borders. Several states (e.g., Louisiana and Oklahoma) moved quickly to prohibit any bank holding-company activity. Others decided to put a cap on the proportion of statewide assets, deposits, or capital that individual holding companies could amass over time. For example, Iowa limited total banking assets held by a single company to no more than 20 percent of the state's aggregate banking assets.

The Bank Holding Company Act did not wipe out interstate banking activity as some authorities had predicted it would. For one thing, seven companies that already held interstate investments in bank and nonbank firms were grandfathered by the new law, and, over time, these companies added to their interstate holdings. (The most notable of these grandfathered interstate firms was First Interstate Bancorp of California, which held stock in banks located in 13 different states.) The Bank Holding Company Act fell hardest on smaller banking companies that had just begun to venture across state lines. Most of these firms simply sold off those banks that would have brought them under federal supervision and regulation. One relatively simple way to escape the impact of the new law was to divest the holding company of all the banks it held, save one, because the law exempted one-bank companies from its regulatory provisions. However, those banking organizations that state authorities most feared—the largest East and West Coast banking organizations and those in the financial centers of the Midwest (e.g., Chicago, Dallas, Detroit, Kansas City, Minneapolis and St. Louis)—made even stronger use of the one-bank-company loophole to expand across state lines. For not only did the 1956 law fail to cover the activities of one-bank holding companies, but also it omitted controls on the nonbank business activities of these same firms.

NATIONWIDE EXPANSION OF BANK-CONTROLLED NONBANK BUSINESSES

The result of the one-bank-company legal loophole in the late 1960s and early 1970s was the rise of bank-centered conglomerate firms that laid claim to leasing companies, mortgage banking firms, finance company units, and other financial-service firms. However, many of these same companies went on to acquire some completely unrelated ventures in meat packing, trucking, manufacturing, and mining—to name but a few of the industries invaded by banking conglomerates. Moreover, the acquired nonbank firms could enter *any* state and expand overseas as well without receiving regulatory approval. Counting their international banking offices (Edge Act corporations) that can legally cross state lines, grandfathered interstate branches, affiliated nonbank banks, and permissible interstate acquisitions of failing banks and thrift institutions, U.S. banking companies controlled more than 7,000 interstate offices even before the states had passed their first interstate banking laws in the early 1980s (Syron 1984, 6).

Opponents decried the risks to banks of venturing into new business fields for which their managements had little expertise. If these nonbank businesses got into serious trouble, it was feared their operating losses soon would erode the scarce capital reserves of the banks involved. The result could be loss of public confidence, bank runs by worried depositors, and financial collapse.

Congress soon responded to this break in the dike of federal and state control over banking by passing the Bank Holding Company Act Amendments of 1970. The 1970 amendments grandfathered some of the oldest nonbank business acquisitions and imposed two important tests on any proposed future business acquisitions:

1. The *closely related test*, which stipulated that any new businesses acquired or launched de novo must be closely related to banking as to be "a proper incident thereto"; and

2. The *public benefits test*, which stipulated that there must be demonstrable benefits (such as the availability of new financial services or the lowering of service prices) that outweigh any costs involved (including the possible diminution of competition).

By and large, the states did not follow the federal government's lead in moving to restrict nonbank business acquisitions. Instead, the majority of states contented themselves with control over bank-branching activity and, in a small number of instances, control over within-state holding-company acquisitions of banks. Nor for a relatively long period of time did any of the states exercise their new authority to permit entry by out-of-state holding companies, though in a few instances grandfathered interstate firms were permitted to acquire new banks within their borders. The notable exception was Maine which saw pressing needs for increasing competition in retail financial services and for bringing more investment capital and more jobs into that state.

THE STATES MOVE TO ENCOURAGE ECONOMIC
DEVELOPMENT VIA INTERSTATE BANKING

Maine enacted a law in 1975 allowing any out-of-state holding company to enter and purchase existing banks or to set up new banking affiliates as long as reciprocal privileges were extended to Maine's bank holding companies. Maine thus became the first state to utilize the Douglas Amendment's built-in loophole that allowed an individual state to permit bank entry from outside if there were apparent local or regional benefits from such a move. For Maine the potential benefit lay in attracting new capital to develop the state and create more jobs for residents. Recognizing Maine's strong need for development capital, its state legislature built a provision into its interstate law to prevent out-of-state banking firms from draining away the state's scarce capital resources. It was six years, however, before a major interstate merger occurred in response to Maine's legislative initiative when, in August 1981, Key Banks of Albany, New York, acquired Depositors Corp. of Augusta. In order to stimulate additional interest in entering the state, the legislature subsequently dropped the reciprocity requirement in its interstate banking law.

One year after the Key Banks acquisition in Maine, two other states — Massachusetts and New York — joined the interstate movement with their own unique banking laws. In 1982 New York invited banking firms from any other state to enter, provided New York banks were extended the same privilege. Other states were in no hurry to accept New York's invitation, however, out of fear of the impact on their local banks if New York City's money-center institutions were to set up shop next door. Reflecting this fear of the giant New York–based banking institutions, no other state with a regional banking law expressly voted to include New York banks as permissible entrants into its territory.

Massachusetts experienced the same fear and, therefore, decided in the same year to permit entry only by holding companies or banks headquartered within the six-state New England region, provided reciprocal entry privileges were extended to Massachusetts banks. In 1983 Connecticut and Rhode Island followed suit, allowing outside entry from anywhere in New England by bank holding companies. Moreover, an anti-leapfrogging provision was included in the Massachusetts law that prevented banks headquartered outside the region from using a grandfathered acquisition anywhere in New England as a lever to pry open the borders of Massachusetts. Lawmakers in these New England states saw the new legislation as a way to bring in new capital for economic development if the region's banks could grow large enough to compete for funds in national and international capital markets. In addition, New England banks might be able to grow to such a size that they could thwart takeover attempts by banking firms from other states.

One further impediment to entry into Massachusetts from outside New England was a divestiture proviso of its interstate banking law that required outside entrants to divest themselves of any bank affiliates outside New England before applying to acquire a Massachusetts bank. Connecticut has a similar law that is now being challenged in court. New Hampshire also had a parallel provision in its interstate banking statute, but has subsequently changed that law to permit bank acquisitions in New Hampshire without the mandatory divestiture of any other banks acquired. Moreover, in January 1989 the Joint Committee on Banks and Banking of the Massachusetts legislature brought forward a new interstate bill for consideration that would allow banking organizations from other states that already had reciprocal interstate banking laws on their books to acquire Massachusetts banks beginning in June 1990. (A summary of interstate banking laws in New England is presented in Table 3–1.)

This discriminatory feature of Massachusetts banking law was not passively accepted by leading banks in the state of New York. Suit was subsequently brought to block implementation of the new Massachusetts law and to strike down a similar statute in Connecticut. On appeal, this suit filed by three petitioners—Northeast Bancorp, Inc., Union Trust Company, and Citicorp of New York—reached the U.S. Supreme Court early in 1985. Named as respondents were three private banking organizations—the Bank of New England Corp. (BNE), Hartford National Corp. (HNC), and the Bank of Boston Corp. (BBC)—plus the Federal Reserve Board, which had previously approved the respondents' interstate acquisitions within New England. The three petitioners opposed these acquisitions on grounds they were not authorized by the Bank Holding Company Act, and, even if they were, the Connecticut and Massachusetts interstate compacts were in violation of the U.S. Constitution (specifically the Commerce and Compact Clauses).

On June 10, 1985, the U.S. Supreme Court announced that it had, without a dissenting vote, affirmed the ruling of the U.S. Court of Appeals for the Second Circuit, upholding the right of any state to decide from what other states it would permit outside entry by banking institutions.[2] Petitioners in this Northeast Bancorp case had argued that the Bank Holding Company Act (in particular, the Douglas Amendment to that Act) did not specifically grant a state the right to lift part of a ban against interstate banking, allowing some banks to enter but excluding others. However, the Supreme Court, after reviewing the legislative history of the Douglas Amendment, ruled that Congress had intended to give the states *flexibility* in regulating the structure of their own banking industries. The Court saw nothing inherent in federal law that would require a state to open itself up to bank entry from every corner of the nation.

Moreover, the nine justices of the Supreme Court saw the New England banking compact as consistent with another key historic goal of federal banking law: retaining local, community-based control over banking. Banks were viewed as quasi-public, quasi-private businesses chartered not just to make a profit, but also to provide vital services—especially the extending of credit, the making of payments, and the safekeeping of property—to their communities. State and local governments had legal grounds pursuant to the public interest to exercise control over where banks could reside in order to offer their services. In addition, these exclusionary interstate banking laws were held not to be in conflict with the federal Constitution because Congress had previously authorized this use of state power. Therefore, such laws were not viewed as an illegal challenge to the federal government's supremacy.

Table 3-1

Interstate Banking Laws for States in the New England Region (as of April 1, 1989)

STATE	STATUS OF LEGISLATION	AREAS OR STATES AFFECTED
Connecticut	Current Law	– Bank entry allowed from 5 other states (Maine, Massachusetts, New Hampshire, Rhode Island, and Vermont) provided a reciprocal privilege is granted to Connecticut banks.
Maine	Current Law	– Entry from banking organizations from any state in the nation is allowed without the need for reciprocity for Maine's banks.
Massachusetts	Current Law	– Reciprocal bank entry is permitted from 5 other states (Connecticut, Maine, New Hampshire, Rhode Island, and Vermont), though a nationwide reciprocal entry law was proposed in the state legislature in 1989.
New Hampshire	Current Law	– Reciprocal bank entry is allowed from 5 other states (Connecticut, Maine, Massachusetts, Rhode Island, and Vermont).
Rhode Island	Current Law	– Bank entry from any state in the nation is allowed provided reciprocal privileges are granted Rhode Island banks.
Vermont	Current Law	– Bank entry is permitted from 5 other states (Connecticut, Maine, Massachusetts, New Hampshire, and Rhode Island), provided reciprocity is granted Vermont banks.
	New Law Effective on February 1, 1990	– Bank entry from any other state in the nation is permitted if Vermont banks are granted reciprocal privileges.

Sources: Financial Structure Section, Board of Governors of the Federal Reserve System, and American Bankers Association, Washington, D.C.

Petitioners in the Northeast Bancorp case had claimed that restrictive state banking laws denied them the "equal protection of the laws" required by the U.S. Constitution. The Supreme Court admitted that regional banking compacts do favor out-of-state companies from within the covered region over banks from other sections of the country. However, the Justices held that Connecticut and Massachusetts could legitimately discriminate in awarding bank entry privileges because they were entitled to consider (and, indeed, had previously considered) "the need to preserve a close relationship between those in the community who need credit and those who provide credit." Thus, the Court ruled, the states could determine if, in their reasonable opinion, acquisitions of banks by firms located outside of their region "would threaten the independence of local banking institutions."[3] The Supreme Court acknowledged the right of a state to weigh the beneficial effects of increasing competition by allowing outside entry against the possible loss of local control and autonomy.

In effect, the Supreme Court, as it has done so often in the past, was placing banking in a unique category from other industries. As Justice Rehnquist stated on behalf of the Court, "with respect to the business of banking, we do not write on a clean slate. . . . Our country traditionally has favored widely dispersed control of banking. While many other western nations are dominated by a handful of centralized banks, we have some 15,000 commercial banks attached to a greater or lesser degree to the communities in which they are located."[4] It is at least doubtful that the Supreme Court would have upheld state compacts granting exclusive entry privileges to some firms and denying them to others if industries other than banking were involved. Indeed, in the case of *Metropolitan Life Insurance Co.* v. *Ward* (470 U.S. [1985]:10–12) the Court struck down an individual state's attempt to levy higher taxes on nonresident corporations compared to resident firms.

The landmark Supreme Court decision in the Northeast Bancorp case literally opened the floodgates of interstate banking legislation. Eighteen months later, at year-end 1986, a total of 36 states had passed enabling legislation, most of these limiting outside entry to banks or bank holding companies from neighboring states. Most states also inserted a reciprocity clause: their own banks or bank holding companies must be given interstate expansion privileges before they will allow banks from another state to come in. As Maine had done a decade earlier, some states embraced outside entry in order to promote local economic development and jobs, but still tried to limit the impact of out-of-state competition on existing banks. For example, South Dakota moved to allow out-of-state entry in order to offer credit-card services. Other states seized on the failing-bank problem and allowed out-of-state companies to enter if they would rescue a troubled local bank and infuse new capital and management into that bank in order to protect its depositors. The idea of giving permission to out-of-state banking firms to

enter in order to absorb failing institutions was reinforced by federal legislation during the 1980s, especially with passage of the Garn-St Germain Act in
1982 and the Competitive Equality in Banking Act of 1987. The former bill
authorized out-of-state banking companies to acquire large troubled commercial and savings banks, while the latter gave the FDIC permission to
arrange interstate acquisitions of troubled institutions (with assets exceeding
$500 million) provided that agency was prepared to supply enough financial
support so that these acquisitions would succeed.

Both South Dakota and Delaware have become leaders in using interstate
banking legislation as a tool for speeding economic growth and development. (See Tables 3–2 and 3–3 for a summary of the Delaware and South
Dakota interstate banking laws, along with the banking laws of other states
located in their regions of the nation.) Sponsors of new banking legislation
in these states perhaps had seen the projections for employment growth
developed by the U.S. Bureau of Labor Statistics. Government estimates of
the growth of employment between 1986 and 2000 call for a 19 percent
increase in total employment or an additional 21.4 million jobs by the end of
the century (as noted by Kutschen [1987]). The service industries as a whole
are expected to add just over 20 million new jobs, with most of this projected
gain accounted for by finance, insurance, and real estate firms (including
banking). These financially oriented industries are expected to add 10 million new jobs (constituting a 44 percent increase) between 1986 and 2000.
More specific estimates call for just over one-quarter of a million (specifically, 262,000) new jobs in banking alone over the 1986–2000 period.[5]

These promising growth statistics have led many states to pursue the goal
of becoming a financial-service center. Several different strategies have been
adopted to achieve that goal, including (1) lowering barriers to outside entry
by some or all suppliers of financial services; (2) reducing or eliminating
restrictions on the offering of some financial services; or (3) reducing or
eliminating taxes on income, services sold, or property owned by financial-
service firms. Advances in communications and information technology
have made it possible for banking firms to establish remote service centers in
distant states and thus serve distant customers.

Probably the best example of these state financial-service initiatives arose
in the state of Delaware. In 1981 the Delaware state legislature passed the
Financial Center Development Act, and the governor signed that bill into
law in February of that year. Bank holding companies from out of state were
invited to charter a single de novo Delaware bank without branches. The
new bank would be required to provide primarily wholesale banking services
(that is, business-oriented financial services rather than retail services to
households) and to have at least 100 Delaware employees by the end of the
first year of its operation. One of the principal goals of this legislation was
to stimulate the growth of bank credit originating in Delaware. This was
accomplished by lifting restrictions on permissible loan rates that Delaware-

Table 3-2
Interstate Banking Laws for States in the West North Central Region
(as of April 1, 1989)

STATE	STATUS OF LEGISLATION	AREAS OR STATES AFFECTED
Iowa	No Interstate Law (though Norwest Corporation has grandfathered acquisition privileges within the state).	————
Kansas	No Interstate Law	————
Minnesota	Current Law	− Reciprocal entry privileges granted to banks in 11 other states (Colorado, Idaho, Illinois, Iowa, Kansas, Missouri, Montana, North Dakota, South Dakota, Washington, Wisconsin, and Wyoming).
Missouri	Current Law	− Bank entry with reciprocity permitted from 8 other states (Arkansas, Illinois, Iowa, Kansas, Kentucky, Nebraska, Oklahoma, and Tennessee).
Nebraska	New Law Effective on January 1, 1990	− Reciprocal entry privileges extended to banks in 10 other states (Colorado, Iowa, Kansas, Minnesota, Missouri, Montana, North Dakota, South Dakota, Wisconsin, and Wyoming).
	New Law Effective on January 1, 1991.	− Nationwide reciprocal entry is allowed.
North Dakota	No Interstate Law (though grandfathered acquisitions by out−of−state firms may be sold to other out−of−state banking firms).	————
South Dakota	Current Law	− Nationwide reciprocal entry is permitted and special−purpose banks may also be owned by out−of state organizations.

Sources: Financial Structure Section, Board of Governors of the Federal Reserve System, and the American Bankers Association, Washington, D.C.

Table 3-3
Interstate Banking Laws for States in the South Atlantic Region
(as of April 1, 1989)

STATE	STATUS OF LEGISLATION	AREAS OR STATES AFFECTED
Delaware	Current Law	— Bank entry is permitted from 5 other states (Maryland, New Jersey, Ohio, Pennsylvania, and Virginia) and Washington, D.C., provided Delaware banks also are allowed to enter these areas.
	New Law Effective on June 30, 1990	— Entry from any other state of the nation is permitted as of June 30, 1990, if reciprocal entry privileges are granted to Delaware banks.
Florida	Current Law	— Reciprocal bank entry allowed from 11 other states (Alabama, Arkansas, Georgia, Louisiana, Maryland, Mississippi, North Carolina, South Carolina, Tennessee, Virginia, and West Virginia) and Washington, D.C.
Georgia	Current Law	— Reciprocal bank entry is permitted from 10 states (Alabama, Florida, Kentucky, Louisiana, Maryland, Mississippi, North Carolina, South Carolina, Tennessee, and Virginia) and Washington, D.C.
Maryland	Current Law	— Reciprocal bank entry privileges are granted to banks from 14 other states (Alabama, Arkansas, Delaware, Florida, Georgia, Kentucky, Louisiana, Mississippi, North Carolina, Pennsylvania, South Carolina, Tennessee, Virginia, and West Virginia) and Washington, D.C.

Table 3-3
Continued

STATE	STATUS OF LEGISLATION	AREAS OR STATES AFFECTED
North Carolina	Current Law	— Reciprocal bank entry is allowed from 12 other states (Alabama, Arkansas, Florida, Georgia, Kentucky, Louisiana, Maryland, Mississippi, South Carolina, Tennessee, Virginia, and West Virginia) and Washington, D.C.
South Carolina	Current Law	— Reciprocal bank entry is permitted from 12 other states (Alabama, Arkansas, Florida, Georgia, Kentucky, Louisiana, Maryland, Mississippi, North Carolina, Tennessee, Virginia, and West Virginia) as well as Washington, D.C.
Virginia	Current Law	— Bank entry allowed from 12 other states (Alabama, Arkansas, Florida, Georgia, Kentucky, Louisiana, Maryland, Mississippi, North Carolina, South Carolina, Tennessee, and West Virginia) and Washington, D.C.
West Virginia	Current Law	— Entry from any other state in the nation is permitted, provided West Virginia banks are granted parallel (reciprocal) privileges.

Sources: Financial Structure Section, Board of Governors of the Federal Reserve System, and American Bankers Association, Washington, D.C.

based banks could charge and allowing these institutions to levy additional noninterest fees on credit-card services. The legislature also imposed a sliding-scale income tax structure in which overall tax rates were lowered significantly below the effective tax rates charged banks in New York, Pennsylvania, and other key banking states.

Two years later, in 1983, the Delaware legislature passed two other banking statutes—the Consumer Credit Bank Act and the International Banking Development Act. The first of these bills permitted bank holding companies headquartered in other states to create "consumer credit banks" in Delaware that could offer consumer loans across the nation. Interestingly enough, the Consumer Credit Bank Act did not impose an employment quota directly on the new consumer-credit firms. However, this 1983 law stipulated that all such firms had to be associated with a credit-receivables processing system that hired a minimum of 250 employees within three years.

Not satisfied with just bringing in domestic banking business, Delaware lawmakers also passed the International Banking Development Act in 1983 which opened the state's borders to foreign banks and to U.S. banks' foreign operations. This was accomplished by forgiving franchise taxes on the net earnings of these firms, lifting reserve requirements on their liabilities, and doing away with interest-rate ceilings on their loans.

The impact of these new laws on the availability of jobs and capital in Delaware and on its banking and financial-services industry was substantial. The growth of loans, deposits, and bank employment at Delaware banks has far outstripped the average growth rate reported by all banks across the United States. Moreover, close to 20 special wholesale-oriented banks were established in Delaware between 1981 and 1987, of which nearly half were set up by New York banks. There is also evidence that at least some of Delaware's existing banks benefitted from the new laws, in part because those banks already controlled by out-of-state holding companies invested additional resources in their Delaware offices in response to the new legislation.

Delaware's interstate banking laws were actually preceded by innovative banking legislation passed the previous year in South Dakota. In 1980 the South Dakota legislature moved to eliminate legal interest-rate ceilings on consumer loans, allowing banks with headquarters in that state to charge household borrowers whatever rate the market dictated. Then, in March 1980, bank holding companies from other states were invited to establish new banks (bearing either federal or state charters) and to center their credit-card operations in South Dakota. As a result of this legislation, several large banks from New York (e.g., Citicorp with its Citibank South Dakota, N.A. of Sioux Falls) made plans to centralize their credit-card operations in South Dakota. Other leading banks in the Midwest and Southwest also acted to set up credit-card operations, resulting in exceptional growth in loans and deposits for South Dakota's banking industry. Moreover, by the late 1980s the majority of South Dakota's largest banks were controlled by out-of-state banking companies.

The economically beneficial impact of the Delaware and South Dakota laws was not on neighboring states, some of which prepared to adopt similar legislation. This pattern of competitive financial behavior between states is a familiar story. During the 1930s, for example, several states quickly copied a Mississippi law that promised significant concessions to out-of-state companies willing to come in and set up operations in Mississippi. Then, as now, many states passed parallel legislation in order to accelerate their own economic development, while others viewed the need for similar legislation as a *defensive* measure — to prevent their own businesses from moving to states with more liberal business laws. For example, New York responded to the challenge from South Dakota and Delaware by passing its own legislation, effective in 1981, to lift legal ceilings on consumer loans and allow banks there to charge special fees for opening consumer credit-card accounts. Nebraska followed suit with a lifting of its loan-rate ceilings and voted to permit out-of-state banking companies to establish a single office in order to conduct credit-card operations. (Tables 3-2 and 3-4 provide summaries of the interstate banking laws of New York and Nebraska, as well as the interstate laws of other states in their respective regions of the nation.)

Several states bordering on or near Delaware — specifically Maryland, Virginia, and Pennsylvania — responded to Delaware's challenge with the passage of competing legislation. Maryland moved in 1982 to enact substantial-

Table 3-4
**Interstate Banking Laws for States in the Middle Atlantic Region
(as of April 1, 1989)**

STATE	STATUS OF LEGISLATION	AREAS OR STATES AFFECTED
New Jersey	Current Law	— Nationwide bank entry into New Jersey is allowed, provided New Jersey banks are granted reciprocal entry privileges from the other states involved.
New York	Current Law	— Nationwide bank entry into New York State is permitted for all those states granting New York banking firms the same entry privileges.
Pennsylvania	Current Law	— Reciprocal entry privileges are extended to banking companies from 7 states (Delaware, Kentucky, Maryland, New Jersey, Ohio, Virginia, and West Virginia) as well as Washington, D.C.

Sources: Financial Structure Section, Board of Governors of the Federal Reserve System, and American Bankers Association, Washington, D.C.

ly higher consumer loan-rate ceilings, so that its banks could charge higher loan rates to individuals and families (up to 24 percent on credit-card loans). Maryland banks also were granted permission to levy charge-card membership fees in 1983, and out-of-state banking firms were given the green light to enter Maryland and launch their own credit-card operations.

Similarly, Virginia lifted interest-rate limits on credit card loans and allowed membership fees to be levied by banks with operations in that state. In the spring of 1983 special-purpose banks owned by out-of-state companies were permitted to apply for charters in order to sell and process credit cards and also to make some business credit and deposit services available. The year before, Pennsylvania had raised permissible credit-card loan rates to a maximum of 18 percent from their previous statutory maximum of 15 percent. Later in 1982 credit-card membership fees were declared to be legal in Pennsylvania, provided they did not exceed $15 annually. (See Table 3-3 for a summary of Maryland and Virginia interstate banking laws and Table 3-4 for a summary of Pennsylvania's interstate banking law and of similar laws enacted by states in the same region.)

Thus, the relatively rapid response of individual states to other states in the same general region of the nation, deregulating one or more banking services, appeared to reduce the expected gains in employment and bank growth of states that initiated such legislation. However, the earliest active states (particularly Delaware and South Dakota) apparently did benefit from their interstate banking legislation, as did consumers and the economy as a whole due to improved efficiency in the allocation of scarce banking resources.

ECONOMIC PROBLEMS IN THE SOUTHWEST AND INTERSTATE BANK EXPANSION

No recitation of interstate banking's history would be complete without a brief discussion of the new banking laws in the energy-dependent Southwest, particularly in the states of Texas, Oklahoma, and Louisiana. (See Table 3-5 for a summary of the interstate banking laws passed by these southwestern states.) Plunging oil and natural gas prices in the mid-1980s resulted in a massive flight of resources (including both people and capital) out of banks, thrifts, and other financial institutions in this troubled Sunbelt region. The oil-price slide hit a low of approximately $9 per barrel during 1986—the same year that Texas' bank failures accounted for a full one-fourth of all bank failures in the United States. By 1988 bank closings in Texas accounted for about half of all insured bank failures nationwide, while just four states—Texas, Oklahoma, Louisiana, and Colorado—accounted for 70 percent of all U.S. bank failures.

To be sure, oil was not the only problem creating turmoil and loss in the banking industry. Agricultural commodity prices also hit new lows, in many

Table 3-5
Interstate Banking Laws for States in the West South Central Region
(as of April 1, 1989)

STATE	STATUS OF LEGISLATION	AREAS OR STATES AFFECTED
Arkansas	Current Law	– Reciprocal bank entry privileges are granted banking firms from 16 other states (Alabama, Florida, Georgia, Kansas, Louisiana, Maryland, Mississippi, Missouri, Nebraska, North Carolina, Oklahoma, South Carolina, Tennessee, Texas, Virginia, and West Virginia) and Washington, D.C.
Louisiana	Current Law	– Nationwide entry allowed if Louisiana banks are given reciprocal privileges.
Oklahoma	Current Law	– Nationwide entry permitted without reciprocity. However, if the banking company entering is from a state not granting reciprocal entry privileges to Oklahoma banks, the entering company cannot expand its Oklahoma activities for at least 4 years.
Texas	Current Law	– Nationwide entry allowed without reciprocal entry privileges granted to Texas banks.

Sources: Financial Structure Section, Board of Governors of the Federal Reserve System, and American Bankers Association, Washington, D.C.

cases well below domestic farm production costs, so that many farmers and ranchers in the Southwest and Midwest simply walked away from their businesses or were foreclosed on by their lenders. Along the Mexican border, U.S. businesses were also severely impacted by the falling value of the peso relative to the dollar, which depressed U.S. sales to Mexican nationals.

The combination of these serious economic problems led very quickly to a fourth problem—business and household bankruptcies that left thousands of commercial offices, warehouses, homes, apartments, and other physical facilities vacant. Loans from banks and thrifts that had placed a high value on oil, gas, and associated real estate projects and had loaned out most of their estimated value now found that such loans were worth only a fraction of their former market value. Forced sales in Houston, the largest city in the South, saw large-scale office facilities and tract homes selling for as low as one-tenth of their appraised value. Just over a quarter of a million workers left Texas between 1981 and 1987, and the state's traditional budget surplus was turned into a record $1 billion budget deficit.

Adding to the economic malaise was a growing awareness among government officials and businessmen and women that states and local governments in the Southwest were going to have to find new sources of funding for both government and private industry. The Southwest had become a "mature oil province"—that is, its estimated remaining oil and gas reserves were declining, now clearly outstripped by the much larger oil fields in the Middle East, Alaska, and the North Sea. Reliance on petroleum revenues for regional growth would no longer maintain the Southwest's standard of living. Its reserve base was falling, perhaps irretrievably if new technology could not come to the rescue, and the market price for each barrel of crude oil recovered was hovering near its cost of production.

This unhappy forecast was not lost on the state legislatures in the Southwest. In September 1986 the Texas legislature passed an interstate banking bill that broke new ground for large states. It allowed banks and bank holding companies to enter from any other state in the nation without requiring the other states involved to extend similar privileges to Texas banks (effective January 1, 1987). The only significant restriction on outside entry in this new law was the requirement that the acquired Texas banking firm must maintain a "separate corporate existence." Although vague, this provision was held by the Texas Attorney General's office to mean that outside banking companies could own Texas banks, but these banks must be "operated" by individuals within the state (with at least half of the directors of an acquired banking firm being residents of Texas).

Oklahoma followed with a similar bill, permitting nationwide entry essentially without reciprocity. However, if the outside acquiring firm was headquartered in a state barring entry to Oklahoma banks, the acquirer could not expand its Oklahoma operations any further until at least four years had passed.

Louisiana was, at first, the only one of the three dominant energy-producing states to limit who or what could come across its borders and purchase the stock of Louisiana banks. The initial bill permitted banks from 14 other states—Alabama, Arkansas, Florida, Georgia, Kentucky, Maryland, Mississippi, North Carolina, Oklahoma, South Carolina, Tennessee, Texas, Virginia, and West Virginia—as well as from Washington, D.C., to enter. However, as the oil-based economic crisis deepened, Louisiana moved closer to Texas and Oklahoma, passing a nationwide-bank entry bill, effective January 1, 1989, but with reciprocity for Louisiana banks still a requisite condition.

THE INTERSTATE BANKING MOVEMENT SPREADS TO NEW REGIONS

The interstate banking revolution that began with Maine, Delaware, and South Dakota soon began to spread out in all directions. In the upper Midwest the states of Illinois, Indiana, Michigan, Ohio, and Wisconsin voted to open up their borders initially to banks from the same region and from other nearby states (such as Iowa, Kentucky, Minnesota, Missouri, Pennsylvania, Tennessee, Virginia, and West Virginia). Later a majority of states in the upper Midwest moved to allow nationwide entry, provided their own banks were also extended entry privileges. The first midwestern state to legalize bank entry from the outside was Indiana, which passed a regional banking bill in April 1985. In November of the same year Illinois passed a similar law allowing entry with reciprocity from the surrounding states. (See Table 3–6 for a summary of these state laws.)

In the South, Alabama, Kentucky, Mississippi, and Tennessee agreed to admit each other's banks, as well as banking firms from selected other states in the surrounding region, including Arkansas, Florida, Georgia, Louisiana, Maryland, North Carolina, South Carolina, Virginia, and West Virginia. This region, too, is moving toward nationwide banking with Kentucky already allowing entry from any other state in the nation, provided Kentucky banks receive similar privileges from other states, while Mississippi is scheduled to convert to entry with reciprocity from 13 other states in 1990. (See Table 3–7 for a summary of interstate banking laws in this portion of the southern United States.)

The states of the Rocky Mountain area also soon followed the lead of Delaware and South Dakota. In fact, today the Rocky Mountain region has one of the highest proportions of nationwide bank entry laws of any region of the nation, and by 1991 all the states in this region (Arizona, Colorado, Idaho, Montana, Nevada, New Mexico, Utah, and Wyoming) will convert to nationwide entry without reciprocity for their own banks. (See Table 3–8 for a summary of these regional interstate banking laws.) The positive response of the Rocky Mountain states to full-service interstate banking was a direct reflection of economic pressures in this region of the nation. These states were severely impacted during the 1980s by declining prices for oil, natural gas, and coal and by a drastic fall in the prices of key metals (especially copper) and agricultural commodities. Faced with rising unemployment and an exodus of businesses, these states sought to attract new sources of capital and employment to the beleaguered region.

A good example of the recent historical evolution of interstate banking in the Rocky Mountain area is provided by the state of Colorado. Effective

Table 3-6
Interstate Banking Laws for States in the East North Central Region
(as of April 1, 1989)

STATE	STATUS OF LEGISLATION	AREAS OR STATES AFFECTED
Illinois	Current Law	– Bank entry allowed from 6 other states (Indiana, Iowa, Kentucky, Michigan, Missouri, and Wisconsin), provided Illinois banks receive similar entry privileges.
	New Law Effective on December 1, 1990	– Nationwide entry allowed on a reciprocal only basis.
Indiana	Current Law	– Reciprocal entry permitted from 11 other states (Illinois, Iowa, Kentucky, Michigan, Missouri, Ohio, Pennsylvania, Tennessee, Virginia, West Virginia, and Wisconsin).
	New Law Effective on July 1, 1992	– Nationwide entry permitted with reciprocal privileges for Indiana banks.
Michigan	Current Law	– Bank entry privileges for banks from any other state in the nation with reciprocity for Michigan banks.
Ohio	Current Law	– Nationwide entry permitted with reciprocal privileges for Ohio banks.
Wisconsin	Current Law	– Reciprocal entry from other states allowed (including Illinois, Indiana, Iowa, Kentucky, Michigan, Minnesota, Missouri, and Ohio).

Sources: Financial Structure Section, Board of Governors of the Federal
Reserve System, and American Bankers Association, Washington, D.C.

Table 3-7
Interstate Banking Laws for States in the East South Central Region
(as of April 1, 1989)

STATE	STATUS OF LEGISLATION	AREAS OR STATES AFFECTED
Alabama	Current Law	– Reciprocal entry permitted from 12 other states (Arkansas, Florida, Georgia, Kentucky, Louisiana, Maryland, Mississippi, North Carolina, South Carolina, Tennessee, Virginia, and West Virginia) and Washington, D.C.
Kentucky	Current Law	– Nationwide bank entry permitted if reciprocal privileges are granted to Kentucky banks and share of statewide deposits does not exceed the maximum legal limit.
Mississippi	Current Law	– Reciprocal entry privileges are granted banks from 4 other states (Alabama, Arkansas, Louisiana, and Tennessee).
	New Law Effective on July 1, 1990	– Reciprocal entry privileges granted banks from 13 other states (Alabama, Arkansas, Florida, Georgia, Kentucky, Louisiana, Missouri, North Carolina, South Carolina, Tennessee, Texas, Virginia, and West Virginia).
Tennessee	Current Law	– Reciprocal entry allowed from 13 other states (Alabama, Arkansas, Florida, Georgia, Indiana, Kentucky, Louisiana, Mississippi, Missouri, North Carolina, South Carolina, Virginia, and West Virginia). However, the out-of-state acquisition of new banks and leap-frogging from another state into Tennessee are both severely restricted.

Sources: Financial Structure Section, Board of Governors of the Federal Reserve System, and American Bankers Association, Washington, D.C.

Table 3-8
Interstate Banking Laws for States in the Rocky Mountain Region
(as of April 1, 1989)

STATE	STATUS OF LEGISLATION	AREAS OR STATES AFFECTED
Arizona	Current Law	— Nationwide entry permitted without a reciprocity requirement for Arizona banks.
Colorado	Current Law	— Reciprocal entry privileges granted to banks from 7 other states (Arizona, Kansas, Nebraska, New Mexico, Oklahoma, Utah, and Wyoming).
	New Law Effective on January 1, 1991	— Nationwide entry allowed with a reciprocity requirement.
Idaho	Current Law	— Nationwide entry permitted without a reciprocity requirement;
Montana	No Interstate Law	—————
Nevada	Current Law	— Nationwide bank entry allowed without reciprocity.
New Mexico	New Law Effective on January 1, 1990	— Nationwide entry permitted without a reciprocity requirement; previously outside entry was permitted only from surrounding states.
Utah	Current Law	— Nationwide entry allowed without reciprocity.
Wyoming	Current Law	— Nationwide entry allowed without reciprocity.

Sources: Financial Structure Section, Board of Governors of the Federal Reserve System, and American Bankers Association, Washington, D.C.

July 1, 1988, under Senate Bill No. 68 passed by the Colorado legislature, banks or bank holding companies from any of seven contiguous states could enter Colorado by acquisition only up until 1993, provided reciprocal entry privileges were granted to Colorado banking firms.[6] However, because the state's anti-branching law was still in force at that time, the acquiring out-of-state banking firm could not set up branches. Moreover, leapfrogging of banking firms from distant states into the seven-state region was prohibited. (For example, a California banking organization having control of banks in Arizona and Utah could not use those acquisitions as a basis for entering Colorado.) However, after January 1, 1991, entry into Colorado from any other state (not just those in the surrounding seven-state region) would be permitted without mandatory reciprocity. This bill was signed into law by Colorado's governor on April 1, 1988.

Until July 1, 1993, no Colorado bank in operation less than five years before the date of its proposed acquisition could be acquired legally. Moreover, no one out-of-state banking organization could hold more than 25 percent of the aggregate deposits of all banks, savings and loans, federal savings banks, and other federally insured depository institutions headquartered in Colorado. The out-of-state acquirer also must have a minimum total-capital-to-total-assets ratio of 6 percent. No savings and loan, federal savings bank, or other similar financial institution from out of state could acquire a Colorado bank before January 1, 1991. Colorado, in fact, is typical of many states in the nation's mid-section that have slowly opened their borders to outside bank entry but have held onto vestiges of the old system of geographic restraints against branching within their borders. These states have allowed outsiders to enter only under terms that give at least some protection to local banks.

In contrast to the relatively slow pace of interstate bank expansion in Colorado and most other states in the Rocky Mountain region, interstate banking in Arizona — one of the strongest economies west of the Mississippi River — has expanded at great speed. Within six months after Arizona's liberal interstate banking bill was passed in October 1986, one-fifth of that state's banks had been acquired by out-of-state institutions, accounting for 30 percent of Arizona's banking assets. While Arizona's second largest bank had been acquired by First Interstate Bancorp of Los Angeles years earlier, within a few weeks of the legalization of interstate activity the state's third, fourth, fifth, sixth, and seventh largest banks were also snapped up by out-of-state investors. This kind of rapid response to interstate laws demonstrates an important principle about the factors likely to spur interstate bank expansion in the future. Key factors that stimulate rapid interstate banking acquisitions include (1) passage of a liberal interstate law that, like Arizona's, does not require reciprocal treatment for a state's banks; (2) maintenance of a strong local economy; and (3) the presence of statewide branch banking, which tends to make a state's banking organizations large enough to be attractive acquisition targets.

States along the West Coast (Alaska, California, Hawaii, Oregon, and Washington) began to move toward interstate banking shortly after the Rocky Mountain states did so. Like the states along the Rocky Mountain chain, Pacific Coast states generally saw little to fear from outside entrants and soon passed nationwide banking legislation, allowing banks to enter from any other state without reciprocity, either immediately or on some specified trigger date in the future. For example, as shown in Table 3-9,

Table 3-9
Interstate Banking Laws for States in the Pacific Region (as of April 1, 1989)

STATE	STATUS OF LEGISLATION	AREAS OR STATES AFFECTED
Alaska	Current Law	– Nationwide entry permitted without necessary reciprocity for Alaska banks.
California	Current Law	– Entry permitted from 11 other states (Alaska, Arizona, Colorado, Hawaii, Idaho, Nevada, New Mexico, Oregon, Texas, Utah, and Washington), provided California banks are granted reciprocal privileges.
	New Law Effective on January 1, 1991	– Nationwide bank entry permitted with no required reciprocity for California banks.
Hawaii	Current Law	– Reciprocal entry privileges exchanged with Guam.
Oregon	Current Law	– Nationwide entry without the need for reciprocity for Oregon banks.
Washington	Current Law	– Nationwide entry allowed, provided reciprocal privileges are granted to Washington banks.

Sources: Financial Structure Section, Board of Governors of the Federal Reserve System, and American Bankers Association, Washington, D.C.

California would allow entry from any of the other 49 states beginning in 1991. The one exception is Hawaii, which has voted to allow reciprocal entry from selected Pacific territories (most importantly, the island of Guam) but not yet from any of the other 49 states. Like the Rocky Mountain region, selected states along the West Coast, especially Alaska, Oregon, and Washington, have faced serious economic problems due to decreases in energy prices and a sluggish demand for housing which has depressed the lumber industry. In the future this group of states will prove to be particularly attractive as entry targets because they give U.S. banks an avenue to rapidly growing trade and commerce around the entire Pacific Rim.

A REPRISE ON THE HISTORY OF INTERSTATE BANKING

Chiseled into the arch above the original building that houses the Smithsonian Museum in Washington, D.C., are these words: "The Past Is Prologue." And so it is with the history of geographic expansion by American banks. Each historic step in the gradual lifting of legal barriers to banks' broadening their markets has involved an intense political struggle and has generally required many years for a consensus to develop in order to make new legislation possible. For example, legal permission for national banks to establish branch offices in their home states was given 63 years after passage of the law that established the national banking system. Bank holding companies were denied permission to cross state lines without an explicit sanction to do so by the states involved more than three decades ago.

Thus, not surprisingly, the advent of full-service nationwide banking from border to border and coast to coast, which took its first halting steps in 1980 and 1981, will not happen even within the next decade or perhaps even within the next generation. The fear of concentrated financial power, rooted deeply in American history, is indeed slowly overcome. That fear, shared by many bankers and consumers alike, will not be alleviated until it is shown to be groundless, until interstate banking organizations prove they are intense competitors that respond aggressively to the public's changing financial-service needs.

Reminiscent of the past as well is the powerful influence of economic conditions in reshaping the structure of American banking. Just as liberalized branching legislation was largely a response to hundreds of bank failures and massive unemployment during the Great Depression of the 1930s, so interstate banking has had its own strong economic roots. Economic decline in the Midwest, associated with an agricultural crisis, and in the Southwest, due to falling energy prices, has brought forth a tremendous demand for new capital in order to stem the rising tide of bank failures. As a primary source of capital, banks were viewed as sources of a powerful spark to reignite the faltering flame of the economy. What appears to have been forgotten is the tendency of the states to copy each other's legislation, particularly when significant economic benefits seem possible. Whatever economic advantage may seem plausible initially is quickly vitiated by the counteractions of other states that wish to preserve and protect their own job roles and tax revenues. But we must turn now in the chapters that follow not to the past of interstate banking, but to its probable impact on the *future*. What is this banking revolution likely to mean to the public and to banks themselves, as revealed by the most recent research studies? While the past is not always a prologue to the future, we can learn great wisdom from recent history, if only to help policymakers avoid stumbling into the errors of the past and to renew our confidence in the continued viability and competitiveness of the American banking system.

NOTES

1. Under the terms of the National Bank Act of 1863–64, national banks were permitted to issue bank notes — then a common way of making loans to their customers — provided these notes were fully backed by bank holdings of U.S. government bonds. This provision of the law created strong bank demand for government securities and, therefore, contributed to the growth of public trading in U.S. government obligations and helped finance the Civil War.

2. See especially *Northeast Bancorp* v. *Board of Governors of the Federal Reserve Sys.* 472 U.S. 159 (1985).

3. Ibid., 17.

4. Ibid., 16–17.

5. Eleanor H. Erdevig (1988, 17–18) notes that 134,000 more jobs are expected in commodity and security brokerage and on the various securities exchanges, while firms processing credit applications and offering marketing investment services are expected to add 495,000 more employees.

6. The seven contiguous states were Arizona, Kansas, Nebraska, New Mexico, Oklahoma, Utah, and Wyoming. Of these states the most likely source of out-of-state bank entrants into Colorado was Arizona.

4

Research Evidence on the Benefits and Costs of Interstate Banking

The generations-old controversy surrounding the geographic expansion of American banking has engendered deep emotions on all sides of the issue. Volumes have been written on the alleged dangers of permitting unlimited bank branching and holding-company activity; they have focused especially on the risks of either diminished or destructive competition between banks, the loss of personal identity and caring service for valued customers, and the draining of scarce funds from local communities, stifling their economic progress, while corporate and governmental borrowers that can afford to pay the highest interest rates receive the credit they demand. On the other hand, proponents of branch banks and holding-company organizations have often painted an idealistic portrait of their contributions to American banking and to the communities they serve. The largest multiple-office banking organizations frequently claim that they offer a wider range of services, provide greater convenience, charge lower service fees, display greater long-run stability, and promote faster economic growth in the market areas they serve.[1]

Unfortunately, there is far less solid research evidence available on these various claims than their proponents and opponents frequently would have us believe. And research evidence on the impact of interstate banking is thin precisely because full-service interstate banking is a relatively new phenomenon in American banking. As we saw in the preceding chapters, interstate bank acquisitions were prohibited to federally supervised banks by the McFadden-Pepper Act in 1927 and by regulatory interpretation stretching back to the American Civil War. Nevertheless, several interstate acquisitions by bank holding companies and a few interstate full-service branch offices had previously been set up and continued to operate under the grandfather provisions of federal law. For the vast majority of American banks, though, interstate full-service banking was a virtual *impossibility* until the 1980s.

These legal restrictions against full-service bank expansion across state lines stifled serious research on the interstate banking phenomenon until the current decade when revisions in state and federal laws (such as the Garn–St Germain Depository Institutions Act of 1982) permitted interstate entry subject to stipulated conditions, such as to rescue a failing bank. Several key research studies have appeared recently, however, including those by Dunham (1986), Evanoff and Fortier (1986), Goldberg and Hanweck (1988), Hunter and Timme (1987), Mester (1987b), Phillis and Pavel (1986), Rogowski and Simonson (1987), J. T. Rose (1986, 1988), P. S. Rose, (1987, 1988a, 1988b, 1988c), Savage (1987), and Trifts and Scanlon (1987), and others. In this chapter we examine the findings of these important studies and their implications for the future of interstate banking in the United States.

POSSIBLE ADVANTAGES FOR BANKS CHOOSING
TO CROSS STATE LINES

One of the most difficult of all questions interstate bank researchers have faced is simply this: *why* do some banks — today a small minority of all U.S. banks — seek to grow and expand beyond their state's borders? What special competitive advantages might banks with interstate networks have over banks not choosing interstate expansion? We should not be surprised to find several different answers to those questions. Moreover, there is a deep controversy brewing in the banking research field over which of those answers, if any, is true.

Barriers to Entry and Excess Profits

One important line of argument about why some banking organizations cross state lines centers on the lure of possible excess profits — that is, a return to bank stockholders that exceeds the normal rate of return earned by firms in a perfectly competitive marketplace. Banking organizations that pursue interstate expansion may be seeking to corner at least a portion of the excess profits that previously sheltered markets have generated for some bank shareholders. As we saw in Chapter 3, the prohibitions against interstate banking contained in the McFadden-Pepper Act and other federal and state statutes represented significant barriers to entry for expansion-minded bankers for more than 50 years. These legal barriers *may* have permitted some commercial banks in the thousands of local county and city markets across the nation to earn relatively large profits without fear of new banks moving into their local markets.

The argument that entry barriers to a given market can result in excess profits for the businesses serving that market is a long-standing theory in economics. Moreover, the theory of market-entry barriers recognizes that there may be several different types of barriers present in any given situation, including natural barriers (e.g., rivers and mountains), technological barriers (e.g., communications and travel over long distances that are prohibitively expensive until cheaper methods are invented), and regulatory barriers (e.g., federal and state government rules that limit branch-office and holding-company expansion by banks). However, regardless of the type of entry barrier present in any given market, the end result should be much the same: entry barriers eliminate some would-be competitors, reducing actual competition, potential competition, or both; prices of goods and services and firm profits will tend to be higher relative to markets without significant entry barriers.

Is there any research evidence that supports the entry-barriers argument? One of the most convincing studies was prepared in the 1950s by economist Joe Bain (1957). Analyzing 20 different manufacturing industries, Bain found that profitability ratios were significantly higher in industries having significant barriers to entry compared to firms in industries with lower entry barriers. Similar findings were uncovered more than two decades later by Federal Reserve economists Savage and Rhoades (1979) who compared bank service prices and profits across local markets in states with varying branching laws. These economists found that unit (single-office) banks selling their services in states allowing entry through branch banking reported smaller profits and paid higher deposit interest rates to their customers than did unit banks headquartered in states where entry by branching was prohibited. Similar findings supporting the theory of entry barriers in banking were unveiled by Edwards (1965), Horvitz and Shull (1964), and Weintraub and Jessup (1964).

If barriers to entry are reduced or eliminated by interstate banking, what then? Theory teaches that profit-maximizing interstate banks will rush into those local markets where the previously sheltered banks are earning superior (excess) profits. Eventually, enough new competitors will appear so that prices and service fees on loans, deposits, and other bank services are driven down toward the levels prevailing in a perfectly competitive market with no significant entry barriers. In theory at least, the public will benefit not only from lower prices but also from a more optional allocation of the nation's scarce resources.

Is there any evidence from recent research to support this line of argument? Have interstate banks selected the most profitable local markets to enter? Have interstate banks created a more competitive environment in those local markets they have entered? Unfortunately, there is, as yet, no direct evidence bearing on any of these questions. The best evidence we have to date comes principally from studies of *intrastate* bank expansion, especially in those states where branching laws have recently been changed. And the results of those studies, including published research by Heggestad and Rhoades (1976), Rhodes (1979), Shull (1972), and Talley (1977), are not particularly encouraging to advocates of interstate banking.

In those local markets entered by branching, the result typically has been either no change or a reduction in the number of competitors. Moreover, in many instances market concentration has *increased*, with the largest banks capturing an even larger share of local deposits and loans. In large measure this research outcome could be attributed to the propensity of branch banks and holding companies to penetrate new markets by acquiring an existing competitor rather than starting a new (de novo) bank. At the statewide level the concentration of deposits and loans in dominant banking organizations did not appear to decline any faster in those states where banks were allowed to expand freely across the landscape compared to states where little geographic expansion was permitted.

These research findings do not *necessarily* imply that the geographic expansion of banks, particularly the spread of interstate banking, must reduce competition. In fact, a few recent studies find the opposite. For example, following a detailed review of the available literature, two economists at the Federal Reserve Bank of Chicago, Evanoff and Fortier (1986), conclude that a relaxation of barriers to bank geographic expansion has generally resulted in increasing competition and more intense rivalry between banking firms. An analysis of important measures of market concentration — the percentage of deposits controlled by the three largest banking corporations and the Herfindahl-Hirschmann index (i.e., the sum of all banks' shares of a given market squared) — revealed that, on average across the nation, local banking markets have experienced *declining* concentrations of deposits in the leading banks. Moreover, the greatest declines in local market concentration seem to have occurred in those metropolitan areas where bank-branching laws had been liberalized.

This conflict in recent research findings leaves us very much in the dark about how full-service interstate banking will affect competition. At the very least, however, the conflict in the research literature provides questionable support for those who argue that interstate bank expansion is likely to promote more intense competition in American banking. Still, recent research that uncovers a relationship between reduction of entry barriers and eventual increased concentration of banking resources with fewer surviving independent competitors, in both local and statewide areas, is consistent with the notion that banks expanding geographically *are* seeking higher profits. The largest American banks appear to be trying to use their comparative advantage over smaller banks (such as their generally superior capacity to develop and market new services, to purchase and employ up-to-date electronic equipment, or to raise new capital at lower cost) in order to reshape local, state, and regional markets more to their liking. If local county and city banking markets are eventually restructured to favor the largest banks, these institutions can pass the benefits of superior profits generated in less-than-perfectly-competitive markets along to their stockholders.

The Conglomerate Power Hypothesis

While the passage of interstate banking legislation in more than 40 states has lowered entry barriers for thousands of local banking markets across the nation, it may be that the spread of full-service interstate banking itself will erect a *new* set of entry barriers, denying the public the benefits of more intense competition among suppliers of financial services. Much depends on whether or not interstate acquiring banks are motivated primarily by the search for greater market power or by other factors.

One of the most controversial issues in the structure and organization of banking in recent years focuses on the possible validity or lack of validity of the conglomerate power hypothesis. This conceptual argument contends that at least *some* large banking organizations covet greater power and reduced competition in the markets they serve. By acquiring either the strongest merger targets or, at least, those target firms with the greatest potential for growth in market share, the interstate banking institution may use its newly acquired market power to carry out predatory pricing that drives smaller competitors from the market and prevents the entry of new firms. Moreover, as fewer banking firms begin to control larger shares of the different markets they serve, understandings may develop among these market leaders, that face each other time and again in many different communities, to share both customers and profits and to avoid competitive rivalry. Thus, entry barriers would rise higher because any banks desiring to enter these same markets would have to face the combined weight of large and widely diversified banking organizations determined to maintain the status quo.

Unfortunately, the research evidence produced thus far does *not* clearly support the conglomerate power hypothesis as an explanation of why some banks choose to enter new states. For example, a recent study by Curry and J. T. Rose (1984) looks at smaller metropolitan and rural areas in seven states — Alabama, Colorado, Florida, Missouri, Ohio, Tennessee, and Texas. A statistical (tobit) analysis of factors believed to affect bank entry in these markets finds *no* statistically significant evidence of barriers to entry from the mere presence of geographically diversified banking organizations in local banking markets. Another study carried out a decade earlier by Rhoades (1974) finds a tendency for firms in industries having a greater proportion of highly diversified firms to report greater profitability. However, a search of more broadly defined industries reveals no significant evidence in favor of the conglomerate power hypothesis.

At the very least, the market power motivation does *not* appear to be a dominant influence on the decision of banking organizations to expand across state lines. This is fortunate because the achievement and exercise of market power would come dangerously close to being illegal under federal anti-trust law, particularly if interstate bankers tried to avoid competition by agreeing on service prices and market shares.

The Signaling Effect

Interstate banking organizations may be seeking to benefit from a signaling effect influencing the behavior of capital-market investors when these organizations announce a new acquisition across state lines. Presumably, the ability to identify promising target firms and secure the approval of all the stockholders involved and the responsible regulatory agencies is tangible evidence of the inherent financial strength of a banking organization. As a result, capital-market investors typically upgrade the value of the stock of an acquiring interstate banking firm, resulting in increasing wealth for their shareholders. Unfortunately, there is, as yet, no agreed-on way to test the signaling hypothesis or to separate its impact from other possible motives that may lie behind interstate acquisitions.

Geographic Diversification

A more plausible explanation for interstate bank expansion is the popular geographic diversification argument. Interstate banks can spread out their public-service facilities and sell services over wider areas, encompassing a variety of different local economies. If branch-office sites are carefully selected, the interstate firm can enter markets across state lines that have different economic features from the local markets the organization already serves. A true geographic diversification effect is achieved if variations in economic activity in one or more local counties or metropolitan areas served are negatively correlated or have a positive, but numerically low correlation with economic activity in other markets served by the same banking organization. The results are a lower risk to the bank's earnings stream, a more stable rate of return for bank stockholders, and a reduced risk of bank failure.

Unfortunately, the research findings on geographic diversification in banking are not particularly promising as an explanation of why banks expand across state lines. Part of the reason may be the restrictions inherent in most state laws that limit bank expansion only to neighboring states, many of which have economic characteristics similar to those displayed by an interstate bank's home state. Moreover, as economists Liang and Rhoades (1988) have observed, acquiring organizations tend to "remake" the banks they purchase to look more like their existing banking affiliates, which may further reduce any benefits that true geographic diversification might otherwise provide.

Pursuit of a Quiet Life

Another viewpoint regarding the motives behind full-service interstate bank expansion is related closely to the conglomerate power theory. It is called the quiet life hypothesis. Allegedly, if a banking organization can achieve greater market power by acquiring banks in distant states, it can exercise that power either to earn superior profits *or* to achieve a position sheltered from the normal risk of loss inherent in a competitive market. A "quiet" existence characterized by low risk exposure may, for some banks, become more valuable than gouging the customers for more revenues and greater profits. Unfortunately, recent research by Hannan (1981), Mester (1987b), Rhoades and Rutz (1982), and others has *not* been supportive of the quiet life argument. It may be that recent federal and state deregulation of the banking industry, coupled with the spreading globalization of financial markets, has left few places where a bank can still enjoy the "quiet life," unchallenged by aggressive domestic or foreign competitors.

Economies of Scale and Scope

One of the most powerful economic arguments favoring large banking organizations is the belief that growth in size causes expenses—specifically, total cost per unit of output—to grow more slowly than output itself. For example, a doubling of bank output may result in *less* than a doubling of total operating costs up to some optimum bank size. Beyond that point, however, unit production costs begin to rise faster than the growth of output, often due to the problem of poor communications within a very large financial-service firm.

These scale economies may be supplemented by another source of cost savings—economies of scope—in which certain productive resources (such as management skills) are spread over multiple products more efficiently than would be the case if the firm were producing just one product. It is the *joint* production of two or more products at less cost than one product can be produced, that gives rise to economies of scope. Thus, it may be cheaper to combine a bank and an insurance agency under one roof, selling loans, deposits, and insurance policies, than to have two firms, one selling traditional banking products and the other selling insurance.

Unfortunately, as Clark (1988) observes, research evidence thus far does not generally support the existence of global economies of scope in banking, though there is some evidence of scope economies with selected pairs of financial products (as noted by Mester [1987a]). As for overall scale economies, these seem to be largely exhausted when a bank reaches approximately $100 million to $200 million in total assets – a moderate-size bank by American standards and a very small bank by world standards. This suggests that the smallest and most specialized banks may operate at a significant cost disadvantage compared to large interstate organizations and will need to approach at least the $100 million asset level to survive in the long run. However, once they reach or are near this optimal-cost point, *any* depository financial institution should compare favorably in production costs and efficiency of operations with the largest interstate banking firms.

In fairness we must note that not all the studies of scale economies conclude that cost savings are exhausted when a bank reaches only moderate size. For example, a preliminary, but fascinating research paper by Federal Reserve economists Shaffer and Edmond (1986) on the cost behavior of billion-dollar U.S. banks – institutions far larger than those studied in nearly all previous bank-cost studies – finds evidence that the most efficient banks lie in the range of about $15 billion to $37 billion in total assets. These researchers use the relatively new technique of hedonic regression and include estimates of the cost benefits of diversification – a form of cost savings not fully available to the smallest banks in the industry. Shaffer and Edmond conclude that diseconomies from bank growth need *not* slow down the expansion of banking organizations across state lines and could benefit bank customers if operating costs can be lowered even for some of the largest banks in the nation.

However, if U.S. banking *is* characterized by only modest scale economies given current technology, as *most* research studies report, there is little reason (from a cost perspective at least) to expect that the largest interstate banking organizations inevitably will come to dominate American banking. The smallest banks, offering only a limited range of services, can still survive and prosper if the majority of research studies are correct in their conclusions.

A SUMMARY VIEW OF INTERSTATE
BANKING MOTIVATIONS

In summary, the findings of recent research studies leave us with few unchallenged opinions regarding the possible motivations behind interstate bank expansion. The conventional wisdom suggests that increased profitability, gains in efficiency and diversification, and possible reductions of competition and operating risk should play dominant roles in shaping mergers and acquisitions among the nation's largest banks. This *may* still be true because the research studies produced to date suffer from a number of serious methodological and data limitations. The least we can say at this juncture is that no clear-cut "winner" has emerged to explain the massive movement underway in American banking toward the new markets that lie on the distant horizon.

RESEARCH STUDIES OF INTERSTATE BANKING EFFECTS AND BEHAVIOR

Although recent research studies provide little undisputed evidence on the factors behind interstate mergers and acquisitions, what does existing research have to say about the *effects* of interstate banking? What benefits and costs does the interstate banking revolution appear to offer banking and the American public? Is there a tangible reward, perhaps in the form of better-quality financial services at lower cost, lying somewhere near the end of the current march toward full-service interstate banking?

Interstate Expansion Strategies

One of the most comprehensive studies ever conducted on interstate bank expansion was carried out by two Federal Reserve economists, Phillis and Pavel (1986), who examined the characteristics of banking organizations targeted for acquisition in interstate mergers during the 1981–85 period. They found that most of these early interstate acquisitions, which were concentrated in the southeastern, northeastern, and New England regions of the United States, reflected a long-run strategic plan by acquiring organizations to increase their ability to produce and deliver *retail* (household) banking services. For example, the loan portfolios of the banks acquired had greater proportions of loans to individuals and families than did the loan portfolios of their interstate acquirers, which tended to emphasize business loans instead. Moreover, reflecting their emphasis on individual consumers rather than on business firms, banks acquired across state lines frequently operated large-scale branch-office networks for which interstate banking institutions were willing to pay a substantial premium over their book value to acquire.

Phillis and Pavel found, too, that interstate bank acquirers possessing large branch-office networks were more likely to purchase banks in other states than were comparably sized banking organizations without substantial numbers of branch offices. Moreover, acquiring banks on average were much larger in size than were randomly selected nonacquiring institutions, which these researchers referred to as "spectators" — banks choosing *not* to play the interstate game. Acquiring banks venturing across state lines averaged 138 branch offices apiece versus 5 offices, on average, for comparable-size banks not pursuing interstate mergers. Acquiring institutions tended also to have a substantially larger share of statewide deposits than did spectator institutions; the acquirer's statewide deposit share was almost 23 times that of the average noninvolved banking institution.

Interstate acquirers depended heavily upon large-denomination money-market deposits (e.g., negotiable CDs greater than $100,000 apiece sold mainly to corporations) as a major source of funding, while their acquisition targets received more of their funding from the relatively small-denomination deposits purchased by households and small businesses. Not surprisingly, acquiring institutions generally were much larger in size than were the banking organizations they purchased. In Phillis and Pavel's sample the acquiring banks held total assets that averaged about $4 billion, compared to just $1 billion in average assets reported by the acquired institutions.

While Phillis and Pavel concluded that interstate bank expansion was predominantly based on an organizational strategy aimed at a larger share of consumer (retail) financial-service markets, at least in the early stages of the interstate movement, Hunter and Timme (1987, 1988) are two researchers who viewed the process of interstate expansion as a response to changing technology and the resulting reduced production costs. They found that recent technological innovations had lowered real production costs among the nation's top 400 banks over the 1980–86 period and significantly increased the required bank size to achieve maximum operating efficiency. In Hunter and Timme's view the largest U.S. banking firms have been excited by the prospect of lowering their real operating costs through the acquisition and deployment of large-scale service production and delivery processes.

While interstate acquisitions might lead to concentrated market power in selected banking markets, these researchers argued that the pursuit of mergers among the largest American banks could stimulate efficient service innovation, resulting in greater convenience and perhaps lower service fees for consumers. After analyzing large-scale holding-company operations in the 1970s and 1980s, Hunter and Timme concluded that the superior economic profits and capital resources of the largest U.S. banking organizations, coupled with recent technological innovation, could generate significant economies of "super-scale" favoring the biggest banks in the nation. Viewed in this context, recent full-service interstate bank expansion owes its origin to expected gains in productivity and operating efficiency traceable to technological breakthroughs in communications and information processing technology.

In two related studies P. S. Rose (1988a, 1988b) examined the financial profiles of banks acquired by interstate companies and the profiles of the interstate acquirers themselves over the 1980–87 period. He finds that banks purchased across state lines, on average, were *not* superior performers during this time period. Quite to the contrary, acquired banks displayed lower-than-average rates of return for their stockholders and increasing risk exposure as the date for their purchase neared. The 105 interstate-acquired lead banks included in Rose's sample reported both lower rates of return on their assets and lower returns on owners' equity capital compared to similar-size banks operating in the same states and metropolitan areas. This finding led Rose to argue that, if profitability was the primary rationale behind the recent revolution in interstate banking, management and shareholders must have been looking at the *expected* profitability of the acquired banking firms, not their *actual* profitability.

Banks acquired across state lines also generally operated with a thinner cushion of equity capital relative to their total assets, suggesting greater exposure to the risk of failure than comparable-size banks not joining interstate networks. Further evidence of this greater risk exposure was found in the form of higher levels of loan losses relative to the safety cushion of long-term (equity) capital contributed by their stockholders. Moreover, the banks purchased in distant states displayed lower operating efficiency and lower employee productivity (measured by the volume of total assets and total revenues generated per employee) compared to banks of similar size head-quartered in the same state, suggesting an "efficiency gap" that may well have played a significant role in identifying these institutions as targets for interstate mergers. Managements of the largest American banks have frequently expressed confidence in their ability to turn unprofitable and inefficient banks into highly profitable operations through a combination of cost-cutting measures, technological updating, more effective promotional campaigns, superior portfolio management techniques, and more realistic pricing of services. Moreover, banks that are performing poorly usually can be purchased for lower prices, and there is likely to be substantially less resistance to the proposed acquisition by the management and stockholders of the target institutions.

When P. S. Rose looked not just at individual banks acquired by purchasers from out of state, but also at the *entire* banking company that was acquired (including *all* of its affiliated firms), the performance differences compared to banks not acquired in interstate transactions were even stronger than before. The profitability (measured by return on assets) of the acquired consolidated banking companies was lower than that of nonacquired banking companies, with a statistically significant difference in four of the five years before their acquisition occurred. Operating revenues over operating costs — an important efficiency measure — was also well *below* the average for similar nonacquired banks. Moreover, each acquired company's average rate of return on stockholders' equity capital was lower than the average equity return of similar-size banks not involved in cross-border mergers, significantly so in the year preceding acquisition. Capital-to-asset ratios — an index of the risk of bank failure — of the banking firms taken over by out-of-state institutions were *below* the average for nonacquired banks, suggesting that acquired banking companies had a thinner cushion against losses on loans and other risk-exposed assets and, therefore, were more likely to fail than similar-size institutions.

What do these findings imply? Do they suggest that American interstate banking firms deliberately pursue high-risk merger targets? Are their managements more risk prone? Not necessarily. More plausible perhaps is the argument that, until very recently in many states, interstate mergers were more likely to be approved (and, therefore, carried a lower regulatory cost burden) if acquiring banks agreed to absorb banking firms that were failing or in serious jeopardy. Thus, the population of interstate acquired firms — at least those acquired during the first decade of the interstate banking movement — is still heavily weighted by troubled banks. In addition, most acquisitions, both in and out of the banking industry, are motivated by *perceptions* of possible increases in the value of acquired firms once new management takes over. Banks that are in trouble frequently can be purchased cheaply and, perhaps, with skilled management, as well as technical and financial assistance from the regulatory agencies (principally the FDIC), can be returned to profitability.

In contrast to P. S. Rose's internal analysis of the features of interstate acquired banking firms, Savage (1987) seeks to identify the external factors — predominantly market structure and economic conditions — that stimulate and explain recent interstate bank expansion. He argues that potential for faster deposit growth and greater overall deposit volume have been key predictors of which states and local areas were entered first by interstate acquirers. For example, Florida has been a leading target entry area for banks along the Atlantic coastline due to its rapid growth and large deposit volume. Florida banks, on the other hand, have been much less inclined to venture outside that state.

Savage suggests that pursuit of scale economies resulting from the growth of individual banks and banking companies is also an important reason for the interstate banking revolution. Potential savings in operating costs have become a more important lure to aggressive banking institutions than ever before due to increasing competition and pressure on earnings as thousands of nonbank financial firms and foreign banking institutions have invaded the traditional service markets of American banks. Moreover, Savage finds little evidence of an adverse trend in the structure of local banking markets toward less competition and more concentrated market power due to mergers and acquisitions across state lines. True, nearly all interstate expansion has consisted of acquisitions of *existing* banks, not the chartering of new banks. Thus, market concentration in local areas has neither increased nor decreased on balance; essentially, one set of stockholders (owners) is substituted for another in an interstate merger. However, at the national level, the proportion of aggregate deposits held by the largest U.S. banking organizations should increase as a result of the interstate banking movement, Savage argues. The continuation of full-service interstate banking will mean that, eventually, American banking will become more concentrated because only the largest money-center banking organizations are likely to take advantage of interstate banking laws.

This concentrating impact on the nationwide banking system may be irrelevant, however, because banking markets are *not* defined or necessarily constrained by political boundaries. Moreover, what matters most to individuals and small businesses is the availability, quality, and price of banking services in the communities where they live and work. An increase in nationwide banking concentration—that is, greater dominance of the largest banking organizations—may actually result in *greater* competition in *local* financial-service markets. If the nation's leading banks eventually come to face off against each other in thousands of local communities across the United States, competitive rivalry between these firms may become intense, and the ultimate beneficiary will be the consumer of banking services. We must keep in mind that competition in business is not a matter of numbers; rather, it is a matter of how firms *behave* as they are confronted with the pricing schedules and marketing initiatives of their rivals. Rivalry in the marketplace may exist in an area served by 200 firms or only 2.

Effects of Interstate Expansion on the Banks Acquired

While there have been few direct tests of the possible benefits to banks from interstate acquisitions, there is at least *indirect* evidence of how investors in the markets for bank stock perceive the gains and losses from both geographic and service expansion by banking organizations. For example, a recent study by Eisenbeis, Harris, and Lakonishok (1984) found *positive* changes in average returns to the shareholders of large bank holding companies engaged in expanding their service offerings over the 1968–74 period. When these institutions formed one-bank holding companies in order to be able to acquire various nonbank businesses, their stock prices rose, generating positive abnormal returns for their shareholders. Moreover, these researchers concluded that geographic diversification by banks, such as through acquisitions of other banks or branching into new areas, would have a greater positive impact on a banking institution's stock price than would product-line diversification through the acquisition of nonbank businesses. Therefore, potentially at least, interstate geographic expansion offers greater opportunities for increasing bank stock values than do service innovation and the mere proliferation of bank service offerings. However, management must still *deliver* superior performance if bank shareholders are to benefit.

Moreover, there is some evidence that stockholders of banking companies targeted for acquisition have benefitted significantly from the large premiums over book value often paid by interstate acquirers. Evidence of this sort was presented recently by Rogowski and Simonson (1987) who explored the impact of recent interstate acquisitions on the premiums paid to complete bank mergers. These premiums typically are measured by the price paid for each share of bank stock less the stock's book value per share divided by that same book value.[2] They began with the working hypothesis that the mere possibility of interstate entry increases the number of potential bidders for banks and leads to higher merger premiums, other factors held constant.

Rogowski and Simonson estimate several regression models in an effort to explain two principal measures of bank merger premiums paid: the price-to-book-value ratio and the deposit premium. The independent variables used to explain these two indicators of bank merger premiums included (1) financial factors (such as rates of return on shareholders' equity capital, capital-to-total-assets ratios, the numbers of long-term bonds held relative to total assets, and the relative asset sizes of acquiring and acquired firms), (2) market conditions (including market concentration and capacity), (3) the medium of exchange used to effect the merger (such as the volume of cash exchanged relative to the purchase price), and (4) the character of the interstate banking law applicable to each merger.

Only two explanatory variables were consistently significant in the Rogowski-Simonson study: the relative size of the participating firms (i.e., the logarithmic difference in total assets between acquiring and acquired banking institutions), and the ratio of holdings of long-term bonds (over five years to maturity) to total assets. The authors argue that the relative size of participating banks is statistically significant because a larger acquiring bank might be more successful at deriving excess value from a smaller acquired firm due to its superior management and/or significant scale and scope economies. The authors conclude that the true impact of interstate banking on bank merger premiums must still be regarded as uncertain, but that at least *some* positive excess premium for stockholders of the *acquired* bank would be necessary to bring about an interstate merger. The average merger premium in interstate combinations may be as high as one-fourth of the book value, on average, of each bank acquired across state lines.

Interestingly, the conclusion that interstate banking legislation tends to increase the size of premiums paid for banks acquired via merger has not been universally accepted. For example, a recent study by Rose (1988c) of more than 500 bank mergers in 45 states found that the presence of interstate banking legislation tended to *lower* average merger premiums. The author cites two possible reasons for this finding:

1. The weakening economies in several states (most notably the midwestern and Rocky Mountain states, hurt by sagging farm and energy prices) that recently passed interstate banking legislation have depressed the market values of the banks in those regions, making them less attractive merger targets; and/or

2. The relative numbers of bidders (acquirers) and acquisition targets in any given state have changed due to interstate banking legislation. (If the number of bidders increases relative to acquisition targets, merger premiums presumably will tend to rise as competition among bidders drives bank stock prices higher; however, the presence of more acquisition targets relative to bidders would tend to lower the

merger premiums paid; when several states enact *reciprocal* banking laws, the number of acquisition targets may rise faster the number of bidders, pushing merger premiums lower. Thus, there is no iron-clad guarantee that bank stock prices and merger premiums will rise when a state opens its borders to interstate banking.)

An earlier study by Pettway and Trifts (1985) of the periodic auctions conducted by the Federal Deposit Insurance Corporation (FDIC) for the assets of failed banks found evidence that excessive bid prices *have* been paid in these auctions. Returns to the winning bidders in FDIC auctions typically have fallen following the public announcement of auction results. However, the small number of observations included in this study argues for additional future research on stockholders' returns from mergers involving failing firms. (In fact, a more recent study by James and Wier [1987] of FDIC auctions of the assets of failed banks finds evidence of abnormal returns reaped by the winning bidders and a wealth transfer from the FDIC to the winning banks.) At least there is the suggestion here that interstate acquirers often pay too much for the banking firms they buy, and this excess payment generally extends the period of time required before the acquiring institution is fully paid back for its initial capital investment.

Still, *some* evidence has emerged recently that the stockholders of *both* acquiring and acquired interstate banks may benefit from interstate mergers and acquisitions, particularly in the case of the largest merger transactions. Weak evidence in this direction is provided by Cox and Grunewald (1988), who examined mergers and holding-company acquisitions for the 1968–83 period. Stronger evidence emerges in a study of 21 interstate mergers ending in 1985 by Trifts and Scanlon (1987). These researchers looked for evidence of positive and statistically significant abnormal returns to the shareholders of acquiring interstate firms, acquired banking companies, or both. Consistent with a large body of research on nonfinancial mergers, Trifts and Scanlon found, in general, that the stockholders of acquired banking companies do gain by scoring above-normal returns that add to the total value of their wealth, while the shareholders of acquiring institutions roughly break even around the announcement dates of their mergers.

However, acquiring banks were *not* viewed by the stock market as a homogeneous group. Acquiring banking organizations involved in the *largest* mergers substantially outperformed those undertaking small acquisitions. Stockholders of acquiring institutions appeared to increase the value of their wealth significantly if the marketplace saw the interstate merger as opening up *substantial* new opportunities for geographic expansion. Clearly, not every interstate bank acquisition will benefit bank stockholders, but those judged to offer a substantial change in an acquiring bank's set of opportunities will, more than likely, result in higher stock prices.

Even stronger and more complete evidence of shareholder gains from interstate acquisitions and mergers has emerged from a review of 37 acquired banking organizations and 153 acquiring banking organizations for the 1982–86 period by De and Millon (1988). These researchers tested two significant events in the recent history of these institutions: the announcement of each interstate merger bid, and the passage of an interstate acquisitions bill in each banking organization's home state. De and Millon uncovered evidence that interstate acquiring bank shareholders, along with stockholders of acquired banking organizations, receive significant returns *above* what would normally be predicted from the amount of risk taken on when the merger or acquisition is announced, regardless of the financing techniques used to effect the acquisition and regardless of the location and size of the banks involved. Moreover, stockholders of target acquired banks receive positive excess returns when their home state's legislature passes a bill allowing out-of-state banking organizations to come in and also when their home state's governor signs that bill into law. The authors concluded that "passage of the interstate banking act in a state constitutes 'good news' for the local banks that are interested in or are potential targets of acquisition by out-of-state banks" (De and Millon 1988, 20). However, these researchers were unable to determine whether the bank stockholder gains observed were due to the benefits of greater geographic diversification, the positive signaling effect from a public announcement, or some other cause.

One of the greatest fears of bankers facing competition from interstate firms is that their banks may be "driven from the market"—that is, forced to accept a declining share of local loans and deposits until their institution is no longer viable. While we have only limited research evidence to date concerning the impact of multiple-office banking firms on market share, the evidence that does exist suggests that most smaller, locally oriented U.S. banks have little to fear from interstate banking organizations, at least in terms of protecting their existing market shares.

For example, Goldberg and Hanweck (1988) recently examined the performance of those banks already operating full-service interstate offices that were grandfathered by the Bank Holding Company Act of 1956. The Douglas Amendment to that holding-company law prohibited a banking company from acquiring controlling interest in a bank across state lines without express state approval to do so. However, 7 domestically chartered companies, operating in 37 states and controlling more than 200 banks, had made their acquisitions *prior* to passage of the Bank Holding Company Act and were, therefore, permitted to retain their existing banks. These grandfathered interstate organizations included First Interstate Bancorp of Los Angeles, First Bank System, Inc. and Norwest Corp. of Minneapolis; Otto Bremer Foundation of St. Paul; General Bancshares Corp. of St. Louis; First Security Corp. of St. Louis; and Credit and Commerce American of Curacao in the Netherlands Antilles (formerly called Financial General, based in Washington, D.C.).

Arguing that interstate expansion is likely to threaten the market share and profitability of noninterstate banks only if it confers real economic advantages (such as reducing risk exposure, increasing operating efficiency, or allowing superior service offerings) to banking firms reaching across state lines, Goldberg and Hanweck plotted changes in the individual bank shares of statewide deposits and the profitability of both interstate acquired institutions and comparable nonacquired banks. A linear regression model was used, with explanatory variables included to capture the effects of bank size, the growth rate of the state involved, bank liquidity, and the character of a state's branching law. They found that the majority of interstate acquired banking firms (23 for the entire period) experienced *decreases* in their statewide deposit shares over the 1960–83 study period. Moreover, while holding-company affiliated banks were significantly more profitable at the beginning of the study period (1960) than other banks in the same state, by the end of the period (1983) there were no statistically significant differences in profitability (measured in terms of either return on assets or return on equity capital) or in portfolio composition between interstate acquired institutions and other banks operating in the same state. There was also evidence that those banking companies with the largest initial deposit size were the banks most likely to suffer a decline in deposit market share later on.

Overall, Goldberg and Hanweck found that, by the end of their study period (1983), the grandfathered interstate bank holding company organizations were "very similar" to their peers. Competition had wiped away any advantages the interstate affiliated banks may have possessed when the period began. Thus, these researchers argued, "lifting the restrictions on interstate banking may not result in the dominance of local or regional markets by large interstate banking organizations" (Goldberg and Hanweck 1988, 67).

Corroboration of this fundamental conclusion about the survivability of smaller, independent banks in the era of full-service interstate banking was recently supplied by J. T. Rose (1988) and by Curry and J. T. Rose (1984). They found that the organizers of new independent banks generally expect their banks to compete effectively against interstate firms. Thus, the intention of most new bank organizers appears to be to operate their institutions indefinitely, rather than selling out their banks at a profit to interstate acquirers as soon as possible. Moreover, Rose and Curry could find no significant evidence that organizers of new independent banks were dissuaded from entry into new markets simply because large, geographically diversified banking organizations were already present there.

WILL INTERSTATE BANKING BENEFIT OR COST THE PUBLIC?

While the shareholders of acquired banking organizations *may* benefit from interstate activity in the form of hefty merger premiums, it is at least debatable whether interstate mergers are likely to benefit the general public, especially *local* consumers of banking services. The range of available services may increase, but what about bank service prices, particularly rates on loans? And will interstate acquirers add funds to or drain funds away from local communities?

Constance Dunham (1986), an economist at the Federal Reserve Bank of Boston, points out that there are important geographic intermediation issues arising out of the expansion of full-service interstate banking organizations. These institutions may drain away local funds, contributing perhaps to a more efficient financial system (i.e., scarce loanable funds will flow more easily to their highest-return uses). However, to the local communities that have funds routed away to distant cities and, therefore, that have less credit available to support local projects, the impact of interstate banking would probably be viewed as decidedly negative. Dunham, however, finds little or no evidence that interstate banking usually increases long-distance geographic intermediation and drains away local funds. Regional, national, and international funds transfers are already practiced by both large and small banks through the correspondent banking system that routes funds and services between banks. Full-service interstate banking appears to have little impact on the functioning of correspondent banks and on the flow of funds between institutions.

To reach such a conclusion, Dunham compiled estimates of what she called the *local ratio*—that is, local uses of funds (principally consumer and smaller business loans) compared to local sources of funds (principally small time and savings deposits). She finds that regional and money-center banks have a local ratio *close to one*, indicating a roughly equal balance between funds gathered from local communities and credit returned to those same communities. In fact, some of the regional and money-center banks studied by Dunham appeared to be *net importers* of local funds (i.e., credit extended to the local community exceeded its local deposits). In contrast, the smaller community banks she examined tended to be *net funds exporters* from their local communities with an average local ratio of *less than one* (i.e., credit extended locally was less than total local funds raised). Thus, Dunham finds little support for the argument that interstate acquiring banks drain scarce capital from county and city market areas in order to make loans to distant businesses and governments.

In a somewhat earlier study that drew on evidence from previous intrastate merger, branching, and acquisition research projects, Dunham and Syron (1984) made several predictions concerning the effects of interstate banking on local communities, nationwide banking concentration, and the offering of financial services. They concluded that, in most cases, local competition will be unaffected or possibly even improved through the spread of full-service interstate banking. One reason for this conclusion was their belief that banking firms acquired by interstate companies will be managed more aggressively and become more prone to rivalry in their local markets, jousting with local competitors and encouraging those competitors also to become more aggressive in pursuing customers. As a result, these researchers recommended permitting full-service banking nationwide, with upper limits placed on the national share of assets that any one banking corporation can hold (such as New Hampshire's rule that a maximum of 15 percent of statewide deposits can be held by any one banking institution growing through acquisitions).

Dunham and Syron concluded that the largest banking organizations will be more likely to expand across state lines. Moreover, they suggested that interstate banking firms will tend to accelerate their internal growth as they seek out both new markets and target firms that either display more rapid actual growth or at least possess the *potential* for more rapid growth in the future. National banking concentration, they argued, *will* increase because local competitors of interstate banks are more likely to pursue their own acquisitions in order to remain competitive in a dynamic and rapidly changing financial marketplace. The net result will be fewer independent banks and a higher percentage of resources controlled by the largest banks in the nation, but not necessarily less competition. Indeed, competitive rivalry may actually increase as more aggressive firms lock horns in thousands of local communities across America.

THE RESEARCH EVIDENCE ACQUIRED FROM INTRASTATE STRUCTURAL STUDIES

Long before studies of interstate banking were attempted, numerous research studies were aimed at bank mergers and holding-company acquisitions within individual states. While these *intrastate* bank mergers are likely to have somewhat different effects than will interstate banking combinations, some states (such as California, New York, and Texas) are so large that the causes and effects of mergers and acquisitions within their borders may be quite comparable to many interstate merger transactions today. What do these earlier studies contribute to our understanding of the causes and effects of the interstate banking revolution?

There is evidence from surveys of bankers involved in intrastate mergers and acquisitions that expected profitability and reduction of risk (in its alternative dimensions of equity-capital, liquidity, and interest-rate risk) are the key motivators of organizational change in banking (P. S. Rose 1987). However, the observed relationships among bank mergers and acquisitions and *intrastate* banking profitability, risk exposure, pricing policies, portfolio mix, and operating efficiency are often weak and tenuous. Frequently these relationships are statistically insignificant or, when statistically significant, are quantitatively de minimus in impact (as observed, for example, by Rhoades [1982]).

One notable exception to the finding of a relatively weak impact from intrastate mergers and acquisitions is the significant difference frequently uncovered between the ratio of total loans to total assets of acquired banks and that of nonmerging institutions (as illustrated, for example, in the studies by Brown [1986], Dunham [1986], and Rose and Scott [1984]). Banks acquired or merged soon report, on average, larger amounts of loans relative to their total assets than other banks. Because the loan-asset ratio is an index of bank risk exposure, this finding suggests that merger-bound banks tend to accept greater risk in their portfolios, either because they are managed more aggressively or because they believe that greater geographic diversification through merger aids in reducing their overall risk exposure, allowing them to take on more loans. There is, however, no consistent evidence of any significant damage to competition in the wake of outside entry into local banking markets by larger banking organizations (as reported, for example, by Curry and J. T. Rose [1984]).

There is also little or no evidence of substantial cost savings — economies of scale or scope — due to favorable changes in single-plant, multi-plant, or product-specific production costs in the intrastate bank merger and acquisition literature. Larger, more diversified banking organizations do *not* appear to possess a substantial operating cost advantage over smaller, less diversified banking firms. As noted by Benston, Hanweck, and Humphrey (1982); Clark (1988); Humphrey (1985); and P. S. Rose (1987), among others, cost economies for the individual banking firm appear to be largely exhausted beyond $100 or $200 million in total assets.

Finally, industrial-organization research focused on local (urban and rural) banking markets finds only limited support for the conglomerate power hypothesis concerning the motivations for intrastate bank mergers.[3] If banks acquire other banks to gain added market power which they use to their benefit and to the detriment of the public, researchers have yet to find convincing evidence to that effect, either inside individual states or across the nation as a whole. Thus, the far more voluminous intrastate acquisition studies carried out before the interstate banking movement began find few tangible benefits from bank mergers and acquisitions, except that merged banks tend to be larger with a longer menu of services and appear to be less prone to failure.

A SUMMARY AND ANALYSIS OF RESEARCH FINDINGS

The body of research studies on American interstate banking is at once enlightening and confusing. That literature finds some completely logical reasons behind recent interstate bank expansion. For example, existing studies suggest that banking organizations are reaching across state lines in order to attract predominantly household customers with checking and savings programs by offering consumer loans and other household-related services. In part, this predominantly retail orientation of interstate banking organizations represents an effort to diversify banking operations by product line and by geography because the lead banks in these organizations are usually wholesale-oriented banks with high proportions of business loans and business deposits in their portfolios. Thus, interstate banking appears to offer the prospect of additional competition in local service markets, particularly in those communities with large numbers of households and small businesses.

Related to the consumer orientation of most interstate acquisitions, these banking firms seem especially interested in household deposits as a source of funding. Deposits made by individuals and families typically are of relatively small denomination, but also generally possess relatively low interest-rate elasticity (i.e., they carry low liquidity risk to the bank). Deposits with low interest elasticity carry lower risk of loss for banks because these funds are less likely than are other bank funds sources (such as large corporate deposits or borrowings in the money market) to be withdrawn when market interest rates climb upward.

Interstate banks appear not only to be searching for deposits of low interest-rate elasticity but also to have identified households and smaller businesses found in larger communities as key targets for their own future growth and survival. For more than a decade now, U.S. banks have been losing their traditional share of global service markets to aggressive banks from abroad, particularly British, Canadian, French, and Japanese banks. Not only have foreign-chartered banks reduced the market shares of U.S. banks in western Europe and around the Pacific Basin, but also these foreign-based institutions have dramatically increased their share of the domestic U.S. market for large-denomination corporate loans. The result is an intensely competitive, wholesale international credit market in which American banks are not always the winners. Many U.S. banks, therefore, have changed their long-run growth strategies, targeting the domestic market for small business and household accounts in the most promising local communities. American bankers seem to feel less challenged by foreign competitors in smaller, localized markets where they share a strong cultural bond with the customers they serve.

This shift of strategy from selling more business-oriented financial services to selling more household-oriented financial services helps us to understand why researchers to date have found little undisputed evidence of cost savings, market power, or diversification benefits from interstate expansion. It may not be true that interstate banks will benefit from their large volume of service operations in reducing production cost per unit, in wielding greater power to control prices or market shares, or in achieving lower risk by entering new states. Rather, interstate banking organizations, operating for the most part from a *defensive* posture, seem to have sought out new markets where they perceive competition to be less intense and profit margins more substantial than in the international banking sector.

There is, as yet, no convincing evidence that interstate banks are more profitable or more successful at defending their market shares than are banks of similar size that are not pursuing interstate mergers and acquisitions. Yet this may not be a result of operating inefficiencies or management miscalculations. Many interstate banking mergers, especially those taking place from the early to the mid-1980s, have involved the absorption of troubled banking firms, often with the assistance of the FDIC. Thus, it is unlikely that future researchers will find evidence of substantial improvement in the performance of interstate banking organizations until the troubled banks they have acquired have been fully assimilated into their acquiring institutions.

In many ways the findings of recent research on interstate banking and its impact on individual banks and the public are disappointing. There are few identifiable benefits, and many of these alleged benefits are disputed by inconsistent findings in the relevant research literature. Interstate banking still shows no undisputed evidence that it enhances economic growth, increases bank profitability, or reduces the risk of bank failure. The one benefit that seems defensible at this point is a probable increase in competition in supplying financial services to households and small businesses. However, this and other possible benefits will accrue only to those local markets that interstate banks choose to enter. Thus far, these markets include most of the nation's largest cities, but little penetration of smaller cities and rural areas has occurred. Therefore, the expected benefits from full-service interstate banking will probably remain small or nonexistent for most American communities for the foreseeable future.

On the other hand, there are also few apparent costs to the American economy from the spread of interstate banking. Little research evidence exists that full-service interstate banking organizations are more risky, are more prone to failure, or lead to reduced competition, higher service prices, or reduced service quality. When the first states legalized bank entry from outside their borders, they appeared to benefit with more jobs and more financial-center activity. For the states that followed later, however, the apparent economic benefits evaporated quickly. At the very least, if previous research is a reliable guide, the American public appears to have little to fear from the spread of interstate banking. The same may be said of American bankers, unless they refuse to compete and battle for every customer or, throwing aside the welfare of their stockholders, refuse to even consider take-over bids that interstate bankers may send their way. The market system *is* the most efficient mechanism for allocating society's scarce resources that has yet to be devised. However, that marketplace works well and benefits the consumer in real terms only if businessmen and women choose to accept the challenge of competition and strive unceasingly to offer better-quality services to each and every customer.

NOTES

1. The reader will find a good discussion of the claims for and against multiple-office (branch and holding-company) banking, along with evidence on both sides of the issue in works by Darnell (1973), McCall and Lane (1980), and the Subcommittee on Financial Institutions (1976).

2. For a discussion of how bank merger premiums are calculated, see Chapter 7.

3. The most detailed study of the possible existence of the conglomerate power motive in financial-institution mergers was prepared recently by Mester (1987b). She concludes that allowing bank acquisitions across multiple markets results in less stability of deposit market shares, greater average savings balances, diminished profitability, lower loan rates, and elevated deposit interest rates — all of these changes consistent with the notion of increasing, rather than decreasing, competition. The prospect of increased savings-account growth is a potentially important clue concerning the motivations for interstate bank expansion because it raises the probability of reduced capital costs and lower liquidity pressures due to the greater proportion of low interest-rate-elastic savings deposits, derived principally from households and small business customers.

5

Public Policy Issues Raised by the Expansion of Banking Across State Lines

Will interstate banking, particularly if it expands to become full-service nationwide banking, generate substantial new regulatory and supervisory issues for federal and state banking authorities? Will the present distribution and scope of supervision and regulation have to be changed in order to protect the public interest? Will there be jurisdictional conflicts between federal and state regulatory agencies as interstate banking spreads? Are any consumer groups likely to be seriously disadvantaged as a result of these structural changes in the industry and, therefore, in need of special regulatory protection? And could regulators be confronted with still more bank failures, straining an already weakened bank regulatory system facing billions of dollars in depositor claims as more bank and thrift institutions collapse?

These are difficult questions to answer because there is little prior experience to draw on. Historically, as we saw in Chapter 3, U.S. banking has been a highly localized industry, serving local neighborhoods, communities, cities, and counties. However, the limited evidence accumulated thus far suggests that any new supervisory and regulatory problems will be *moderate*. Acquisitions within the same region of the nation generally will fit comfortably under the same federal supervisory and regulatory agencies as before.

For example, mergers and acquisitions bringing together Florida and Georgia banks and bank holding companies would come under the supervision of the Federal Reserve Bank of Atlanta and also the southeast regional office of the Comptroller of the Currency (if national banks are involved) or the banking commissions of the two states involved (if state-chartered banks are merging). Most frequently, it is the acquirer's federal supervisory agency that is most directly involved in an interstate merger or acquisition, along with the state banking commission in the home state of the acquired institution.

POSSIBLE DAMAGE TO COMPETITION IN SERVING
MIDDLE-MARKET BUSINESS FIRMS?

One potentially important issue for bank regulators and, ultimately, for the U.S. Congress was noted recently by Federal Reserve economist Constance Dunham (1986). This issue centers on the possible damage to middle-market business firms—those businesses with annual sales of, for example, $50 million up to about $250 million—as interstate acquisitions combine banks with headquarters in neighboring cities. The danger is that acquisitions of this kind can reduce the level of competition in providing banking services to firms of this particular size. Because middle-size companies tend to deal in broader financial-service markets—covering several cities or an entire region—the merger of even geographically separated banks can reduce the number of financial-service suppliers to these companies. Economic theory suggests that, as the market for financial services directed at middle-range businesses becomes more concentrated, this could lead to higher prices for credit and other banking services and to poorer service quality for thousands of these firms.

This possibly damaging outcome from interstate mergers for business customers points to the need for greater vigilance on the part of the federal regulatory agencies and the U.S. Department of Justice. These agencies have been charged by Congress with the responsibility of assessing the competitive impact of any proposed bank merger or acquisition. Federal law, beginning with the Sherman Act of 1890 and the Clayton Act of 1914, requires all regulatory agencies that are affected by a business merger or acquisition to determine the probable effects of that proposed combination on competition in serving the public. Both the Bank Merger Act of 1960 (as amended in 1966) and the Bank Holding Company Act of 1956 (also amended in 1966) require each banking agency to determine whether a proposed merger or acquisition would have a "substantially adverse" impact on competition in the market areas to be served. If so, the request to merge must be denied, and the Justice Department will bring suit in federal court to stop the transaction if that becomes necessary.

KEY REGULATORY ISSUES THAT MUST BE FACED
UNDER INTERSTATE BANKING

Will concentration increase in the middle market for business services as more interstate acquisitions are permitted, linking city to city? Will this increase in competition threaten the competitiveness and survival of tens of thousands of medium-size businesses that depend on the middle market for credit, payments, and other financial services?

Historically, the primary focus of the federal bank regulatory agencies and the Department of Justice has been the probable impact of a proposed banking combination on the "most damaged market," defined as that highly localized geographic area around the bank's office or offices (usually represented by county, city, or metropolitan area boundaries) where the major portion of customers served is made up of individuals, families, and small businesses. Interstate banking will demand from regulators a much *broader* view of this "most damaged market" concept, however. Federal and state agencies must begin to place greater emphasis on the access of middle-size businesses to their most vital financial-service requirements — short-term inventory financing, long-term loans for the purchase and repair of plant and equipment, trust and agency services, cash and portfolio management services, marketing advice, and other operating needs.

This change of focus admittedly would impose a greater burden on economists employed by the bank regulatory agencies and on lawyers at the Justice Department because they might now have to closely examine the multiple local areas that would be involved when an interstate merger application is filed. For example, a merger between banks in Kansas City and Minneapolis, Dallas and New Orleans, Los Angeles and Phoenix, Atlanta and Miami, or Boston and Hartford may appear to have little adverse impact on the supply, pricing, or quality of financial services purchased by households or small businesses tied closely to their respective local communities. But for medium-size business firms that may regard banks in *all* cities in a given region as potential suppliers of the services they need, regulatory approval of such a merger presumably would eliminate some actual competition from the middle market. If large numbers of such mergers are sanctioned, the result may be a wastage of scarce resources, excess profits for banks serving these broad regional markets, and a diminished supply of the vital resource of credit, priced at excessively high loan rates. This eventuality would place middle-size businesses at a decided disadvantage relative to the largest corporations in the race for scarce capital funds.

The Department of Justice relies heavily on its calculation of concentration ratios in the metropolitan area or areas (usually the local Standard Metropolitan Statistical Areas [SMSAs]) in which merging banks are located. The concentration ratio for a given market indicates the proportion of banking resources controlled by the largest firms serving that market. Several years ago the Department of Justice and the three federal bank regulatory agencies — the Federal Reserve Board, the Federal Deposit Insurance Corporation, and the Comptroller of the Currency — adopted the *Herfindahl-Hirschmann index* to measure market concentration.

Once a market's boundaries are defined, economists within these agencies will calculate the percentage share of total deposits that each banking firm in the local market area controls. Then each firm's market share is *squared* in order to give greater emphasis on the shares held by the largest banks serving that market. Finally, the squared market shares are summed to derive one index number for the whole market area. Thus,

$$\text{Herfindahl-Hirschmann Index (HHI)} = \sum_{i=1}^{k} \left(\begin{array}{c}\text{Market Share of Total Deposits} \\ \text{Held by Each Bank Serving a} \\ \text{Given Market}\end{array}\right)^2$$

where k banks serve the market in question.

If there is only one bank serving the market area under examination, the single bank's market share is, of course, 100 percent, which becomes 10,000 when squared. A market in which the HHI exceeds 1,800 is considered "highly concentrated" according to guidelines announced in 1982 by the Department of Justice. If a bank merger proposed in a highly concentrated market would cause the HHI to increase by more than 200 points, such a merger may be challenged by the Justice Department (as noted by Connor [1985] and Di Clemente and Alemprese [1983]).

Markets in which the HHI lies between 1,000 and 1,800 are classified by the Justice Department as "moderately concentrated." A change of 200 or more points in the HHI due to a proposed merger in such a market may or may not be challenged by the Justice Department; however, that agency will consider other factors before reaching a decision on whether to file suit in federal court and block the proposed transaction. Proposed mergers in unconcentrated markets with a Herfindahl-Hirschmann Index of less than 1,000 points are not likely to result in a Justice Department suit to stop the acquisition.

The point that must be made here, however, is that the mere calculation of the Herfindahl-Hirschmann index in the local market of the acquired banking institution will *not* usually be adequate to protect medium-size business customers from a loss of competing service alternatives. Bank regulators will not be able to determine how much damage (if any) will be done to the business middle market if the merger is approved by the bank regulatory agencies and the Department of Justice.

One way to approach this difficult problem is to survey middle-size businesses in the markets touched by a proposed bank merger. The key questions to ask would center on whether or not these firms view banks in *both* cities involved in the merger as viable competitors for loans, deposits, and other financial services needed by these businesses. If a significant number of firms do view banks in both merger cities as feasible sources of supply for banking services, the regulatory agencies need to recalculate the HHI for a market that encompasses *both* cities involved in the merger and perhaps other communities as well.

AN INCREASE IN NATIONWIDE
BANKING CONCENTRATION

Public concern over the possibility of less competition for the accounts of middle-market businesses at the regional level is only one of several major policy problems that interstate banking may place on our doorstep. Another key regulatory issue centers on a probable increase in banking concentration nationwide. Inevitably, the rise of interstate banking organizations will drive some (hopefully only a few) smaller banks into bankruptcy or into mergers with larger banks. The industry gradually will consolidate its resources into a few dominant organizations, though thousands of smaller independent banks are expected to survive, and many of these will remain profitable by identifying and serving well the customers in their own special niche.

Currently, nationwide banking concentration in the United States is the lowest of any industrialized country in the Western world. The top five U.S. banking corporations presently control less than 20 percent of total banking assets in the nation, and that approximate concentration ratio has held steady for at least the past half century. This five-bank concentration ratio compares with five-bank concentration ratios in Canada and France of about 80 percent, while in Great Britain the five leading banks hold about 70 percent of that nation's banking resources (as noted recently by Baer and Pongracic [1984]). Banking concentration has actually declined in Canada and Great Britain since 1970 due to substantial penetration of British and Canadian home markets by dozens of foreign banks, especially those based in Japan and the United States. Many economists expect to see a similar concentration-moderating trend in the United States due to the growing penetration of American commercial and real estate loan markets by British, Canadian, French, and Japanese banks, as well as by smaller numbers of banking institutions from other leading nations in Asia, Europe, and the Middle East.

Thus, interstate banking need not lead to a highly concentrated banking industry in the United States. In fact, recent studies by Miller (1988) and Kaufman, Mote, and Rosenblum (1983) project that, even if full-service interstate banking becomes possible everywhere, the number of surviving U.S. banks is likely to exceed 2,000, with perhaps two dozen nationwide financial conglomerates and the rest consisting of numerous smaller, retail-oriented banking firms. Moreover, even if the national concentration ratio *does* rise, the United States clearly has a long way to go before its level of concentration even approaches that of other leading market economies. Indeed, between 1970 and the mid-1980s national banking concentration was stable while local concentration generally declined. Much depends on the character of government regulation and especially on the maintenance of freedom of entry for new domestic financial-service firms and for foreign banking companies that desire a share of U.S. markets. Greater freedom of entry into the banking business will help greatly to keep both local and national banking concentration within reasonable limits. While existing geographic restrictions on branching and holding-company activity do help to keep individual banks relatively small and the national banking concentration relatively low, such restrictions also tend to increase the banking concentration and stifle competition in the local communities across the United States where the majority of banking customers live.

The lesson that emerges from a study of other national banking systems that have allowed their banks to branch nationwide is that fewer independent banks, in all probability, will survive, particularly if merger policies are relatively liberal. However, government policy can counteract this by

1. Allowing both bank and nonbank firms to develop and sell a broad range of financial services;
2. Permitting foreign banks to enter under terms and conditions that allow them to be fully competitive with domestic banks;
3. Ensuring that domestic banks are granted the same service powers as the foreign banks that have penetrated domestic markets; and
4. Offering full access to the nation's payments system to all financial-service firms and not just to a privileged few.

Allowing free entry into *any* financial-service market usually rapidly deconcentrates that market. With unrestricted entry by financial firms the public has a better chance to enjoy the benefits of competition—improved service quantity and quality and reasonable prices (that are close to the true cost of production) for all financial services brought to market. Even if the U.S. continues with the relatively liberal merger policies put in place by the administration of President Ronald Reagan during the 1980s, banking concentration need not increase significantly or damage the intensity of competition in local financial-service markets, provided federal and state governments agree not to put further impediments in the way of bank entry into new markets and pledge not to stand in the way of the development and offering of new banking services anywhere in the nation.

Finally, we must keep in mind that if national banking concentration *does* increase significantly in the wake of full-service interstate banking activity, there *will* be some benefits from having fewer, but large banking organizations. One positive contribution centers on the cost and efficiency of the nation's payments system. Electronic payments flowing through ATM networks and automated clearinghouses should become more efficient, reducing float time in clearing and collecting checks and decreasing the enormous costs associated with the current U.S. payments system which processes about 40 billion checks a year. With fewer banks, more checks will be written and received by customers of the same bank, and less external processing of checks will be required. The entire payments process will speed up—a trend helped along by the superior ability of larger banking organizations to purchase and install automated processing equipment and electronic payments systems. Passage of the Expedited Funds Availability Act by Congress in 1987 provides added incentive to accelerate the nation's payments process and improve its operating efficiency, so that the resulting cost savings can be passed forward to bank customers in the form of lower service fees and more rapid access to deposited funds.

Nationwide full-service banking will benefit many customers because the largest U.S. banks will be able to consolidate the processing and record keeping of customer credit and deposit accounts. This will simplify computer records and programming demands, minimize the duplication of computer hardware and software, and improve overall reliability and accuracy. However, full-service interstate banking may require some significant restructuring within the Federal Reserve System which processes daily a substantial proportion of the nation's checks, records and transfers ownership of billions of dollars of government securities, and loans millions of dollars of reserves to banks that have temporary cash deficiencies. If major banking organizations go nationwide with a full menu of services, they will be able to choose which Federal Reserve Bank to access for services, and, thus, the 75-year-old, geographically dispersed organizational structure of the Federal Reserve System may become increasingly irrelevant to the service needs of the nation's banks. Indeed, as noted by Humphrey and Berger (1988), some nationwide banks may choose to compete aggressively with the Fed by offering the same full line of services, eroding the key role that the nation's central bank plays in the daily functioning of the American banking system.

In summary, a significant long-run increase in nationwide banking concentration is *not* inevitable because of the interstate banking revolution, though it is highly probable. Increases in banking concentration across the nation can be substantially moderated with an intelligent national banking policy, and even if industrywide concentration does rise significantly, the intensity of banking competition in local communities will *not necessarily* be damaged. Indeed, competition in local markets may actually increase if the legal barriers to interstate banking come down completely because every local banking market then will be under the threat of entry from outside. That threat can drive prices and excess profits down and bring actual or potential competition from *new* service suppliers to bear. As Federal Reserve Board economist Stephen A. Rhoades (1985) notes: "Interstate banking alone will have little impact on concentration in local banking markets. The anti-trust laws and the manner in which they are applied are likely to have far greater repercussions in that sphere" (1985, 30).

Both local and national banking competition, as well as the pricing, quantity, and quality of services, will be improved if American policymakers promote

1. Greater freedom of bank entry from outside the nation and from outside each local community market (which will be enhanced more and more as time goes by due to automation and advances in communications technology that inevitably will bring distant market areas closer);

2. Greater freedom from productlike restrictions (especially for the critical service areas of credit, savings, and payments), so that any financial firm can develop and offer new financial services wherever effective demand for those services exists; and

3. Vigorous enforcement of the nation's anti-trust laws against attempted service price collusion or bank market-sharing agreements wherever they might arise.

THE POTENTIAL LOSS OF STATE GOVERNMENT CONTROL

Another key regulatory issue accompanying interstate banking lies at the level of the individual state. Most states have not intervened in the acquisition of their banks by holding companies operating within the same state. Although some states insist on information reports from holding companies operating within their borders, most states have not been overtly concerned about the possible impact of bank holding companies on depositor safety, service quality, service availability, or competition. Further interstate acquisition activity, however, may intensify the concerns of some states over what is happening to their own banking industry as a result of continuing entry from outside and rising levels of statewide banking concentration.

Unfortunately, if state boards, commissions, and legislative bodies attempt to gather enough information to pass judgment on proposed new interstate bank acquisitions, they are likely to face substantial information and resource constraints. Few state agencies have access to detailed data regarding the performance of out-of-state banking organizations. Procurement of the data they will need for an adequate, continuing evaluation of structural changes in each state's banking industry will be costly, in terms of both staff time and money.

Many states, then, could face an imposing tradeoff problem: Should they abandon responsibility for controlling and monitoring the state's banking industry and its services to local citizens and hand that responsibility totally to the federal government? Or should each state vigorously assert its own right under the Constitution to become an active gatekeeper at its own borders, serving as a significant determining factor in the kind and quality of banks and banking services each state's citizens receive? If the answer to the latter question is "yes," can the state afford the cost in human and financial capital (funded either by local taxpayers or by local banks) to gain effective supervision and control over its own banking structure?

Each state must, then, make its own judgment as to whether the benefits to its citizens justify the costs of monitoring the banking industry. In some cases state interposition in the regulatory approval process could so impede outside bank entry that it would damage the state's opportunity for faster economic development and greater availability of jobs. In many instances it will be better for each state's long-run interest to leave the private marketplace alone rather than adding still another tier of regulation (and another hurdle in the form of new legal entry barriers) for interstate banking organizations to confront.

THE SURVIVAL OF KEY REGULATORY AGENCIES

Another regulatory issue that interstate banking will almost certainly intensify concerns the future role of the Office of the Comptroller of the Currency (the Administrator of National Banks) in the American banking system. In terms of history the Comptroller's Office is the oldest bank regulatory agency in Washington, D.C., created by the National Bank Act of 1863 to accept and rule on applications for new national bank charters and to supervise the activities and risk exposure of existing federally chartered banks. It has a reputation for being a forward-looking agency, genuinely concerned that banks be allowed to offer sufficient new services and to expand into new markets as the public's demands for financial services change.

Each national bank contributes funds to help sustain the federal supervisory and examination system — the source of the Comptroller's annual budget. As more and more national banks are merged out of existence, fail, or are converted from federal charters into state charters, however, the Comptroller's source of funding begins to contract. Other things being equal, the national banking system shrinks in size, and a less thorough and effective job of monitoring national banks is likely to be done. Ultimately, the Comptroller's influence in the counsels of government regulation of the banking system will wane. Indeed, this process of regulatory deterioration is already underway. Ultimately, Congress must decide what future role the Comptroller's Office should play in a banking system currently in turmoil and definitely in transition toward a new system that may well require a new regulatory structure.

THE POSSIBLE NEED FOR *MORE* BANK SUPERVISION
AND EXAMINATION

One reason there is concern over the possible demise of the Comptroller's Office is the potential need for more, not less, supervision and examination of banks as full-service interstate banking spreads. The argument here is largely inductive — based on the hard lessons of the past brought on by a combination of economic adversity (particularly the decline in energy and commodity prices) and deregulation of banking, both occurring roughly together in the decade of the 1980s. As Day (1988) observes, "government gave financial institutions new powers without providing the resources to detect and punish abuses" (p. 10). This thought is echoed by FDIC Chairman William Seidman, responsible for the supervision of nearly 8,000 state-chartered banks; he observed, "we didn't realize that deregulation required more supervision, not less" (quoted by Day [1988, 10]). Indeed, that error proved costly, particularly to the FDIC which in 1988 suffered the first operating loss in its history. The federal deposit insurance fund declined nearly 23 percent between year-end 1987 and year-end 1988. The $14.1 billion held in reserve by the FDIC at the close of 1988 represented less than 1 percent (specifically, 0.83 percent) of the total volume of all insured deposits in the United States.

More than four-fifths of the banks that have failed in recent years did not face a formal, on-site examination during the 12 months preceding their closing. This record reflects budget cuts recommended by officials in the Reagan administration and approved, at least tacitly, by the Congress. Moreover, the industries involved—particularly banks and savings (thrift) institutions—lobbied for cuts in the regulators' staffs. Logically, it seemed that with fewer regulations to enforce, there was less need for bank examiners and other agency staff. Through the early and mid-1980s, for example, the FDIC's examination force declined about 18 percent, before climbing nearly 45 percent from its mid-decade low as bank failures mounted and the agency's much-publicized troubled bank list reached record lengths. The other federal supervisory agencies displayed similar fluctuations from historically low employment rolls at first to high-watermark staffing levels later on. However, percentagewise, their changes in work-force size were not as dramatic as those encountered by the FDIC.

The notable exception to this trend of declining agency work forces was the Federal Reserve System; its total employment role actually rose significantly during the 1980s, in part because federal deregulation handed new responsibilities to the Fed, especially in providing check clearing, discount window loans, and other services to nonmember banks. With a higher volume of services demanded, the Fed was allowed to staff up in order to meet that anticipated demand. However, the Fed examines only state-chartered member banks—today about 1,100 banking institutions—on a regular basis, as well as overseeing all bank holding companies, so it accounts for only a fraction (less than 10 percent) of the banks that require regular examination of their safety and soundness.

The fundamental flaw in the reductions of supervisory and regulatory compliance staff among the federal banking and thrift agencies was, of course, the a priori conclusion that fewer regulations required fewer overseers. What administration and congressional advocates of this untested hypothesis failed to take into account was that, with fewer regulatory rules and fewer regulatory personnel, there was less risk that bank managers, shareholders, and staff would be caught and penalized for willful violations of banking standards. Banking became a more "wide open" industry that sanctioned extreme risk taking, which led, in turn, to a significant rise in problem banks. Thus, the federal supervisory agencies found themselves on the horns of a real dilemma: more troubled institutions to monitor and fewer trained professionals to spot serious problems in time to repair the damage. Coupled with increasing competition from domestic financial firms and foreign banks, the eroding regulatory process became a formula for disaster, particularly for those financial institutions (most notably, savings and loan associations) already weakened by economic forces.

THE LONG-RUN IMPLICATIONS FOR PUBLIC POLICY

None of the foregoing regulatory issues is easily resolved. And the depth of thought that has gone into these issues — particularly of the published variety, accessible to interested citizens who must ultimately decide the future of banking regulation — is yet alarmingly small. Much more analysis needs to be brought to bear on these vital issues of public policy if the ongoing interstate banking revolution is to serve the public interest and promote greater public confidence in American banks and the nation's banking system.

The issue of new policies for banking supervision is especially critical. Bankers are no different from the managers of any other type of business firm: when regulations are liberalized or lifted, they move to take advantage of the new rules and profit from greater freedom of action. The result, predictably, is a wider distribution of risk exposure within the industry. Some institutions remain safe and prudently managed, while others are willing to take on added risk (in effect, "betting the bank") in an effort to maximize returns and outperform the earnings of their competitors. Those banks that succeed put tremendous competitive pressure on others to follow their example; thus, the pursuit of greater risks for greater stockholder rewards and enhanced managerial perquisites carries within it the seeds of a general conflagration in which more banks and bank customers than those directly involved will suffer substantial losses.

Moreover, as Federal Reserve economists Paul Calem and Janice Moulton (1987) remind us, as American banks grow through full-service interstate mergers and acquisitions, their sheer growth in size may threaten the safety and soundness of the banking system. The failure of any of these largest banking organizations can send shock waves through the financial system of much greater magnitude than the failure of smaller banks not belonging to an interstate network. Failures are of greater consequence in banking than in most other industries because bank failures can produce chain reactions, affecting other banks as well because of the historically close relationship between banks that hold deposits with each other and frequently share the risk of making large loans. Thus, regulatory scrutiny of the soundness of individual banks and of the willingness of bank management to accept greater risk exposure can become more, not less, important in the interstate banking era than ever before in the nation's history.

Those banking institutions that lie at the extreme end of the risk distribution probably need to be routinely examined at least once a year, rather than once every 36 months — the rule that characterizes the present system. There is already in place in the form of a computerized monitoring system developed by the FDIC a policy tool to screen banks on a regular basis as their financial reports are filed. A few critical performance ratios (such as the rate of growth of equity capital, return on assets, real estate loans as a percentage of the total loan portfolio, etc.) are calculated to detect those banks that are "outliers" and, therefore, may require closer and more immediate regulatory scrutiny.

Such a policy tool is in desperate need of being refined and perfected for it would help both federal and state regulatory agencies to focus their scarce resources on those banks most in need of close supervisory attention. Certainly, the public's keen interest in a safe and sound banking system deserves at least that kind of attention and concern at all levels of government today. The welfare of banks is not independent of the welfare of their local communities and states. As the primary purveyors of business and consumer credit and the principal repository of the public's savings, commercial banks have an impact on local business sales, the availability of jobs, and the quality and scope of government services that is not only profound, but also perhaps more powerful than that of any other American industry. To abandon regulatory responsibility for monitoring bank condition, levels of competition in local, national, and regional markets, and the degree of public confidence in the nation's banking system is unacceptable public policy. And the advent of full-service interstate banking — no matter how far this organizational revolution extends across the American landscape — will not relieve us of the burden of that responsibility. The continuing crisis in the savings and loan industry reminds us that we ignore the new issues of public policy accompanying the spread of full-service banking only at our peril.

6

Entering New Interstate Markets: How Do Bankers Decide Which States to Enter?

What types of markets and states are interstate organizations likely to pursue as nationwide banking becomes more and more feasible? Why do interstate banking organizations choose some markets and avoid others? Both research studies and the public statements of bankers provide some interesting evidence on how banking markets are evaluated for possible future entry. First, we look at the evidence provided by published research, then at the information supplied by interstate bankers themselves, and, finally, at the economic and demographic characteristics of the states that have attracted the most bank entries from out of state in recent years.

THE RESEARCH EVIDENCE ON WHAT STIMULATES BANK ENTRY

One way to determine how bankers evaluate and choose among their target markets is to examine closely the characteristics of market areas they have entered in the past. Several important studies by Curry and J. T. Rose (1984), Hanweck (1971), Lister (1979), P. S. Rose (1980), Woodard (1976), and Woodard and Goldsberry (1984) have analyzed the acquisitions of large, multi-bank holding companies and have found five common features in the new markets these organizations eventually chose to enter. Each of the markets chosen appeared to display exceptional performance in one or more of the following dimensions:

- Size of the target market (usually measured by total deposits or by total population)

- Level of per-capita wealth or income
- Population per banking office
- Growth rate of the target market (typically measured by the percentage change in deposits, personal income, or population)
- Unemployment rate of the target market

Markets of larger deposit or population size more readily attract new bank or branch-office entry, as do higher levels of wealth and income. Moreover, areas with a relatively high population count per bank or banking office are often viewed as "underbanked" and, therefore, as promising targets for entry. Faster-growing cities, counties, and regions invite bank entry where that growth is economically relevant to banking organizations. For example, rapid growth in population may not be matched by growth in business sales, personal incomes, and savings—all of which are watched closely by bankers because the latter directly impact on the demand for credit and for deposit services. However, where there is evidence that wholesale and retail sales, as well as household incomes, are advancing along with population, banks are likely to penetrate such markets rapidly, either through new branches where state law permits or through holding-company acquisitions.

Another factor often considered in making market-entry decisions is the structure of a banking market. The word *structure* in this case is borrowed from the science of economics and refers to such characteristics of a banking market as the number of banking and nonbank financial-service firms present there, the degree of concentration of assets or deposits in the hands of the largest firms in the market, and whether or not the number and concentration of firms serving the market are increasing or decreasing over time. The structure of a market really has *two* dimensions:

1. The market's *static* structure, as indicated by the number of firms and the relative site distribution of firms that serve that market today; and

2. Its *dynamic* structure, or how the number of firms and their relative size rankings are changing over time.

Banking markets that are highly concentrated in the hands of only a few large firms may be viewed as having little real interfirm rivalry and, therefore, little actual competition occurring in a *static* sense. However, if new firms are starting to enter in large numbers, the market may be progressing in a *dynamic* sense toward more intense competition and interfirm rivalry. Quite obviously, bankers must pay close attention to *both* the static and the dynamic aspects of a potential new-entry market because a market that looks favorable for entry today may look quite otherwise in a fairly short span of time.

More concentrated markets in which the largest banking firms control a high percentage of total assets or deposits tend to discourage entry from outside, as suggested in recent studies by Hanweck (1971) and J. T. Rose (1977). Because of the high degree of control those large banks may exercise, it will be more difficult for a new bank to enter and eventually acquire a significant share of the target market. Similarly, if concentration is increasing, most bankers are likely to conclude that a given market is gradually becoming *less* attractive to enter. More firms serving a market imply greater competition, while fewer banks and related nonbank financial-service firms suggest a lesser degree of competition or, perhaps, a banking market that is "underbanked"; thus, a new bank might do very well in that particular state or region.

Other factors that we might normally expect to be important in deciding what new banking markets to enter—for example, high bank profits—generally have *not* been found by most researchers to be significant characteristics of those banking markets most frequently entered. While we might expect that most banks would "line up" to enter markets where the established banks are earning superior profits, previous research does not generally find this factor to be important, perhaps because high profits and high concentration usually go hand in hand. If banks are averse to highly concentrated markets, any profits observed may simply not be high enough to offset the damaging impact that the concentration of power in the hands of a few entrenched financial firms can have on a new bank trying to get started.

A number of other research studies have explored the criteria used to enter a new market with a branch office. Presumably the criteria for establishing new banks and for establishing new branch offices of an existing bank are *similar* to each other for most banking firms. However, the two need not be identical. For one thing, a new branch office normally represents a smaller investment of physical capital and human resources than does a brand-new banking corporation. A new branch may be able to survive in an economic downturn, provided the home office keeps it afloat through injections of new capital until its local market recovers. Moreover, the home office can provide some services (such as data processing, portfolio trading, and loan review) that a new bank would have to support on its own. It is also easier to convince federal and state regulators of the necessity of closing a single branch office if it does prove unprofitable than would be true if the controlling company wanted to close a bank completely and sell all of its assets.

Recent studies by Hannan (1981, 1983) find evidence that market size relative to the number of banking offices is a key factor in the establishment of new branch offices. Specifically, Hannan found that an increase in the ratio of total deposits in the local market (in this case, counties in Pennsylvania) to the number of banking offices present stimulated the construction of new branches. Hannan also discovered a "price effect" in new branching activity. Banks establishing new branch offices seemed to be attracted to "high-price markets" where loan rates averaged above the norm and deposit interest rates were relatively low. In contrast, neither market growth nor the structure of local banking markets (especially the concentration of deposits) proved to be significant determinants of branch-office entry in his study. There is, however, countervailing research evidence (e.g., Alhadeff and Alhadeff 1976) that markets with the foregoing characteristics—large deposit totals per office and high service prices—also tend to be characterized by high entry barriers, so that it is more difficult to successfully start a new bank or branch office in those particular areas.

Because many banking companies will cross state lines through holding-company acquisitions, it may well be that earlier studies of the specific factors that cause holding companies to enter new markets are the most relevant ones for predicting future interstate full-service bank expansion. These studies (especially those by Rhoades [1976] and Boczar [1975]) find holding companies generally more interested in the financial performance of banks in their target markets, especially their profitability. As expected, markets where banks report higher-than-average profitability stimulate *more* holding-company acquisitions. Holding companies also seem to avoid more concentrated banking markets, perhaps because they are less likely to generate adequate profitability there on a long-term basis. More rapidly growing markets, however, appear to invite more holding-company entry, as do higher levels of personal income per capita, which suggests that bank holding companies look favorably on markets where increased sales of retail (household) banking services are more likely—an assumption that is consistent with the findings of studies comparing holding-company banks to non-affiliated institutions (e.g., P. S. Rose and Scott 1979) where the former typically hold larger proportions of consumer and real estate loans than is usually true of banks not affiliated with holding companies.

Unfortunately, the sparse research literature on interstate banking acquisitions leaves largely unexplored a number of factors that might have a significant impact on the market entry decision of an interstate banking organization. Among the key issues overlooked thus far are those centered on possible market power motivations, efficiency and productivity factors, corporate control issues (such as the acquisition of mismanaged assets), desired portfolio adjustments, debt capacity, capital costs, and pricing policies. Moreover, existing research studies tend to be primarily descriptive in nature, rather than being primarily oriented toward the testing of a wide range of factors that may influence the decision to choose one local market over another and one state over other states. Therefore, we must look beyond prior research studies to *new* sources of information on the reasoning process used by expansion-minded interstate banking firms.

WHAT INTERSTATE BANKERS EVALUATE IN ASSESSING POTENTIAL NEW MARKETS

Evidence gathered by the author from numerous interviews with CEOs and planners inside interstate banking organizations on both the East and West Coasts and in the Midwest points to a wide array of market selection techniques in the industry. However, *most* interstate acquirers appear to pass through the following steps at one time or another in the merger and acquisition process:

1. A long-run market strategy is selected which determines what proportion of future acquisitions will be made in areas already served versus new market areas not entered before;
2. Specific states and regions are targeted for eventual entry, based on recent and projected demographic and economic data;
3. Within the states and regions targeted for future entry, certain local markets (i.e., metropolitan areas, counties, etc.) are selected for more detailed study; and, finally,
4. A few banking organizations within the targeted local markets that meet certain broad criteria (such as deposit size or the number and placement of branch offices) are selected for detailed study as potential acquisition targets.

Entering Old Markets and Expanding into New Market Areas

Interstate banking firms must confront a fundamental choice: should they build further within those markets they already serve and are familiar with, or should they launch off into new, uncharted waters? Most tend to build further in market areas they already serve through affiliated bank or non-bank businesses, particularly in areas where they have ample prior experience in making loans. For example, Citicorp of New York has announced its intention to enter California once that state permits nationwide entry for full-service banks in 1991. However, Citicorp already has a sizable presence in California markets with approximately 100 branch offices, due to its previous acquisition of the troubled savings and loan Fidelity Savings of San Francisco in 1982.

Leading interstate banks have tended to develop regional strategies that focus on a limited group of neighboring states. For example, recently several of California's largest banks, led by BankAmerica, pulled back a portion of their international and East Coast operations in favor of a Pacific Coast strategy which focuses heavily on the neighboring states of Arizona, Oregon, and Washington. In the Midwest the $7 billion Huntington Bancshares, Inc., of Chicago announced banking acquisitions in four neighboring states in 1986 — specifically, Indiana, Kentucky, Michigan, and Ohio. The most important of these acquisitions were in the suburbs surrounding Detroit, Indianapolis, and Cincinnati.

Not only do interstate banking organizations display strong regional preferences, usually for locations in those states having close proximity to their home state, but also they are highly selective in the local communities they choose to enter. There is a strong bias against acquisitions of banks situated in rural towns and small cities not associated with major urbanized areas. Many intrastate and interstate bank holding companies have confined all or nearly all of their acquisitions of bank and nonbank affiliates to SMSAs — Standard Metropolitan Statistical Areas, which are counties of at least 50,000 residents with an integrated urban character.

An example of this strong urban bias is found in a recent report by Bennett (1987) that the leading Midwest holding company, Huntington Bancshares, is interested in further acquisitions in the Detroit area and would like to confine further acquisitions in the midwestern states to metropolitan areas rather than rural communities. Another prominent example is the situation in Texas, a state that contains more rural banks than any other. Texas first allowed out-of-state holding companies to enter in 1987. And, thus far, the new entrants have bypassed that state's many rural areas to concentrate their attention on the leading banking firms in Dallas and Houston. An earlier study by P. S. Rose (1976) of all U.S. holding-company acquisitions in the early 1970s showed a similar strong bias toward major metropolitan areas characterized by rapid growth in population and personal income.

One major problem with acquiring many *rural* banks is their small average size, particularly the small amount of capital they can contribute to the acquiring institution. Acquisitions of relatively small rural banks may cost nearly as much as those of larger urban institutions; yet the resources they bring to the acquiring organization are often too small to justify the costs involved. Moreover, small rural banking institutions have a higher failure rate, which exposes the acquiring firm itself to greater risk of loss.

The Diversification Effect

Making new interstate acquisitions in those states and regions where a bank is already represented or with which it has become familiar from previous customer contacts carries a positive economic advantage: it saves on information costs. That is, management does not require the extensive "tooling up" that entering an unknown state requires; nor does the acquiring bank face the burden of convincing local businesses and households that the new owners will strive to provide a full menu of needed services, reasonably priced and conveniently available. The problem with the strategy of "staying at home" in interstate banking, however, is that, first of all, it may prevent the bank from taking advantage of yet-to-be-discovered profit opportunities. Second, it is a banking strategy that may not generate the risk-reducing benefits of geographic diversification for the acquiring organization.

Simply acquiring more banks in the same states may do little to develop a portfolio of local markets that generate service sales and revenue flows that are relatively uncorrelated or, best of all, negatively correlated with each other. For example, an interstate banking organization in heavily industrialized Michigan may get substantial risk-reducing benefits for its earnings stream if it acquires banks in Texas, an energy- and service-based economy. Falling bank revenues in Michigan may be offset by rising bank revenues in Texas and vice versa.

Still, most banks have not chosen strategic plans that maximize the potential benefits of geographic diversification in order to shelter their institutions from risk. Good examples dot the landscape of the Southwest in recent years. For example, when world oil prices fell sharply in the mid-1980s, First City Bancorp, based in Houston, decided to switch its emphasis from energy lending to real estate investments in Houston and other nearby cities. Obviously, this was anything but effective geographic diversification. When energy prices fell, so did real estate values in the Houston metropolitan area and in other cities of the Southwest. Other leading Texas bank holding companies, such as MCorp and First RepublicBank Corp. of Dallas, also found themselves top-heavy with property loans in the Dallas–Fort Worth metroplex, as well as in Houston.

We must hasten to add that the risk-reducing benefits of geographic diversification in banking may be more apparent than real. One reason is that no matter where a bank is located, its acquirers do *not* usually treat it at arm's length with little or no involvement in the bank's internal affairs. Acquiring a new bank is not the same behavioral process as buying stock on the New York or Tokyo exchanges. Stock purchased from a securities exchange is usually a relatively passive event: the stock is simply held for a time and then sold to another investor. The stock investor, unless he or she has controlling interest, does not usually become involved in the management of the firm in which stock is held. However, when a holding company buys a bank, it is typically not a passive investment. As economists Liang and Rhoades (1988) observe, the new owner may rush in to install new operating policies, new goals, and new management. Often the newly acquired banking organization is remade into the image of its acquirer. Whatever geographic diversification benefits might have been within the acquirer's grasp may be systematically destroyed.

ECONOMIC AND DEMOGRAPHIC ASPECTS OF
THE INTERSTATE BANKING MOVEMENT

While interstate banking provides plenty of examples of hasty and ill-conceived decisions and strategies, it is also clear that a majority of the mergers and acquisitions crossing state lines today reflect long-range strategies based on economic and demographic trends, as well as on trends in the financial condition and operating characteristics of the nation's banks. Interstate banking acquisitions have not spread randomly and uniformly across the continent. They have been concentrated in *selected* local markets (cities and counties) and in *selected* states and regions, reflecting the influence of strong economic, demographic, financial, legal, and regulatory factors.

This selectivity in choosing states and regions to enter is a rational response to recent economic developments. Until the 1980s the 50 states were becoming more and more equal over time in per-capita personal income — a trend that held there from the 1930s through the late 1970s. However, that 45-year trend toward income equality was reversed over the most recent decade, and state income inequality has risen sharply ever since. As Coughlin and Mandelbaum (1988) have noted, by 1987 the inequality in state per-capita personal incomes had risen to the degree of inequality evident two decades earlier in 1966. While the earlier long-term trend in U.S. per-capita incomes saw high-income states slowing their growth rates and low-income states growing faster, the more recent trend has seen high-income states growing faster and low-income states growing more slowly, worsening any previous discrepancies in personal income levels across the nation.

The states with the fastest growth in recent years include Connecticut, Delaware, Florida, Maryland, Massachusetts, New Hampshire, New Jersey, New York, Rhode Island, and Virginia — states in which interstate banking also has progressed rapidly. Also contributing to the new income inequality trend were 9 states — Idaho, Indiana, Louisiana, Montana, New Mexico, North Dakota, Oklahoma, Utah, and West Virginia — with below-average per-capita incomes that grew very slowly during the most recent period. With one or two exceptions (especially in Indiana and Utah), interstate banking activity in these states was subdued to nonexistent.

Interestingly enough, all the states experiencing the most rapid per-capita income growth through 1987 were situated along the Atlantic Coast, as noted by Coughlin and Mandelbaum (1988). Low-income states, on the other hand, were scattered across the rest of the nation. Even though there is a long-term trend in the United States, spanning more than two decades now, toward a shift of manufacturing activity to the Sunbelt states, this industrial shift has not carried along with it a significant increase in per-capita incomes, as was true in earlier years. Moreover, the so-called Frost-belt states in the northeastern tier of the nation have experienced a dramatic turnaround in basic industries, computers, construction, and medical and financial services.

On a regional basis most interstate banking acquisitions have been concentrated in five of the nine regions of the nation as designated by the U.S. Census Bureau. These active banking regions include (1) the South Atlantic region (Delaware, Maryland, Virginia, West Virginia, North Carolina, South Carolina, Georgia, and Florida); (2) the New England region (Maine, New Hampshire, Vermont, Massachusetts, Rhode Island, and Connecticut); (3) the Middle Atlantic region (New York, New Jersey, and Pennsylvania); (4) the East North Central region (Ohio, Indiana, Illinois, Michigan, and Wisconsin); and (5) the Pacific region (Alaska, California, Hawaii, Oregon, and Washington). As Table 6-1 indicates, four of these five regions are the most populous areas in the United States.

For example, the East North Central region contained nearly 42 million people in 1987, according to a U.S. Census Bureau estimate. The South Atlantic region ranked a close second with nearly 41.7 million residents. Moreover, U.S. Census Bureau projections suggest that the South Atlantic region will have the largest number of people by 1990, with a resident population of nearly 44 million. The Middle Atlantic and Pacific regions contained an estimated 36 to 37 million residents apiece. Therefore, market size measured by population appears to have become a major force propelling interstate bank mergers and acquisitions. This population-based motivation for interstate banking activity is consistent with several recent research studies (cited earlier in this chapter and in Chapter 4) that conclude the desire of bankers to penetrate more dynamic local markets for retail (household) banking services has been a driving force fueling interstate mergers and acquisitions.[1] Population density also ranks high in the most active interstate banking regions. As Table 6-2 indicates, the Middle Atlantic group of states — New Jersey, New York, and Pennsylvania — ranked first in population density with 375 persons per square mile in 1987, followed by New England with 204 persons per square mile. The East North Central and South Atlantic regions, including such active interstate banking states as Delaware, Florida, Georgia, Illinois, and Ohio, ranked third and fourth in population density, respectively. With a more dense population, retail shopping activity tends to be more intense, which generates a higher volume of checkable deposits from households, a larger volume of business loans to stock inventories, and more installment loans to individuals and families who may require bank credit to purchase big-ticket items, such as automobiles, furniture, and household appliances.

Four of the five leading interstate banking regions contain an above-average proportion of residents of retirement age (i.e., over 64 years old). (See Table 6-3.) In particular, the Middle Atlantic and New England regions rank second and third among all U.S. regions in the percentage of residents over 64 years of age, closely followed by Florida and the whole South Atlantic region. In contrast, the regions of most intense interstate banking activity tend to have relatively low school-age and infant populations (i.e., under 18 years old). (See Table 6-3.) For example, the Middle Atlantic region, encompassing New Jersey, New York, and Pennsylvania, ranks ninth and last in the proportion of children under 18 years of age, followed by the

Table 6-1

Population Size and Growth of the Principal Regions of the United States

Region	Total Population, 1987 Census Estimate (in thousands)	Population Rank	Percentage of Resident Population Growth, 1980–87	Rank of Population Growth Rate	Population Projections to 1990 (in thousands)	Projected Population Rank by 1990
East North Central Region (Indiana, Illinois, Michigan, Ohio, and Wisconsin)	41,904	1	0.5	9	42,055	2
South Atlantic Region (Delaware, Florida, Georgia, Maryland, North Carolina, South Carolina, Virginia, West Virginia, and Washington, D.C.)	41,684	2	12.8	4	43,742	1
Middle Atlantic Region (New Jersey, New York, and Pennsylvania)	37,433	3	1.8	8	37,499	4
Pacific Region (Alaska, California, Hawaii, Oregon, and Washington)	36,533	4	14.9	2	38,265	3
West South Central Region (Arkansas, Louisiana, Oklahoma, and Texas)	26,910	5	13.3	3	27,937	5
West North Central Region (Iowa, Kansas, Minnesota, Missouri, Nebraska, North Dakota, and South Dakota)	17,634	6	2.6	7	17,722	6
East South Central Region (Alabama, Kentucky, Mississippi, and Tennessee)	15,290	7	4.3	5	15,597	7
Mountain Region (Arizona, Colorado, Idaho, Montana, Nevada, New Mexico, Utah and Wyoming)	13,167	8	15.8	1	13,995	8
New England Region (Connecticut, Maine, Massachusetts, New Hampshire, Rhode Island, and Vermont)	12,844	9	4.0	6	13,078	9

Source: U.S. Bureau of the Census.

Table 6-2

Demographic Features of the Principal Regions of the United States

Region	Population Density per Square Mile, 1987 Census Estimate	Rank of Population Density	Percentage of Population over 64 Years of Age, 1986	Relative Rank in the Percentage of Citizens over 64 Years of Age	Percentage of Population Under 18 Years of Age	Relative Rank in the Percentage of Citizens Under 18 Years of Age
East North Central Region (Indiana, Illinois, Michigan, Ohio and Wisconsin)	172	3	12.0%	6	26.7%	4
South Atlantic Region (Delaware, Florida, Georgia, Maryland, North Carolina, South Carolina, Virginia, West Virginia and Washington, D.C.)	156	4	12.8	4	25.1	8
Middle Atlantic Region (New Jersey, New York and Pennsylvania)	375	1	13.4	2	24.3	9
Pacific Region (Alaska, California, Hawaii, Oregon, and Washington)	41	7	10.8	7	26.3	5
West South Central Region (Arkansas, Louisiana, Oklahoma, and Texas)	63	6	10.4	8	30.1	1
West North Central Region (Iowa, Kansas, Minnesota, Missouri, Nebraska, North Dakota, and South Dakota)	35	8	13.5	1	26.3	5
East South Central Region (Alabama, Kentucky, Mississippi, and Tennessee)	86	5	12.2	5	27.4	
Mountain Region (Arizona, Colorado, Idaho, Montana, Nevada, New Mexico, Utah, and Wyoming)	15	9	10.2	9	29.0	2
New England Region (Connecticut, Maine, Massachusetts, New Hampshire, Rhode Island, and Vermont)	204	2	13.3	3	26.2	7

Source: U.S. Bureau of the Census.

Table 6-3
Age Distribution of the Population in Selected States (States Listed by Population Size)

State	Percentage of Population over 64 Years of Age in 1986	Relative Rank in the Percentage of Citizens over 64 Years of Age	Percentage of Population Under 18 Years of Age in 1986	Relative Rank in the Percentage of Citizens Under 18 Years of Age
California	10.6%	38	26.3%	27
New York	12.8	18	24.6	44
Texas	9.5	46	29.5	8
Florida	17.7	1	22.5	50
Pennsylvania	14.6	2	24.0	46
Illinois	12.0	27	26.5	26
Ohio	12.3	22	26.5	24
Michigan	11.4	35	27.0	19
New Jersey	12.9	17	24.0	45
North Carolina	11.5	33	25.6	37
Georgia	10.0	43	28.1	10
Virginia	10.5	40	24.9	42
Massachusetts	13.6	10	23.0	49
Indiana	11.9	29	26.8	21
Missouri	13.7	7	25.8	35

Source: U.S. Bureau of the Census.

South Atlantic states and New England. Because older residents, rather than young families, tend to have the greatest volume of savings and also rank high in income levels, these demographic characteristics provide an attractive target market for banks planning their interstate strategies.

At the level of the individual state, substantial interstate acquisition activity has occurred in eight of the ten most populous states in the nation, led by Florida, North Carolina, New Jersey, Ohio, and Michigan. (See Table 6-4.) While several of these most populous states have *not* experienced rapid population growth in recent years (for example, Ohio and Michigan were estimated to have lost population between 1980 and 1987), these slower-growing states represent large, established banking markets, particularly in

Table 6-4
Population Growth, Density, and Projected Growth of Leading States in the United States

State	Total Population, 1987 Census Estimate (in thousands)	Population Rank	Percentage of Resident Population Growth, 1980–87	Rank of Population Growth Rate	Population Density per Square Mile, 1987	Rank of Population Density	Population Projections to 1990 (in thousands)	Projected Population Rank by 1990
California	27,663	1	16.9%	6	177	12	29,126	1
New York	17,825	2	1.5	43	376	6	17,773	2
Texas	16,789	3	18.0	5	64	29	17,712	3
Florida	12,023	4	23.4	4	222	10	12,818	4
Pennsylvania	11,936	5	0.6	46	266	8	11,827	5
Illinois	11,582	6	1.4	44	208	11	11,612	6
Ohio	10,784	7	−0.1	47	263	9	10,791	7
Michigan	9,200	8	−0.7	48	162	14	9,283	8
New Jersey	7,672	9	4.2	29	1,027	1	7,899	9
North Carolina	6,413	10	9.0	16	131	17	6,690	10
Georgia	6,222	11	13.9	11	107	21	6,663	11
Virginia	5,904	12	10.4	13	149	16	6,157	12
Massachusetts	5,855	13	2.1	40	748	3	5,880	13
Indiana	5,531	14	0.7	45	154	15	5,550	14
Missouri	5,103	15	3.8	33	74	27	5,192	15

Source: U.S. Bureau of the Census.

the two product lines emphasized by most interstate banks in recent years: household credit, deposits, and other consumer-oriented financial services; and credit services for small and medium-size businesses.

We can refine our analysis of population growth by drawing on U.S. Census Bureau estimates for leading metropolitan areas around the nation. The most rapidly growing metropolitan areas in terms of population in recent years have been concentrated in states experiencing substantial interstate banking activity. For example, Florida—a state that figured prominently in interstate banking activity during the 1970s and 1980s—contained 5 of the 15 fastest-growing U.S. metropolitan areas: Fort Myers, Palm Bay, West Palm Beach, Orlando, and Daytona Beach. Texas, which became a prime interstate target in the late 1980s, was home to five of the top 15 metropolitan areas in rate of population growth: Austin, Fort Worth, Arlington, McAllen, and Brownsville. California followed with three of these leading metro centers: Riverside, Stockton, and Bakersfield.

Not unexpectedly, states and regions that rank high in total personal income and income growth also rank high in terms of interstate bank acquisitions, as Tables 6–5 and 6–6 reveal. For example, the New England region ranked number one in both the level of per-capita personal income and the recent growth rate of that income measure. The South Atlantic and Middle Atlantic states also ranked high in personal income levels and reported growth in total income and in per capita income that has been especially rapid in recent years. The linkages among income levels, income growth, and bank deposits are well established. As family incomes rise, consumption of goods and services also increases, which requires larger checking account balances and a rise in savings deposits that may need to be called on at any time to sustain a family's standard of living. Not so transparently clear, but accurate is the close linkage between bank borrowing and household incomes. Higher-income individuals and families borrow more, not less, on a per capita basis. Part of the reason is education, which increases an individual's awareness of his or her opportunities to use credit and grants the capacity to prudently manage when and where borrowing is advisable.

A new measure of economic activity and of the comparative sizes of the economy in each state—the Gross State Product—was announced in the summer of 1988 by the Bureau of Economic Analysis of the U.S. Commerce Department. Analogous to the measure of the nation's annual income and

Table 6-5
Growth and Volume of Personal Income in the Principal Regions of the United States

Name of Region	Percentage of Change in Personal Income, 1985–86	Rank of the Change in Personal Income	Region	Dollar Volume of Personal Income per Capita (1986)	Rank of Per-Capita Personal Income
New England	8.4%	1	New England	$17,166	1
South Atlantic	7.7	2	Middle Atlantic	16,508	2
Pacific	7.5	3	Pacific	16,351	3
Middle Atlantic	7.0	4	East North Central	14,467	4
East South Central	5.9	5	South Atlantic	14,088	5
West North Central	5.8	6	West North Central	13,992	6
Mountain	5.7	7	Mountain	13,203	7
East North Central	5.6	8	West South Central	12,735	8
West South Central	1.6	9	East South Central	11,243	9

| Average for Entire United States 6.3% | | | Average for Entire United States $14,641 | | |

Sources: U.S. Bureau of the Census and U.S. Department of Commerce.

Table 6-6
Leading States in the Growth and Size of Per-Capita Personal Income

State	Percentage of Change in Personal Income, 1985–86	Rank of Change in Personal Income	State	Dollar Volume of Personal Income per Capita, 1986	Rank of Per-Capita Personal Income
New Hampshire	10.1%	1	Connecticut	$19,600	1
Arizona	9.3	2	New Jersey	18,626	2
Georgia	8.7	3	Alaska	17,796	3
Maine	8.7	4	Massachusetts	17,722	4
Massachusetts	8.4	5	New York	17,111	5
Florida	8.3	6	California	16,904	6
Connecticut	8.1	7	Maryland	16,864	7
Virginia	8.0	8	New Hampshire	15,911	8
Nevada	8.0	9	Illinois	15,586	9
New York	7.9	10	Nevada	15,437	10
California	7.9	11	Virginia	15,408	11
South Dakota	7.7	12	Colorado	15,234	12
North Carolina	7.7	13	Delaware	15,010	13
Rhode Island	7.6	14	Washington	15,009	14
Washington	7.5	15	Minnesota	14,994	15
Average for Entire United States	6.3%		Average for Entire United States	$14,641	

Sources: U.S. Bureau of Economic Analysis and U.S. Bureau of the Census.

production activity, the Gross National Product (GNP), the Gross State Product (GSP) measures the value of goods and services produced by an individual state during a designated interval of time (with data now available on the GSP annually back to 1963). It is quite likely that banking firms pursuing interstate banking strategies will follow the GSP estimates closely in the future because these estimates help pinpoint those states and regions generating the largest volume of transactions from producing and selling new goods and services—transactions that will generate new loan demand and create new deposits. The GSP figures displayed in Table 6-7 are a further indication of why states such as California, New York, Illinois, Pennsylvania, Florida, Ohio, New Jersey, and Michigan have played major roles in the interstate banking movement. They contain the nation's biggest economies and, therefore, the most potential for attracting profitable bank loans and deposit accounts.

A key economic dimension that must be factored into all plans and strate-

Table 6-7

Volume of Economic Activity by State, Measured by the Gross State Product (GSP)

State Name and Rank	1986 GSP (in billions of dollars)	Percentage of Total U.S. GNP 1986	State Name and Rank	1986 GSP (in billions of dollars)	Percentage of Total U.S. GNP 1986
1. California	$534	12.6%	6. Florida	$178	4.2%
2. New York	363	8.6	7. Ohio	176	4.2
3. Texas	304	7.2	8. New Jersey	155	3.7
4. Illinois	210	5.0	9. Michigan	153	3.6
5. Pennsylvania	184	4.3	10. Massachusetts	116	2.7

Source: U.S. Bureau of Economic Analysis.

gies for future interstate bank expansion is the vulnerability of selected states and regions to economic cycles, especially losses due to recessions when family and business incomes fall and unemployment rises. This is an especially important issue for manufacturing-based economies such as those in Illinois, Michigan, Ohio, and Wisconsin. These particular economies (as noted in a recent report prepared by Carlson [1988] for the Data Resources, Inc., a forecasting service) are particularly vulnerable to swings in interest rates. Rising interest rates tend to decrease manufacturing investment and reduce the availability of jobs from manufacturing firms. States located in the Pacific Northwest face similar exposure to interest-rate changes due to heavy manufacturing activity and the prominence of the lumbering industry, in which sales volume fluctuates with the demand for construction of new homes and commercial buildings. Both of these regions face significant vulnerability to economic recessions and are likely to lag somewhat behind other states and regions in the future magnitude and scope of interstate banking activity.

Finally, it is almost certain that the condition of a state's banking industry influences which states will be targeted for future entry, though there is great uncertainty and debate over how to measure the industry's overall condition. Table 6–8 provides some relevant data on the two most common measures of bank profitability—return on assets (ROA) and return on equity capital (ROE)—and of bank risk exposure—net loan chargeoffs to average loans and leases and equity capital relative to total assets. Return on assets, which is the ratio of net after-tax income to total assets, is an index of bank operating efficiency in using scarce resources to generate net income for the institution's stockholders. Return on equity capital is a direct measure of stockholder returns, showing how much after-tax income was generated for each dollar of capital provided by the bank's owners. Net loan chargeoffs

Table 6-8
Average Bank Profitability and Risk by State (as of 1987)

States	Measures of Bank Profitability		Measures of Bank Risk Exposure	
	Return on Assets	Return on Equity Capital	Net Loan Chargeoffs to Average Loans and Leases	Equity Capital to Total Assets
Alabama	1.11%	11.27%	0.61%	9.73%
Alaska	(0.82)	(31.13)	1.69	8.73
Arizona	(1.02)	(5.90)	1.33	7.50
Arkansas	1.01	11.12	0.87	8.99
California	0.70	8.09	0.73	7.94
Colorado	0.14	2.47	1.60	8.22
Connecticut	0.86	7.22	0.18	9.82
Delaware	1.40	12.59	2.48	8.92
District of Columbia	0.55	5.10	0.55	6.67
Florida	0.34	5.46	0.56	8.89
Georgia	1.19	12.35	0.52	9.34
Hawaii	1.13	10.61	0.32	11.12
Idaho	0.36	6.52	0.93	7.53
Illinois	0.93	11.22	0.70	8.41
Indiana	0.85	10.11	0.64	8.25
Iowa	0.82	9.04	1.22	8.86
Kansas	0.64	7.82	1.51	8.46
Kentucky	1.07	11.55	0.66	9.00
Louisiana	(0.52)	(7.29)	2.45	7.80
Maine	1.24	16.71	0.15	7.59
Maryland	1.08	12.82	0.21	8.67
Massachusetts	0.85	12.23	0.19	6.62
Michigan	0.97	12.47	0.36	7.66
Minnesota	0.74	8.93	1.08	8.31
Mississippi	0.96	10.48	0.85	8.93
Missouri	0.82	9.67	0.77	8.22
Montana	0.53	6.74	1.67	8.09
Nebraska	0.84	9.41	1.42	8.83
Nevada	1.13	10.20	1.06	7.12
New Hampshire	1.00	13.51	0.14	6.84
New Jersey	1.05	14.31	0.26	7.14
New Mexico	0.53	6.85	1.30	7.62
New York	0.91	11.30	0.35	8.71
North Carolina	0.56	7.22	0.32	10.19
North Dakota	0.71	8.03	1.88	8.89
Ohio	1.02	11.94	0.49	8.54
Oklahoma	0.14	1.79	2.38	8.12
Oregon	0.63	9.49	0.97	7.55
Pennsylvania	1.18	12.99	0.22	9.05
Puerto Rico	0.52	6.59	0.50	9.00
Rhode Island	0.75	8.09	0.61	6.55
South Carolina	0.95	9.15	0.38	11.02
South Dakota	0.85	8.99	1.38	9.27
Tennessee	1.11	12.93	0.64	8.33
Texas	(0.40)	(3.78)	2.00	7.44
Utah	0.14	2.80	1.79	9.63
Vermont	1.15	15.09	0.21	7.59
Virginia	1.22	13.79	0.35	9.04
Washington	0.71	8.38	0.57	7.96
West Virginia	1.04	11.14	0.46	9.29
Wisconsin	0.92	10.76	0.45	8.53
Wyoming	0.26	2.23	2.05	8.12
National Average for All U.S. Banks	0.74	8.70	1.04	8.34

Source: Federal Deposit Insurance Corporation.

reflect the amount of bank loans declared to be worthless and removed from the bank's books *less* any recoveries of funds from loans previously considered worthless. The higher the proportion of loans charged off relative to a bank's total portfolio of loans, the greater the credit-risk exposure of the bank and the greater the likelihood that it will fail. The ratio of equity capital to total assets also is an index of the risk of bank failure because banks with less equity capital relative to their assets have a smaller financial cushion to absorb operating losses. A low equity-capital ratio means more of the bank's assets are funded by debt rather than owners' equity with a greater danger that any debt incurred cannot be repaid.

The averages reported in Table 6–8 for all banks in a given state provide us with evidence that recent interstate acquisitions have been tilted toward those states with the highest levels of bank profitability and with low to moderate loan losses and failure risk. A good example is Illinois with a 0.93 percent ROA—well above the national average of 0.74 percent in 1987—and an 11.22 percent ROE—again substantially higher than the 8.07 average for all U.S. banks. At the same time, Illinois' loan loss record falls below the national mean. As we saw in Chapter 1, Illinois is among the leading states in the number of recent interstate bank acquisitions. Other states with high bank profitability and relatively low risk exposure include Massachusetts, Michigan, New Hampshire, and New Jersey which also have attracted a volume of interstate banking activity substantially higher than in most of the other regions of the United States.

AN OVERVIEW OF THE CRITERIA FOR CHOOSING STATES AND COMMUNITIES TO ENTER

In this chapter we have taken a broad overview of the factors that bear on the decision of a banking organization to expand across state lines. The principal factors propelling bank expansion uncovered by recent research include market size; growth rate of personal income, population, and deposits in target market areas; total deposits; and number of banking offices per capita. An increase in any of these determining factors appears to increase the likelihood of bank entry through branching or acquisition, both within states and across state lines.

Each interstate banker interviewed by the author appears to possess an inherent bias favoring his or her own region of the nation. These regional strategies place heavy emphasis on planned bank acquisitions in *neighboring* states about which interstate acquirers have superior knowledge concerning the market conditions and the particular banks targeted for merger. However, these regional acquisition strategies can substantially reduce the benefits of risk-reducing diversification that might have been obtainable had interstate acquirers targeted areas with widely different economic and demographic characteristics and with cash flow patterns that are different from those of the banks they have acquired in the past.

Clearly some states are missing out in the expansion of interstate banking. These states, predominantly in the Rocky Mountain region and in the Midwest, have struggling economies with serious weaknesses in their agricultural and energy sectors. Interstate banks appear to rely heavily on *expected* increases in bank earnings and, therefore, are most interested in states and regions with improving and growing economies. Indeed, this drive among interstate banking firms to pursue target banking organizations operating in rapidly growing economies, with above-average production and income levels, reflects the intense level of financial-services competition around the globe and in thousands of local communities across the United States. Remaining competitive in global financial markets requires a strong deposit base that only the most diversified and economically stable markets inside the United States can provide.

NOTE

1. See especially Dave Phillis and Christine Pavel (1986). The author recalls a fascinating interview with a bank planner on the West Coast regarding his bank's possible interest in expanding into the Rocky Mountain region. When the author mentioned the possible benefits and costs of expanding into the state of Wyoming, this banker dismissed that possibility with a glance out the window of his 11th floor office: "Why, I can see more people from here than live in the entire state of Wyoming!"

7

Methods for Analyzing and Selecting Banks for Interstate Acquisition: How Do Bankers Choose Their Target Firms?

Once a region, state, or local area is selected for entry by acquisition or merger, how do interstate organizations in the United States choose their corporate targets? What leads interstate banking firms to bypass one bank or bank holding company and target another located in the same city for acquisition? While different banking institutions use different approaches to the bank selection process, certain key factors appear to be common reference points for the majority of interstate bankers.

PURCHASE PRICES AND PREMIUMS

A key factor in every acquisition of a bank or bank holding company across state lines is the price that must be paid, especially the premium over book value. The so-called *merger premium* is simply

$$\text{Merger Premium} = \frac{\left(\begin{array}{c} \text{Price per Share} \\ \text{Paid by} \\ \text{the Acquirer} \end{array} - \begin{array}{c} \text{Book Value per Share} \\ \text{of the Acquired Bank} \\ \text{or Holding Company} \end{array} \right)}{\begin{array}{c} \text{Book Value per Share} \\ \text{of the Acquired Bank} \\ \text{or Holding Company} \end{array}} \times 100$$

Some financial analysts prefer a simpler form of the merger premium measure known as the *price-to-book ratio*:

$$\begin{array}{c} \text{Price-to-} \\ \text{Book Ratio} \end{array} = \frac{\text{Price per Share Paid by the Acquirer}}{\begin{array}{c} \text{Book Value per Share of the Acquired Bank or} \\ \text{Holding Company} \end{array}}$$

Acquirers are generally willing to pay a premium above an institution's book value because they believe that the market value of a targeted bank or bank holding company as a going concern is greater than its book value. Financial theory suggests that the market value of a firm — bank or nonbank — reflects the expectations of investors that the merger target will generate a stream of earnings which, when the future value of that earnings stream is discounted into current dollars, will equal the current market value of the firm. Thus, an acquiring banking organization will only bid for a target firm if it expects to recover its invested funds plus receive adequate compensation for risk bearing during the planned holding period.

Most acquiring interstate banking companies wind up bidding not only more than the book value of the targeted firm, but also more than its current market value because of an expectation that the target's future value will rise *above* its current market value. The expected increase in the target firm's future value is often due to *synergistic effects* — that is, cost savings due to superior management. The new and larger merged firm may be able to produce more efficiently and purchase raw materials, capital, and services in greater volume at a better price. The premiums paid for most U.S. bank mergers in recent years have ranged somewhere between 50 percent over a bank's book value up to 200 percent, or even more. For example, when Horizon Bancorp of Morristown, New Jersey, was acquired by Chemical Banking Corp. of New York early in 1989, Chemical paid a reported 50 percent more than Horizon's book value. Presumably this merger premium was paid willingly because Chemical saw Horizon's nearly $4 billion in deposits and 127 branch offices as adding significantly to the former's high-ranking position as a leading consumer-oriented bank in the Middle Atlantic region.

In terms of price-to-book ratios, these have ranged from 1.5 times book value up to about 3.0 times the target bank's book value. For example, Alberts (1986) reports that Banc One Corp. of Columbus purchased American Fletcher Corp. of Indianapolis for 2.4 times book value in 1986, while Citizens and Southern Bank of Atlanta paid 1.8 times book value for Landmark Banking Corp. of Florida in 1985. As a result of recent inquiries, economists and financial analysts (especially Guenther [1989] and Matthews [1987b]) estimate that the average acquisition premiums have been 70 percent over book value in the New England region and about 60 percent over book value in the Southeast region of the nation. In the Midwest, bank merger premiums have averaged about 90 percent over book value, though the range of observed premiums in this region of the nation has been very wide and volatile due to the large number of failures among midwestern banks.

Unfortunately, in most instances, the merger premiums paid appear to have been *excessive*. As Cates (1985) notes, shareholders of acquiring banking organizations have benefitted from most mergers far less than have the shareholders of acquired banks. Moreover, book value is a treacherous standard to use in measuring the earnings-generating potential of a bank today. It is based on past history and not on the current resale value of the bank's assets and liabilities. Book value generally is a pale reflection of the value the owners would receive if the bank's assets were liquidated and the institution were closed.

In somewhat different (but equivalent) terms, the stockholders of an interstate acquiring bank will benefit from a merger or acquisition across state lines if that transaction will increase the market price per share of the acquiring bank's stock. The theory of finance holds that the price per share of bank stock can be calculated from the following formula:

$$\text{Market Value (Price) of a Bank's or Bank Holding Company's Stock} = \frac{\text{Expected Stream of Future Dividends Paid to Each Stockholder}}{\text{Discount Factor for Each Dollar of Expected Future Dividends (Reflecting the Degree of Risk to the Firm's Earnings Stream)}}$$

This simple formula indicates that a bank or banking company can increase the value per share of its stock if it can convince investors that completing a proposed interstate merger will (1) increase the future stream of stockholder dividends the acquiring firm will pay out, or (2) reduce the risk associated with that dividend stream, as reflected in a lower discount factor applied to each dollar of dividends received.

As we noted above, an interstate merger may ultimately increase a bank's earnings (and, therefore, its ability to pay higher stockholder dividends) or reduce its risk exposure through such steps as

1. Increasing the efficiency of operations at the interstate acquiring firm, at the acquired firm, or at both by
   a. Eliminating the duplication of labor or physical facilities (e.g., by having *one* trust department instead of two),
   b. Updating the operating facilities of the acquired bank by using the latest service production technology, and
   c. Purchasing supplies and equipment in greater volume and, therefore, receiving price discounts on those purchases;
2. Increasing the revenue-generating capacity of the acquiring or acquired bank or both by
   a. Pricing and marketing existing services more effectively to meet the needs of the customers the banks serve,
   b. Opening up new markets and developing new services not previously offered, and

    c. Expanding the banks' use of financial leverage (i.e., increased debt capital relative to equity);

3. Reducing the risk exposure of the merged interstate banking firm through

    a. Increased product-line diversification by adopting new services with cash flows that behave differently from the cash flow generated by the existing menu of services offered by the acquiring bank or bank holding company, and

    b. Increased geographic diversification by acquiring banks and bank holding companies in new markets not already served by the acquiring firm, but having economic conditions that behave differently over time from those in the markets the acquiring firm already serves.

    The key question most bankers ask as they contemplate a future interstate merger or acquisition is this: what impact will the transaction have on earnings per share (EPS) of the acquiring banking firm? That is, what will the effect of the proposed merger be on

$$\text{Earnings per Share (EPS)} = \frac{\text{Bank or Holding Company's Net Income after Taxes}}{\text{Total Number of Shares of the Bank or Holding Company's Common Stock Outstanding}}$$

    If EPS is expected to rise in the wake of the acquisition, the bank's tradeable stock becomes more attractive to investors in the capital market and its market price rises. However, an expected decline in EPS makes the banking company's stock appear less attractive to profit-seeking investors, and its stock price will fall, *ceteris peribus*.

    We should not forget, of course, that shareholders of the banking firm about to be acquired in an interstate merger are guided by a similar beacon. They, too, look at earnings per share — specifically, at the EPS they expect from their own banking institution in the future versus the EPS they expect to receive if they accede to the acquiring bank's offer and surrender their old shares for new shares. If the EPS expected from the new shares offered by the acquirer significantly exceeds the EPS anticipated from the old shares, the interstate acquisition is likely to proceed to a successful conclusion.

    This does not mean, however, that the interstate merger itself will be profitable in the long run for the shareholders of *either* banking firm. Earnings expectations are nothing more than forecasts, based sometimes on rational analysis and at other times on speculation or intuitive feelings. And forecasts are often wrong. One ratio used widely by financial analysts, however, does help us pin down the conditions necessary for a favorable outcome from an interstate merger — the stock-price-to-earnings (P/E) ratio. That is,

$$\text{P/E Ratio} \quad = \quad \frac{\text{Price per Share of Bank or Holding Company Stock}}{\text{Annual Earnings per Share of the Bank}}$$
$$\text{or Holding Company}$$

When a banking firm with a relatively high P/E ratio acquires a firm having a lower P/E ratio, the shareholders of *both* the acquiring and the acquired companies will receive more earnings per share of stock (EPS) if the combined company's total earnings do *not* decrease after the interstate merger is completed. However, if the P/E ratio for the acquired banking firm exceeds the P/E ratio for the acquiring institution, the EPS of the merged company will decline to a figure that is lower than before the interstate acquisition took place due to dilution of earnings.

Shareholders of acquiring interstate firms are especially concerned about diluting and, thus, weakening their share of earnings and ownership in the acquiring organization. If the purchase price paid for the acquired bank is relatively high, shareholders of the interstate acquiring firm will soon feel the burden of the merger transaction. For example, if the acquired firm is purchased for cash, the acquirer will have to issue a substantial volume of debt simply to raise the needed cash. However, repaying this debt plus interest will drain the acquirer's net income, threatening to reduce stock-holder dividends. On the other hand, if stock is *exchanged*, so that share-holders of the acquired firm receive stock from the interstate acquirer, the higher the purchase price, the more stock must be given. This further reduces the total ownership share held by existing shareholders and requires that total earnings be spread over more outstanding shares, reducing earnings per share for every bank stockholder.

The fate of EPS in any interstate merger or acquisition, then, rests on the size of each participating bank's net after-tax income and the P/E ratio for *both* acquired and acquiring institutions. Specifically,

$$\begin{array}{c}\text{Degree of Financial} \\ \text{Success of an} \\ \text{Interstate Merger} \\ \text{or Acquisition}\end{array} = \frac{\left(\dfrac{\text{Acquiring Bank's Stock Price per Share}}{\text{Net Income after Taxes of the Acquiring Bank}}\right)}{\left(\dfrac{\text{Acquiring Bank's Stock Price per Share}}{\text{Net Income after Taxes of the Acquired Bank}}\right)}$$

As we have seen, the shareholders of *both* interstate acquiring and acquired banks are usually better off if the ratio of stock price to net income for the acquiring banking firm exceeds the acquired bank's ratio of stock price to its net income.

The one factor that the analysis above does not consider is the possibility that an interstate merger will generate true synergistic effects in the form of reduced operating expenses or improved operating efficiency. As a result, the net after-tax income of the *combined* organization will expand at a faster rate than before the interstate merger took place. If there is a high probability that net income will increase at a faster pace after the merger, the interstate acquirer will be able to offer the acquired firm's shareholders more stock or more cash to tempt them to accept the acquirer's offer. Bank managers today recognize the necessity for carrying out a simulation analysis of several possible outcomes from a proposed interstate merger — especially alternative possibilities for the acquired and acquiring banks stock prices and net incomes — to determine (1) how much risk there is that an interstate merger will fail in its objectives, and (2) the length of time it will take for the acquiring bank or holding company to retrieve its initial investment in the acquired banking firm.

As full-service interstate banking firms enter new market areas, they tend to drive up the price (and the merger premiums) of target banks. The higher prices mean that some bidders are eliminated from the market because they face increased risk that either the target banking firm's earnings will be too low or the time required to recover their investment in the firm will be too long to make the interstate merger profitable. Banking organizations that forecast lower future growth in targeted areas are soon outbid by those acquirers willing to accept more risk.

A recent example was provided by Bennett's (1987) analysis of the interstate strategies of Huntington Bancshares, Inc., of Chicago. Several Indiana bank acquisitions apparently desired by Huntington did not occur because the prices for the target banks had risen too high relative to their earnings potential as seen by Huntington's management. In Texas, on the other hand, the sharp decline in oil prices in the mid-1980s produced "bargain-basement" prices for some of the state's leading bank holding companies. For example, NCNB Corp. of North Carolina acquired the state's largest holding company, First RepublicBank Corp., for a premium of only 7 percent over Republic's book value, well below the average premiums paid for acquired banks in other states. In fact, NCNB paid nearly twice that figure for those banks and holding companies it was acquiring in the southeastern region of the nation where its headquarters is located.

While we have concentrated in the foregoing paragraphs on earnings per share (EPS), the stock-price-to-earnings ratio (P/E), and the merger premium as key indicators of the most desirable interstate acquisition targets, many bankers also look at other key measures of strength in a target firm. (See Table 7–1.)

RELATIVE SIZES OF INTERSTATE ACQUIRING AND ACQUIRED BANKING FIRMS

The asset or deposit size (and, therefore, the base of resources that will be available for future acquisitions) of the acquiring interstate institution also

Table 7-1
Measures of Financial Strength in a Proposed Interstate Merger

$$\text{Operating Earnings Per Share} = \frac{\text{Net Operating Earnings}}{\text{Shares of Common Stock Outstanding}}$$

$$\text{Ownership Dilution Ratio} = \frac{\text{Number of Shares of Common Stock of the Acquiring Banking Company Issued to Shareholders of the Acquired Banking Firm}}{\text{Total Common Stock Outstanding of the Acquiring Banking Company}}$$

$$\text{Price-Earnings Ratio} = \frac{\text{Current Market Price Per Share of Common Stock Outstanding}}{\text{Current Earnings per Share of Common Stock}}$$

$$\text{Earnings Dilution Ratio} = \frac{\text{Net After-Tax Income}}{\left[\begin{array}{l}\text{Number of Shares of the Acquiring Banking Company's Common Stock Before the Acquisition} + \text{Number of New Shares of the Acquiring Banking Company Issued to Shareholders of the Acquired Firm}\end{array}\right]}$$

$$\text{The Core Deposit Ratio of the Interstate Acquisition Target} = \frac{\text{Total Core Deposits (=Demand Deposits + Savings Deposits + Fixed-Rate Time Deposits under \$100,000 Apiece)}}{\text{Total Liabilities of the Banking Firm Targeted for Acquisition}}$$

$$\text{Benchmark Interstate Merger Price} = \text{Merger Premium Over Book Value Paid in Recent Mergers and Acquisitions in the Same Market Area}$$

$$\text{Book-Value Ratio} = \frac{\text{Book Value of the Acquired Banking Firm}}{\text{Book Value of the Acquiring Banking Firm}}$$
(tangible assets plus one-half of bad-debt reserves less tangible liabilities)

$$\text{Net Present Value of the Interstate Merger or Acquisition Target} = \frac{\text{Projected Net Cash Flow from the Acquired Banking Firm in Year One After Acquisition}}{(1 + \text{Acquirer's Required Rate Return})^1} + \frac{\text{Projected Net Cash Flow from the Acquired Banking Firm in Year Two}}{(1 + \text{Acquirer's Required Rate Return})^2}$$

$$+ \dots + \frac{\text{Projected Net Cash Flow From the Acquired Banking Firm in the Final Year the Acquiring Firm has Control}}{(1 + \text{Acquirer's Required Rate of Return})^n}$$

$$\text{The Exchange Ratio} = \frac{\text{Market Value Per Share of Acquiring Banking Firm}}{\text{Book Value Per Share of Acquired Firm}}$$

plays a major role in targeting banks and banking companies for future acquisition. As an illustration, recently Huntington Bancshares, Inc., with about $7 billion in total assets, reported an interest in finding another banking firm in the Midwest region to acquire that had no more than $2 billion in assets and, preferably, that was in the $1 billion range. This strategy would call for targeting a bank no larger than about 30 percent of the acquirer's asset size.

There is a popular theory among managements of larger money-center and regional U.S. banks that one of two strategic models must be chosen and carefully followed in the next phase of interstate banking. Either leading regional banking institutions must expand via acquisition to reach efficient operating size if they are to survive in the long run as an independent banking firm, or they must be content with their current internally generated growth, but be prepared to be acquired and to seek the best possible terms of acquisition for their managements and shareholders. There is considerable disagreement among researchers in the banking field, however, as to the particular size threshold above which a banking organization achieves adequate size for both efficiency and long-run survival as an independent company. Moreover, as Matthews (1987a) suggests, that size threshold will change, even in the absence of inflation, with continuing breakthroughs in the technology of financial-service production and delivery. The critical size range today probably exceeds $30 billion in assets and, with the information and communications technologies now under development, may soon approach $100 billion in total assets.

Moreover, surviving interstate banks, regardless of their size or original location, will be forced to gravitate toward a limited set of geographic nodes in the future—particularly the cities of Atlanta, Boston, Chicago, Los Angeles, New York, St. Louis, and San Francisco. Based on current trends, these nodal interstate banking centers will be characterized by

1. Excellent communication and transportation linkages throughout the home region and with other regions of the nation and the globe, such that transportation costs (in terms of both time and money) are minimized.
2. Access to adequate supplies of excellent managerial and professional talent in order to be able to make rapid, but far-sighted decisions.
3. Superior living environments in terms of educational and social/cultural facilities and opportunities for management and staff.

Expansion from these nodal points at first is more likely to be in the form of acquisitions of those banking firms tightly clustered around nodal cities. Then interstate acquirers will spread out from those nodal points in a series of roughly concentric circles that encompass larger and larger marketing areas of the nation.

CHOOSING AN APPROPRIATE THRUST OR FOCUS
FOR INTERSTATE EXPANSION

Each interstate banking firm generally launches its interstate acquisition program with a particular focus—a strategic objective that fits with the acquiring institution's long-range plan. Recently, William Petersen (1987) analyzed the differing strategies of U.S. banks that are regional leaders. He found five broad strategies at work across the nation:

1. An overall corporate strategy that emphasizes effective and efficient coordination among unit divisions of a banking corporation in order to gain an advantage over competitors.
2. Product-oriented strategies, whereby the principal goal of the banking firm is to offer specific services in targeted markets or to offer high-quality services.
3. Distribution strategies that stress selling techniques to maximize returns from producing and selling banking services, multiple service sales to each customer to promote customer loyalty, expansion of overall sales volume to lower production costs, and efforts to increase market share to secure advantageous pricing of services offered.
4. Technology-based strategies aimed at lowering production costs and raising barriers to entry by outside banking organizations in order to pursue higher long-term profits.
5. Service-oriented strategies that emphasize the identification and satisfaction of customer needs and define market segments toward which the bank can target its sales promotion efforts.

As we saw in Chapter 4, after reviewing existing research evidence on interstate banking, interstate managers usually have elected to expand their organization's presence in primarily retail service-oriented markets by offering attractively packaged personal financial services to families, wealthy individuals, and young up-scale business managers and professionals. This has resulted in an emphasis on careful evaluation of branch office locations held by acquired banking institutions and selective closing of branches that appear to duplicate existing facilities or to be underperforming relative to the interstate acquirer's standards.

The other major focus of U.S. full-service interstate banking acquisitions in recent years has been the middle market—loans, deposits, and other services sold to medium-size business firms (usually defined to include those businesses with sales of at least $50 million per year up to perhaps $250 million annually). Firms below this middle range generally are believed to represent a market that almost *any* local bank, regardless of its size, can serve; therefore, interstate banking organizations do not view themselves as having any special advantage in serving the smallest businesses.

On the other hand, businesses larger than middle size purchase their services in the most intensely competitive financial markets around the globe, where aggressive foreign banks struggle against the top U.S. banking institutions. This global corporate service market is driven almost exclusively by *price*; as a result, U.S. banks have lost a major share of the corporate market to foreign banks (especially the Japanese banking conglomerates) due to the greater efficiency and lower profit margins that foreign banking institutions frequently can offer. Most American bankers seem convinced that the middle market, along with retail services to households, offers the greatest potential for profitable interstate expansion. However, there is also a general perception in the banking industry that successful penetration of the business middle market requires an acquirer to purchase at least a medium-size bank (holding about $1 billion or more in total assets) in each strategically located metropolitan area within the region or regions the full-service interstate organization has decided to serve.

The predominance of retail and middle-market banking strategies among U.S. interstate banking institutions today reflects a fundamental tenet of bank management philosophy that is generations old. Its principal axiom is "stick to the business you know." This strategy allows a transfer of more of the knowledge gained in the bank's existing markets to those new markets entered via interstate merger. It allows greater scale economies in advertising, in the hiring and training of new personnel, and in facilities design and construction, and often in service production and delivery as well. One reason these cost savings are possible is the growth in production and sales volume for established service lines that use pre-tested production and delivery methods in new interstate markets. This strategy helps to explain a host of recent interstate combinations, such as Chemical Bank of New York's acquisition of Texas Commerce Bancshares. Both of these institutions are well respected in the business middle market and in the retail banking services in their respective regions of the nation.

IMPLICATIONS OF STRATEGIES FOR CHOOSING INTERSTATE ACQUISITION TARGETS

The most important decision an interstate banking firm can make is the choice of target banks or holding companies to acquire. That decision is likely to have profound effects on the banking firm's stock price, earnings, future growth, and ultimate survival as an independent banking organization. The key factors that shape the interstate company's acquisition decision center on the prices that are required to effect acquisitions across state lines (including the premium over book value that must be paid to consummate each merger), the earnings performance of both acquiring and acquired banks, the prospect of substantial dilution of earnings and ownership in the acquiring institution if too much is offered to shareholders of the acquired firm to make the transaction succeed, the relative asset sizes of the participating institutions, the geographic proximity of target banks and their acquirers to regional trade centers, and the character of the institutions acquired (in terms of mix of services and clientele).

The foregoing factors are particularly telling in most interstate bank mergers because they provide us with clues as to why so many interstate mergers and acquisitions are *not* a financial success. One common problem is the payment of excessive acquisition prices and merger premiums which cannot be easily or quickly absorbed by the shareholders of the acquiring firm. As bank management consultant Jon Moynihan (1984) has observed, value destruction can be confidently predicted in the wake of an acquisition if premiums of 60 percent or more over a target bank's market value are paid by the acquirer. Earnings per share become severely diluted because the acquiring bank has had to give so many new shares or so much cash to the acquired bank's shareholders. Moreover, frequently, earnings do not grow sufficiently after the interstate acquisition to keep earnings per share growing. Equally troublesome, if a flood of new shares must be issued to allow the merger to succeed, is the fact that the ownership share of the combined organization controlled by the acquiring firm's shareholders will shrink. These shareholders may find it more difficult to win support for their ideas about the firm's future growth and performance.

Too many interstate bank acquirers seek the wrong "fit" in terms of an acquisition target that is not complementary to the character of their banking organization. A wholesale-oriented bank may reach out for smaller retail banks, only to find that it lacks the management techniques and professional skills to control its acquisitions and keep their earnings growing. Interstate acquisitions are most likely to succeed where *both* the acquiring and the acquired firms have substantial experience and resources invested in *similar* service lines. In interstate banking this has generally occurred where large wholesale-oriented banks have acquired banks active in financial-service markets for middle-size businesses or where large money-center banks with a strong reputation for selling quality retail (household-oriented) banking services have acquired smaller banks with substantial retail-service menus as well. While these two strategies would appear to subvert the benefits of risk-reducing product-line diversification in banking, the research evidence currently available suggests that diversification benefits — particularly diversification benefits from selling services with uncorrelated cash flows — are relatively minor in commercial banking today.

As Moynihan (1984) has also noted, interstate banking organizations with consistently superior performance must know where their greatest skills lie and how those skills can be brought to bear to improve the performance of each acquisition *before* that merger is launched. They must have management information systems that reveal at all times how each unit is performing relative to other units and that guide daily, weekly, monthly, and annual management decisions. Acquisition activity should be directed mainly at banks with a superior track record of performance, not at inferior banks unless management can *clearly* see how an inferior institution can be turned around. Moreover, once a suitable bid price for a new acquisition is determined based on realistic cash-flow estimates, the top-performing interstate bank will not bid significantly more than that price or make promises it cannot keep.

Successful banking continues to depend on the skills and commitment of management and a successful track record of experience in serving customers. Without question, banking markets and regulations have changed drastically in our own time, but the fundamentals of successful bank management have changed little, if at all.

8

Overcoming the Key Management Problems of Interstate Banking

As interstate banking legislation has spread in domino fashion from state to state, American banks have gained significant new opportunities for growth and expansion. However, the falling legal barriers to full-service interstate bank expansion have *not* lessened the problems that often come with growth through merger and acquisition. In fact, many of these problems have *increased* because the number of actual and potential competitors has grown substantially as a result of federal and state deregulation of banking. Moreover, deregulation has removed the shelter that American banks once enjoyed from the pressures of the financial marketplace. When banks relied on government regulations to price their deposits and loans, to prevent new competitors from entering their territory, and to guarantee their deposit liabilities to the public, the banks' rate of return to their owners and the value of their stock were determined as much by government support as by the strong winds of competition between banks and other financial-service firms. Now that federal and state deregulation has lifted many of those constraining regulations and has made banking a more risky business, management must grapple with many new problems occasioned by interstate mergers and acquisitions.

The key problems that American banks face today from interstate expansion include

1. Trying to anticipate and prepare for future changes in federal and state legislation,
2. Finding adequate capital when it is needed to strengthen the institution and to provide a base for future growth,
3. Finding and dealing with unexpected and prospective costs once an acquisition has been made,

4. Winning acceptance by the new communities entered, and

5. Overcoming conflicts between the managements of acquiring and acquired institutions.

ANTICIPATING AND PREPARING FOR CHANGES IN FEDERAL AND STATE LEGISLATION

Full-service interstate banking has progressed rapidly since the initial steps into the new banking era were made by Delaware and South Dakota at the beginning of the 1980s. As we saw in Chapter 1, 46 states passed some form of interstate banking legislation between 1980 and 1989. Yet many of the "big prizes" still remain closed to the most aggressive banking organizations—most notably California where its nationwide banking bill will not become effective until 1991. Other attractive "prizes" in the interstate chess game remain effectively closed to most acquirers due to economic recessions and serious unemployment (as in Colorado and Texas), regional banking compacts (as in the New England region) that admit banking firms from states not likely to be a serious competitive threat due to the relatively small size of their leading banks (as in Maine), or local economic conditions.

On the horizon, however, are some major changes in state entry barriers that represent significant opportunities for expansion to new regions, but also serious competitive challenges to home banking organizations. For example, California's scheduled 1991 opening to banks along the East Coast promises to sharply intensify the competitive climate for financial services in that state and around the Pacific Rim. Leading California banks, such as Wells Fargo, BankAmerica, Security Pacific, and First Interstate, probably have less to fear from the elimination of California's entry barriers than do medium-size and smaller banks that must prepare for acquisition or for intensified competition and lower profit margins. The largest California banks already compete with leading East Coast institutions in the global market for corporate banking services. Moreover, many of the largest banks from New England, New York, Florida, Georgia, and even the Midwest already have an established presence in California through affiliated non-bank firms. For example, Citicorp operates close to 100 Citibank branch offices as a result of its acquisition of troubled Fidelity Savings of San Francisco in 1982.

In contrast, the Rocky Mountain region is *not* currently viewed as a prime area for near-term interstate acquisitions. The author's interviews with senior managers, economists, and bank planners on both coasts and in selected mountain and plains states suggest concern over the future economic prospects for most of the Rocky Mountain states, especially Colorado, Montana, and Wyoming because their economies have faltered due to declining or low coal and oil prices and to severe long-run problems in agriculture.

An added problem, perhaps even more serious, is the relatively small population in most states in the Rocky Mountain region. As we noted in Chapter 4, most interstate acquisitions to date have centered on areas with large retail banking and mid-size business markets. Such sites are few and far between along the Rocky Mountain chain and in much of the Midwest. The exceptions include Arizona, Illinois, Indiana, Minnesota, New Mexico, Ohio, Texas, and Wisconsin where there are several large concentrations of population and signs of economy recovery—both of which will bring in significant new interstate competition in the years ahead.

FINDING ADEQUATE CAPITAL TO PROVIDE
A BASE FOR FUTURE GROWTH

Bankers generally believe that the most serious constraint against future full-service interstate expansion by many otherwise-qualified banking organizations will be lack of capital. Billions of dollars of long-term debt and equity capital will be needed to fund new acquisitions, strengthen affiliates that are in trouble, and develop new services demanded by customers in both old and new markets. Many of the super-regionals and money-center holding companies have had their capital seriously eroded by huge loan losses related to international lending and severe recessions in key domestic sectors—oil and gas, farming, commercial real estate and construction, and lumber. Other banking institutions that have managed to preserve at least minimally acceptable levels of capitalization have seen their credit ratings fall and, commensurately, their borrowing costs driven substantially higher, making the cost of interstate expansion programs difficult to justify from a near-term economic vantage point. While this does not necessarily mean that interstate expansion plans must be tossed away, many banking companies are definitely "on hold" until the economic fundamentals—especially the cost and availability of long-term capital—change for the better.

Recent changes in U.S. and international bank capital regulations will undoubtedly play a major role in determining which U.S. banks are able to be real "players" in the interstate banking movement and which must remain primarily "spectators," sitting on the sidelines. The International Lending and Supervision Act was passed by Congress in 1983, committing the United States to continued support of the International Monetary Fund (IMF) which has helped prop up heavily indebted, lesser-developed nations, such as Argentina, Brazil, and Mexico. However, U.S. bankers were able to win federal government support of the IMF (and, therefore, new capital to buoy up some of their largest international borrowers) only on the condition that leading American banks adhere to more restrictive regulations on foreign lending and bank capital. Specifically, federal regulators required U.S. banks with international loans to set aside special capital reserves to meet possible defaults on their foreign credits. Minimum capital standards, including a requirement that U.S. banking organizations maintain a ratio of total capital to total assets of at least 6 percent, were imposed on *all* banks.

Unfortunately, the capital positions of many of the nation's leading banks and bank holding companies had fallen substantially below that percentage figure when the new regulations were put in place. The most difficult new capital standard to meet was the requirement that primary capital—the permanent portion of a bank's financial structure, including common and perpetual preferred stock, retained earnings, capital reserves, and mandatory convertible debentures—be raised to a minimum of 5.5 percent of total assets, a requirement that sent numerous banks and bank holding companies into the security markets to shore up their capital positions.

These new and more stringent capital requirements were further intensified as a result of a series of meetings of the Basel Group—central bankers, secretaries of the treasury, and other financial experts from 12 industrialized countries in the West, including the United States, Austria, Belgium, Canada, Great Britain, France, the Federal Republic of Germany, Italy, Luxembourg, the Netherlands, Switzerland, and Japan. These nations agreed to minimum ratios of 4 percent for primary capital to assets and 8 percent for total capital to assets. Moreover, a plan was developed to evaluate the composition of a bank's assets and assess higher capital requirements on those banks that are holding riskier assets (including off-balance-sheet contingent agreements, such as standby credits that may drain a bank's resources if one of its customers cannot pay).

Facing new and more stringent domestic capital requirements and the prospect of tough international capital regulations, leading money-center banks—including Citicorp, Chase Manhattan, and BankAmerica—were forced to deduct millions of dollars against their current earnings in order to build up their loan-loss reserves against the possibility of devastating defaults on international loans. These loan-loss allocations put downward pressure on the stock prices of major U.S. banks. However, for American banks the resulting decline in stock prices was magnified in October 1987 when stock exchanges around the world were hit with the greatest single-day selloff of equity shares in history.

This combination of adverse market and regulatory developments has forced several leading U.S. banks to move toward strengthening their equity capital positions—to satisfy heightened regulatory requirements, to retain their current stockholders, and to avoid a significant escalation in future borrowing costs due to the concerns of capital market investors over the banks' risk exposure. These pressing capital requirements have prevented several prominent U.S. banks, such as Manufacturers Hanover of New York, from adopting a more aggressive program of full-service interstate expansion and have made it easier for key regional banks around the nation—such as NCNB and First Union Corp. of Charlotte, North Carolina; U.S. National in Portland, Oregon; and BancOne of Columbus, Ohio—that do not face as heavy a burden of regulatory pressure to increase their capital. These regional banking organizations have been relatively free of huge capital deficiencies and, thus, can often afford to pursue new assets and aggressively expand their share of the nation's banking resources.

There is evidence, however, that the balance of power in interstate banking may be shifting away from the leading regional acquirers toward the nation's largest money-center banks. The profits of these industry leaders rebounded sharply and pushed toward record levels in the late 1980s, while several regional interstate acquirers began to experience serious loan quality problems and unexpected increases in operating expenses, particularly in New England, the Southeast, and the West. Moreover, a highly favorable regulatory decision by the Federal Reserve Board in February of 1989 opened to the largest money-center institutions—such as Chemical Bank, Citicorp, and Chase Manhattan—a new and potentially significant source of revenue. The Fed ruled that bank holding companies could apply for permission to underwrite corporate notes and bonds and would be granted permission to do so after a case-by-case review. This new service power, as a practical matter, is really only of use to the largest New York, California, and possibly Illinois banks, but it carries the potential for significant future profitability for these dominant U.S. banks.

DEALING WITH UNEXPECTED AND
PROSPECTIVE COSTS AFTER ACQUISITION

Every merger, interstate or not, holds at least some surprises for the management and stockholders of the acquiring institution. The willingness of some banks to be acquired may reflect more than just the desire of their stockholders to maximize wealth and income. The selling of a bank or a holding company may be viewed as the least troublesome route out of some serious internal problems, such as aging senior management for whom no adequate replacements have been found or deteriorating office facilities that will soon need to be renovated or abandoned. Problems that previous management and ownership have left unresolved and that new ownership and management must eventually deal with are called *prospective costs*.

One of the most prominent examples of prospective costs in recent years has centered on the loan portfolios of acquired banks. After the merger when new management examines in detail the acquired institution's loan file, the volume of nonperforming and uncollectible loans may grow far beyond management's initial estimates. One prominent example occurred following the recent acquisition of First Railway and Banking Company by First Union Corp. of Charlotte, North Carolina—a leading regional holding company. Within a few months, more than $60 million of old loans had to be charged off the acquired bank's books.

Another serious problem interstate banking organizations must deal with in the period ahead is the cost of "brick-and-mortar" branch offices and other physical facilities. Deregulation and the intense competitive pressures it has brought have forced banks to make more efficient use of each dollar of their capital resources. As the decade began, among the most important cost-saving measures launched by many banks (including such industry leaders as BankAmerica and Wells Fargo) was the closing of unproductive and unprofitable branch offices.

Advances in the technology of service delivery and information processing have shifted the bulk of daily banking transactions (especially the processing of payments and other funds transfers) to automated systems that span both time and distance more efficiently than do paper transfers and physical labor. This is advantageous from one point of view: it has freed bankers from a repetitive daily routine, so that more time is available now to meet the specialized financial needs of their most important customers. From another vantage point, however, the ascendancy of automation has forced bank managers to re-evaluate their traditional physical production and delivery facilities and has necessitated painful decisions regarding the immediate closing or gradual phase-out of some local branch offices, often at the risk of substantial customer ill will.

At the same time, the decision about which automated operating system to adopt after an interstate merger occurs has climbed high on the list of key merger issues to resolve. It is a ticklish problem from an employee morale standpoint because the management and employees of all the banks involved in an interstate merger may have devoted years of effort to developing their own unique systems. Yet a single unified operating system is usually essential in order to give senior management the kinds of information it needs to make quick, informed, and effective decisions for all the affiliated bank and nonbank firms that make up today's larger interstate banking organizations. Moreover, most large branch and holding-company organizations today have developed centralized employee training programs to provide greater efficiency and to make possible the easy movement of management and staff from one affiliate or branch unit to another unit without the necessity of retraining. A unified operating system is essential to make a bank's strategic operating plan work.

In the 1986 four-state mega-merger led by First Union Corp. of Charlotte, North Carolina, the transition to a unified automated operating system was carefully planned from beginning to end. As described by Adams (1986), the process of synthesizing existing technologies into one operating system began with a key decision—the choice of the best core operating system (which, in this case, belonged to the parent company, First Union)— and then the establishment of multiple project teams, each holding weekly meetings and focusing on a different problem area. As many as 70 committees in some states worked on everything from check clearing and items processing to service delivery to customers at the level of each branch office, backed up by a detailed looseleaf guidebook assembled by senior management. Yet when local circumstances required flexibility, the movement toward a unified postmerger branch operating system was modified to allow local units to *gradually* blend their unique systems into the overall operating plan, helping to avoid "culture shock" on the part of local customers who might become confused by a rapid changeover in ownership and management philosophy and drift away to other banks. In this huge First Union acquisition, the different banks involved practiced functioning as a merged unit, with *joint* planning and problem-solving committees working together nearly six months before the actual merger took place.

A related problem that constitutes a rapidly growing source of bank operating expense today is the upward spiral in rental fees for commercial space in downtown buildings, especially along the East and West Coasts. Rental fees per square foot have risen rapidly in such leading cities as New York, Chicago, Los Angeles, and San Francisco. Many existing leases on bank headquarters and branch offices today were contracted years ago when office rental prices were much lower. However, as these leases come up for renewal in the 1990s, many U.S. banks will face a serious dilemma in deciding whether to renew existing lease agreements at a higher level of overhead expense or to abandon a significant number of branch offices.

A good example of the flavor of recent management thinking concerning this overhead problem appeared in September 1988 when Chase Manhattan Corp. announced plans to relocate close to one-third of its New York City work force (which then numbered about 16,000) to Newport across the Hudson River in New Jersey. Chase officials indicated the proposed change would probably bring substantial savings in utility costs and rental fees. An added advantage centered on the lower costs of protecting employees from crime risk, particularly those who must work late hours. However, such relocation decisions nearly always incur some loss of customer good will and the risk of retribution from area businesses and units of government. In this instance, as reported by Lowenstein (1988), the bank was concerned about the possible loss of a number of large government accounts, including the right to manage New York City's public employee pension plan.

The pressure to abandon existing branches or to move to lower-cost office sites is likely to grow as deregulation and technological change continue to impact on the roles performed today by neighborhood branch offices. A recent study reported by Bryan and Allen (1988) for McKinsey & Company, Inc. suggests that the majority of banking transactions are no longer related to customer walk-up or drive-through contact with local bank branches. Instead, more banking business today arises from off-premises transactions, such as customer purchases at the grocery store paid for via point-of-sale computer terminals, the use of remote money-dispensing machines (ATMs) and telephone or mail services, and communications through home and office computers linked to the bank's own computer system.

Increasingly, bank branch offices must look to their traditional role in attracting relatively low-cost deposits as the principal justification for their continued existence. However, deregulation of federal deposit interest-rate ceilings (completed in the spring of 1986) has sharply narrowed the spread between a bank's cost of borrowing local deposits and its cost of borrowing in the international money market. Full-service bank branches can survive from a strictly economic perspective only if they can expand the revenue productivity of the services they sell or lower production costs through such devices as cross-sales of new and old services, expanded use of automation, more efficient construction techniques, and improved employee education programs that increase productivity within the bank.

It may also be possible to use political leverage to win concessions from county, city, and state governments for those banks that threaten to close or move their office facilities. For example, when the National Broadcasting Company threatened to move its headquarters to New Jersey, New York City reportedly deterred that move by promising NBC approximately $100 million in tax savings covering a period of 35 years.

WINNING ACCEPTANCE BY THE
NEW COMMUNITIES ENTERED

Both intrastate and interstate mergers and acquisitions create problems in maintaining the allegiance and loyalty of the customers of both acquiring and acquired institutions. Loan customers who have been turned down by one of the merging banks and have become customers of the other bank involved may feel that their relationship is threatened. Credit and deposit customers of the acquired firm may be concerned that the bank personnel they have come to know will leave, voluntarily or otherwise. These customers may feel alienated, and a search for a new bank and a new banking relationship will often begin on the heels of a merger announcement.

One approach to dealing with concerned customers is to establish a merger hotline several weeks before the merger is to take place. Incoming calls can be routed to the bank officer or staff member who is most qualified to answer the customers' questions. Alternatively, selected bank personnel can be specially trained to handle incoming calls in a manner that quiets customer fears and preserves the merging bank's good will in the community. A good model of this approach was provided by Sovran Bank, N.A. of Richmond, Virginia, which was formed by the merger of Virginia National Bank and First & Merchants Bank. Marketing specialists at Sovran established a Merger Information Center that ultimately handled close to 22,000 calls, helping to resolve customer problems and cutting down on the large number of questions directed at bank tellers, which delayed the processing of routine transactions. Moreover, the persistence of long teller lines could cast doubt in the minds of customers that the merger would ultimately benefit the bank's customers in any tangible way.

Sovran also put informational material in the monthly deposit statements mailed to its account holders. These information sheets answered the most frequent questions that bank employees had previously encountered, including

1. What happens to my funds if I hold accounts at both banks involved in the merger?
2. Will I have to pay for newly printed checks, or can I continue to use the checks I have?
3. Will ATM cards be affected?
4. What about check cashing? How will that be impacted by the merger or acquisition?

Many banks also have discovered the importance of establishing close relationships with newspaper, radio, and television reporters in the local areas they serve. Senior-level managers can be encouraged to be open to frequent press interviews and to look for public and private opportunities to explain what the merger is all about and how it is likely to impact on both the individual customer and the community as a whole.

Moreover, there is growing awareness that bank employees, like the bank's customers, need special attention once an interstate merger goes public. Some banks that have established customer hot lines have encouraged their employees to use those same lines themselves to seek out answers to their concerns about an impending merger. Frequent pre-merger meetings of senior management with small groups of employees and division heads also are recommended. Underlying such efforts is the knowledge that if bank employees, particularly those who come into direct contact with customers, are fearful of a merger's consequences, that fear will be communicated, often in subtle ways, to the customers. In this case, the risk of losing important customer accounts and damaging community good will becomes very real.

Frequently, the key step that management must take to calm the feelings of customers, employees, and stockholders is to convey the image of continuity. That is, the interstate acquirer must demonstrate that it will continue to support the local community and value existing customer relationships *after* an interstate acquisition as the acquired bank did before the acquisition. That feeling of continuity with the past can be preserved if management and staff continue to play visible roles in the local community through civic organizations and bank sponsorship of worthwhile community programs and if familiar advertising themes are not changed abruptly.

The same feeling of continuity can also be enhanced by *gradual* changes in bank personnel and directorships, whenever possible, following a merger. Interstate bank management must recognize that whether an acquired bank had a successful or an unsuccessful record of performance prior to its purchase, the chances are better than even that it has a superior knowledge of its local community than does the acquirer. To dispose of the management and staff of an acquired institution right away risks local alienation, inappropriate advertising to fit the local market's needs, and failed performance. No matter how large and sophisticated an interstate system becomes, its management and directors must recognize and affirm that the central support of a successful service marketing program rests in the hands of the management and staff of each local banking office. It is not enough to erect a one-way communications channel from a centralized marketing program, which dictates marketing slogans and initiatives, to the interstate firm's local offices. Successful bank marketing programs also can emerge from neighborhood and regional offices where the reservoir of knowledge about local service needs usually is greatest of all.

There is no substitute for a planning program and a planning routine that rest on input from the *local* level. Local bank plans should include marketing objectives and an outline of how the local affiliate bank or branch office intends to set in motion its own marketing plan and monitor its own progress toward the interstate firm's marketing objectives. Too many banks acquired by interstate banking organizations in recent years have abandoned their own internal planning programs. This key managerial mistake may help to explain the sub-par financial performance of many banks acquired across state lines that we discussed earlier in Chapter 4.

Mergers involving large banking organizations, which include most interstate acquisitions, may create waves of reaction in the public sector that extend well beyond the customers of the banks involved. Local and state government officials may become involved, depending on the public's perception of the costs and benefits of each combination. Many bankers have learned to make courtesy calls on local and state officials to explain why the interstate merger is being pursued and what its expected benefits are for the local community and region, as well as for the customers and shareholders of the banking firms involved.

A good example was the 1984 merger of the Trust Company of Atlanta and Sun Banks of Orlando, Florida, which had elected to merge under the aegis of an Atlanta-based holding company. Fearing loss of customer good will in the sensitive Florida market, these institutions chose Orlando as the appropriate site to announce the merger, and officials from both institutions met that same day with Governor Bob Graham of Florida and, later, with Governor Joe Frank Harris of Georgia. A somewhat different strategy was adopted in the merger of First Wachovia Corp. of Winston-Salem, North Carolina, and First Atlanta Corp. The newly combined organization divided its headquarters and senior management staff between Winston-Salem and Atlanta. The management and staff in each of these two cities appear to be complete unto themselves and control only the subsidiaries within their own states.

Interestingly enough, First Atlanta accepted the Wachovia merger bid even though Wachovia offered a price for its stock that was about 10 percent less than the price offered by North Carolina National Bank (NCNB), based in Charlotte. NCNB's unwillingness to compromise on the location of the combined firm's headquarters may have been a factor in the decision of First Atlanta's shareholders to accept a lower dollar offer from Wachovia (as noted in a recent article published by the American Bankers Association [1987]).

The NCNB organization encountered another aspect of the community acceptance problem in the wake of its expansion into the Southwest by acquiring First RepublicBank Corp. of Dallas, the largest of the region's banking firms. The most serious miscalculation by NCNB centered on a failure to anticipate the strong degree of risk aversion among large depositors in the Southwest that had developed as a result of record numbers of bank and savings and loan failures. When NCNB acquired First Republic it converted Republic's affiliated banks into *branches* of its Dallas unit, NCNB Texas National Bank. Under FDIC regulations this newly created branch-office system could offer depositors only a maximum of $100,000 in federal insurance, no matter how many of its Texas offices received their deposits. In contrast, under the old First RepublicBank holding-company system, a million-dollar deposit could be split up into $100,000 units among different affiliated banks, and each deposit was covered for the *full* $100,000 in insurance. The result was twofold: (1) significant amounts of deposits flowed out of NCNB Texas branches into competing banks, and (2) the average interest rate on money-market CDs paid by NCNB's Texas unit rose sharply. The higher interest rates posted by NCNB's management aroused angry reactions from other leading bank executives in the region and closer regulatory scrutiny from the Texas state banking commission. Some other banks in the region began portraying NCNB staffers as "outsiders," hoping depositors would switch their funds to locally owned institutions (as reported by Apcar [1988]).

California banks selling services in New York City report evidence of a "status effect" among customers in that city. New York businesses and households often prefer to deal with a major Manhattan bank as a sign of their personal and corporate status in that huge market. Banks from outside Manhattan can offset this insular advantage of the city's leading banks by adopting costly customer incentives — for example, by offering lower-priced or higher-quality services. This status effect can become a significant economic entry barrier that must be paid for by outside entrants every day. As a strategic planner from a large West Coast bank explained to the author, "Every market has its own personality. When we consider a new market area for entry, we ask if our institution's personality fits that particular market." This West Coast bank adopted the strategy of, wherever possible, using *local* managerial talent to rent space and sell services in new markets. Thus, when it ventured into China, it bought a Chinese firm staffed by Chinese employees; it did the same thing with its new affiliate in West Germany.

OVERCOMING CONFLICTS BETWEEN THE MANAGEMENT OF ACQUIRING AND ACQUIRED INSTITUTIONS

Many financial analysts argue that the biggest hurdle in the path of successful interstate mergers is the meshing of philosophies and objectives of the management and ownership of the two companies involved. As attorney and merger consultant Arthur Burck (1984) has observed:

What usually is not comprehended — often until too late — is that mergers are not abstract jig-saw puzzles or mathematical formulae; basically they involve complex human beings with fixed ways, attitudes and prejudices, and differing talents; even under the best circumstances it is difficult to take two disparate and separate groups and blend them into one happy, motivated, and smooth-functioning team. . . . (1984, 658)

A similar observation was made recently by psychologists Smye and Grant (1989). They point out that mergers are often pursued because the financial aspects of the transaction appear to be acceptable, but the parties involved may not have considered the impact on the managements and staffs of the merging institutions. Different management styles and different employee compensation schedules that are not successfully meshed may produce serious internal conflicts, resulting in declining productivity and higher employee turnover. The interstate merger process itself, like banks themselves, must be closely and carefully managed every day.

There may be good reasons backing a decision to let some managers of acquired banking institutions leave, voluntarily or otherwise. Frequently, management effectiveness diminishes as an organization grows because larger banks demand different managerial skills than do smaller banks. Most banks add new services as they grow. The effective marketing and production of those new services may be better accomplished by a *new* management team. But there are good methods of discharging existing management and staff that minimize the damage to employee morale, and there are poor methods that can seriously undermine employee productivity.

A good illustration of this problem occurred when Wells Fargo purchased Crocker National Bank in California. Wells Fargo reminded the latter's management that the two banking institutions had not agreed to a merger of "equals," but rather that Wells Fargo had "purchased" Crocker. That statement implied that Wells could make wholesale changes in its newly acquired affiliate, which it subsequently did. Hundreds of employees were let go in what some industry observers dubbed the "neutron bomb" approach to merger and acquisition—i.e., the numbers of people employed are stripped down to the bare minimum needed to run the firm efficiently, but the buildings are left standing!

Discharging employees to cut labor costs may be destructive of the goals of an interstate merger. For one thing, if the acquired banking organization is very large, management changes may need to be made in the executive staff of the *acquiring* bank as well as in the acquired bank's management and staff. In this instance the resulting combined institution may require skills in integrating information systems and in managing personnel that *neither* of the merging firms possesses. Moreover, rather than firing existing employees, it may be better from an employee morale and productivity standpoint to simply allow the normal job turnover rate to take care of any surplus staff. For example, Smye and Grant (1989) note that about half of the business executives in acquired firms usually move on to new jobs during the first year following a merger.

Some acquiring organizations have pursued an optimistic "courting" approach to the managements and employees of their target firms. For example, NCNB extended pay raises and yellow roses to employees of its Texas affiliate, the former First RepublicBank Corp. of Dallas. This approach seemed particularly appropriate in the NCNB Texas case because the incoming North Carolina management team feared Texas customers would react negatively to a non-Texas institution acquiring what had been that state's largest banking organization.

After presidential elections are held in the United States, the new president selects a sizable transition team to work with the currently elected president so that the change of power and authority is as smooth as possible and there are no serious discontinuities in American foreign policy. This same transition-planning approach is essential if the personnel side of interstate mergers is to be successful at minimum cost to the acquirer. Experts usually recommend holding *joint* planning sessions before the merger date to bring any differences in goals, management styles, or compensation schedules out into the open where they can be fully explored and resolved before the acquisition is consummated. As business journalist Adams (1986) reported, following his review of the First Union Corp. of Charlotte's chain mergers, bringing in banks from South Carolina, Georgia, and Florida during 1986, the key to merging different organizations using different techniques, as well as differing management styles, is to "focus not on machines, but people, suppressing egos at the top and massaging them at the bottom" (1986, 28).

An added side benefit to holding joint planning meetings before a merger is consummated is the fact that management and staff of the two merging institutions then gain valuable experience in how to integrate their approaches and their work into a single, coordinated unit. Smye and Grant (1989) also recommend setting up focus groups at different levels within the banks involved at which employees from both banks meet to discuss concerns and possible philosophical differences. Eventually, management and staff begin to define problems and set goals in terms of "we" instead of "them" and "us."

AN OVERVIEW OF INTERSTATE ACQUISITION PROBLEMS AND THEIR IMPLICATIONS

Every interstate merger or acquisition brings its own unique set of problems; some of them are temporary problems that are worked out in the transition period, while others represent long-term difficulties that may never be fully resolved. Financial analysts have likened a business merger to a marriage between two people. Each party brings with it a unique litany of problems and beliefs that must be resolved quickly if the marriage is to succeed. There is an old saying about marriages that "the first year is the hardest." And so it can be with interstate bank mergers and acquisitions as well, unless each of the problems discussed in this chapter is addressed fully and management remains alert to new problems that inevitably seem to appear.

There is growing awareness in American banking that interstate mergers and acquisitions represent a *process* with key signposts along the way that must be heeded if that process is to yield beneficial results for all concerned. The interstate acquisition process begins with a clear statement of institutional goals and a logical analysis of how proposed mergers and acquisitions will serve those goals. Once the decision is made to negotiate a merger or acquisition, planning must begin immediately on how to carry out the transaction as smoothly as possible. Management of the interstate acquiring firm must decide if each of the problem areas we have touched on in this chapter—changes in federal or state legislation that open up new territories for expansion, capital shortages, unexpected and prospective costs, community acceptance, and conflicts between old and new management—represents a significant issue in the merger at hand. A careful strategy must be worked out in advance of the consummation of an interstate merger for dealing efficiently with each of these possible problem areas.

Events of the past decade have centered the banking community's attention on two of these problem areas—possible capital shortages and managerial conflicts—as being, potentially, the *most* troublesome. Fortunately, progress on the first of these problems—the issue of capital shortages—has been substantial, with most of the largest U.S. banks having significantly improved their capital ratios in recent years. Reserves built up in response to problems with energy credits and international loans and more conservative internal loan and portfolio management policies have combined to strengthen the capital position and lower the risk exposure of the biggest U.S. banking organizations.

However, the problems that arise by amalgamating the managements of acquired institutions into the networks of interstate acquiring organizations remain a key issue for the future. It is a problem particularly difficult to evaluate and resolve because there are no formulas and no regulatory guidelines to help steer the newly merged banking organization into a safe harbor. Those interstate banking organizations that ignore issues of management conflict and employee morale and that do not plan for their resolution are flirting with a potential firestorm that can eventually consume even the best banking organizations in the nation.

9

Interstate Goals and Outcomes: What Bank CEOs See as Their Problems and Accomplishments from Interstate Expansion

As the number of interstate bank acquisitions continues to grow and as these acquisitions spread into nearly every state, the impact of interstate banking on the banks involved, on their competitors, and on the public at large should become much clearer. Certainly the viewpoint of bankers themselves, especially those who have made recent interstate acquisitions, as to the successes and failures of their expansion programs is important evidence on both the public and the private aspects of the interstate banking movement. For example, do interstate banks develop and offer more new services than other banks? Do they improve the quality of service offered to the public? Are interstate banking organizations safer institutions with lower risk of failure? Examining the opinions and judgment of the chief executive officers (CEOs) responsible for their institutions' geographic strategies can help us pinpoint the problems of bank performance and public welfare that may lie ahead as the interstate banking revolution spreads across the United States.

Over 100 banking firms making interstate acquisitions during the years from 1980 into the first quarter of 1989 were contacted with questions about the possible impact of interstate acquisition activity in general and of their own most recent acquisition in particular. Officers of the surveyed institutions were asked questions in 10 broad areas of management, institutional performance, and strategy. In particular, they were asked to

1. Assess the public interest aspects of the interstate banking movement — for example, whether or not interstate banking is likely to change the probability of bank failures, yield more services for the consumer, improve service quality, affect

banking competition, drain scarce capital from local communities, or change the prices charged for financial services.

2. Identify the most influential characteristics of states and market areas chosen for entry.

3. Describe the most influential characteristics of those banking firms targeted for acquisition.

4. Identify the most promising states for future entry, as viewed by the CEOs of these interstate banking organizations.

5. Rank those states considered to be the most promising for entry from highest to lowest.

6. Indicate those states viewed by interstate bankers as not particularly promising for entry in the foreseeable future.

7. Describe what services each interstate organization will emphasize (if any) as it expands across state lines.

8. Identify the possible advantages full-service interstate banking organizations will have over institutions not planning expansion across the nation.

9. Specify what changes (if any) were made in policies and practices of banking institutions acquired across state lines.

10. Indicate whether or not they, as the CEOs of interstate acquiring organizations, are satisfied with the outcome of their most recent acquisitions.

THE PUBLIC INTEREST ASPECTS
OF INTERSTATE BANKING

Chief executive officers of interstate organizations appear to believe strongly in the potential for public benefits from the interstate movement. As shown in Table 9-1, close to half of all CEOs responding believe that interstate banking will reduce the likelihood of bank failures, principally because the larger and more geographically diversified banks that are created through interstate expansion will be better protected against business recessions and local economic adversity. While economic activity in one state may decline, there is less likelihood that the economies of every state where these institutions sell their services will be depressed as well. However, an equivalent number of bank CEOs disagree that interstate banking will reduce the likelihood of future bank failures. Probably this is because so many failing firms have been acquired across state lines, and a high proportion of these continue to perform poorly, often because regulators waited so long before declaring the acquired institutions insolvent and forcing them into an interstate merger.

A majority (71 percent) of the responding CEOs also believe that the average consumer will benefit from the availability of more financial services through interstate banking. To be sure, offering new services in any market is both expensive and risky. However, larger and more geographically

Table 9-1

Bankers' Evaluation of the Likely Public Interest Aspects of Interstate Banking

Interstate Banking Will:	Percentage of Respondents Who		
	Agree	Disagree	No Opinion
Reduce the Likelihood of Bank Failures	43%	43%	14%
Result in More Financial Services for the Average Consumer	71	21	8
Result in Improved Service Quality	64	36	0
Result in More Concentrated Banking Markets and Reduced Banking Competition	29	71	0
Drain Scarce Capital from Local Communities in Order to Make Large Corporate and Foreign Loans	7	93	0
Result in Lower Prices or Interest Rates Charged for the Following Services:			
Consumer Installment Loans	43	50	7
Small Business Loans	36	57	7
Large-Denomination Corporate Loans	57	43	0
Credit Guarantees	29	57	14
Checkable Deposits	43	50	7
Cash Management Services	57	43	0
Trust Services	57	43	0

diverse banking organizations can reduce the risk of service innovation due to their abilities to hire skilled management, to undertake extensive advertising programs, and to test market new services in selected areas without hastily committing the whole organization to a new service line that may not succeed. Moreover, as the history of branch banking suggests, services offered through the home office usually can be made accessible through *any* branch office in the system more easily than is true of single-office (unit) banks or smaller branch banking systems.

These CEOs also believe, by a considerable majority (64 percent), that bank service quality will be improved as full-service interstate banking spreads across the nation. Presumably larger and more stable banks can afford to hire competent management and staff to monitor and maintain the quality of service production and delivery. They also can afford more frequent technological updating that can usher in greater accuracy, efficiency, and speed in making service delivery to the customer. Still, a substantial proportion of responding bank executives—about 36 percent or just over one-third—disagree with the premise that service quality would improve under interstate banking. This group reflects the widely held opinions that one bank's services are usually much the same as another's and that real changes in service content are difficult, if not impossible, to achieve in most markets.

Interestingly enough, however, most responding interstate bankers do *not* expect that most service prices will be lowered or that interest earnings on deposits will be increased in the wake of full-service interstate bank expansion. Only about one-third of those responding expect lower interest rates on small business loans, and just under 30 percent believe prices will be lowered on check-guarantee services. About two-fifths of the interstate bankers replying expect reduced prices on checkable deposits, and the same proportion believes consumer loan rates will fall. Interest rates on large corporate loans are expected to be lowered by a slight majority (57 percent) of responding bankers, perhaps as much due to strong foreign bank competition for domestic corporate customers as to the gradual spread of interstate banking. The same conclusion held for cash management and trust services, with almost three-fifths of responding bankers believing the fees charged for these services will decline. Both cash management and trust services are heavily used by large corporations, and interstate banks would, therefore, face stiff competition even in U.S. markets from British, Canadian, French, and Japanese banks.

Perhaps not surprisingly, few of the responding interstate bank CEOs are prepared to accept two possible *negative* outcomes of interstate banking: (1) the potential for reduced competition and greater concentration of power in the financial marketplace, and (2) the draining away of scarce capital funds from local communities. Only about one-quarter (29 percent) expect an increase in market concentration, and only one CEO in every 14 forewarns of a draining of funds away from local communities into corporate and foreign loans. By a wide margin, bank executives view full-service interstate bank expansion as a *positive* step for the industry and for the public, with the principal benefits centered on more and better quality services for the public.

ASSESSING STATES AND LOCAL MARKET AREAS
FOR POSSIBLE INTERSTATE ENTRY

What do bankers look at in deciding whether to enter new states and local market areas? What features of a state or region appear to attract interstate bankers the most? As indicated in Table 9-2, the most important feature of a potentially good target market, according to bank CEOs, is rapid or above-average population growth, followed closely by growth in personal income. Approximately four-fifths of all responding bank CEOs see population and income growth as dominant features of their target markets. Above-average growth in a state's or region's personal income suggests increasing demand for household financial services and, therefore, an increasing demand for cash and installment loans. Moreover, more rapid growth in personal in-

Table 9-2
Characteristics of States and Local Market Areas that Influence Bankers' Acquisition Decisions

Characteristics of States and Local Market Areas	Percentage of Respondents Indicating the Characteristic Most Influential in Choosing States and Local Market Areas
Rapid or Above-Average Growth in Population	86%
Rapid or Above-Average Growth in Personal Income	79
Availability of a Large Volume of Core Deposits from Households and Businesses	71
Rapid or Above-Average Growth in Total Deposits at Existing Financial Institutions	64
High or Above-Average Ratio of Population per Banking Office	64
Rapid or Above-Average Growth in Retail Sales	29
Rapid or Above-Average Growth in Residential and/or Nonresidential Construction	29
Other Influential Factors: (including competition, population density, population size, and stability of the economy)	7

Note: Figures in the table total more than 100 percent because respondents were allowed to choose more than one characteristic.

come often translates into increased retail and wholesale sales activity, accelerating the demand for business loans.

The availability of a large volume of core deposits from households and businesses ranks third in importance as an attractive feature of targeted interstate markets. Just over 70 percent of the CEOs replying to the survey identify access to these relatively low-cost, interest-rate-insensitive sources of bank funds as a key barometer of a worthwhile state or local market for entry. Deregulation of banking, especially the lifting of federal interest-rate ceilings on deposits by the federal government during the 1980s, appears to have tempered bank pursuit of core deposits. Many bankers believe that deregulation of interest rates has sharply reduced the available stock of core deposits as it has made most depositors more sensitive to differences in interest rates and service fees between one bank and another.

Demographic characteristics other than population growth also rank high in separating markets targeted for future interstate entry from those that are likely to be avoided by interstate acquirers. As expected, a majority of responding bankers (64 percent) believe that an above-average ratio of population to the number of banking offices operating in a state or region is influential in making a decision to enter or not to enter. The continued expansion of population relative to banking facilities available appears to open up the doors of opportunity for profitable bank expansion. Population growth generates both new loan and new deposit demand. A few responding bankers also mention population density as an indicator, with greater numbers of people per square mile offering the potential for greater bank profits and growth. A state or local area with greater overall population size is also viewed as more likely to experience future bank entry.

Rapid growth in deposits is viewed almost as favorably as strong population growth, with nearly two-thirds of responding bank executives viewing this as a favorable feature of a target market. If total deposits are growing at an above-average rate of speed, this suggests that entering interstate banks will have access to the funds they need to accommodate growing loan demand, possibly with less need to rely on the volatile and often expensive international money market for funding. A small portion of bankers point to stability of the local economy as an important characteristic of a desirable market and a desirable area to enter. Other factors mentioned by responding bankers include the market shares held by existing financial institutions in the targeted area, the quality of bank management in a state or local community, the size of the local economy, the availability of alternative investments, the speed with which the number of commercial loans is growing, the existence of real opportunities for diversification, the size of household income, and the target area's growth and economic conditions as compared with those of the acquiring institution's current market areas.

Competition also is identified by less than 10 percent of the respondents as having a negative effect on future entry. It seems evident from the personal interviews conducted by the author with officers of leading interstate banking firms that the management of these firms does not generally shy away from or seek to avoid competition. These organizations typically are headquartered in intensely competitive local and regional markets and expect more of the same in those markets they most desire to enter in the future.

CRITERIA USED TO CHOOSE TARGET BANKING FIRMS FOR FUTURE ACQUISITION

What features of a banking organization may lead to its eventual acquisition by an interstate acquirer? How can a bank better position itself to be looked at seriously as a target for an interstate takeover? As Table 9-3 suggests, not surprisingly above-average historical profit performance stands at the top of the list. Of bank CEOs responding to the survey, 64 percent name this feature as most influential. Banks and holding companies with an exceptional track record of profitability, along with other requisite features, will be given a serious look by most out-of-state banking firms. Interestingly enough, however, these CEOs do not rate *potential* profitability as highly as they do a favorable record of historical profitability. Apparently they prefer to have evidence that a target bank has been profitable in the past, rather than speculating on higher future profits that, clearly, may not materialize.

Not surprisingly, in a period of great concern with bank stability and failure risk, the quality of the loan portfolio of an acquisition-targeted bank also ranks high with these CEOs. Banks and holding companies reporting above-average loan quality are identified by just over 70 percent of the respondents as presenting a desirable profile for future acquisition. This has been a serious stumbling block to entry into and acquisition of banks in the Rocky Mountain area, the Southwest, and the Midwest where recessions in agriculture, energy, and mining have led to sharply deteriorating loan quality. Major interstate acquirers already burdened with their own loan-quality problems from the international sector and from commercial real estate transactions have little enthusiasm for acquiring banking organizations that are also struggling with serious loan-quality problems.

Acquiring bankers also respond positively to *potential* opportunities for bank growth when there is evidence of "unexploited marketing opportunities." Half of the CEOs responding see these untapped selling opportunities as important to their acquisition decisions. Just over 40 percent of the respondents react favorably to the prospect of reducing operating costs in those target banking firms that appeared to have high costs and operate inefficiently. Presumably the acquiring institution would bring in new and better management and operating costs would fall. Because service production and delivery problems are within a banker's control, while profits earned depend on the customers and general market conditions, as well as

Table 9-3
Characteristics of Target Banking Organizations that Most Influence Bankers'
Acquisition Decisions

Characteristics of Target Banking Organizations	Percentage of Respondents Indicating the Characterstic Most Influential in Targeting a Banking Organization for Acquisition
Above–Average–Quality Loan Portfolio	71%
Above–Average Historical Profitability	64
Relatively Large Holdings of Core Deposits	57
Evidence of Unexploited Marketing Opportunities	50
Superior Location and Condition of Physical Facilities	43
Evidence of Inefficiencies and Excessive Operating Costs That Better Management Could Eliminate	43
Low Current Profitability, but Above–Average Potential for Future Profitability	14
Above–Average Capitalization (ratio of equity capital to total assets or to risk assets)	7

Note: Figures in the table total more than 100 percent because
respondents were allowed to choose more than one characteristic.

management decisions, it is not surprising that bankers respond favorably to
a problem in a target firm that appears to be correctable with good management decision making and technological updating.

Despite the concern of leading international banks with the adequacy of
their capital as a defense against loan losses, especially following the Basel
Agreement of 1988 which made international capital regulation possible,
interstate banks do not appear to view their bank acquisitions as a key
source of future equity capitalization. Few respondents (only 7 percent) see
an above-average ratio of equity capital to total assets or of equity capital to

risk assets as contributing to a favorable financial profile for a bank they would consider acquiring. For one thing, many of the targets for interstate acquisition are simply too small to have a substantial impact on the capital adequacy or the future capital availability of acquiring institutions. Also, many full-service interstate acquisitions in the early and mid-1980s were centered on banks in financial trouble with weak levels of capitalization. These troubled firms would not be likely to make a significant contribution toward reducing an acquirer's risk exposure, at least for some considerable period of time in the future.

As might be expected from the findings reported in Table 9–2, the availability of core deposits – usually small in denomination with little sensitivity to interest-rate movements – continues to rank high as an indicator of promising acquisition targets. Banks and bank holding companies with relatively large holdings of core deposits are flagged by over half (57 percent) of the respondents as desirable targets for future takeovers. Core deposits help these banks keep their funding costs low and relatively stable. Lower-cost deposits obviously aid the bank in maintaining a favorable spread of operating revenues over operating costs. More stable funding costs promote greater stability in bank earnings, which lowers stockholder risk and increases the value of the bank's stock in the market, other factors held equal.

The location and condition of a bank's physical facilities also turn out to be an important feature in assessing an interstate acquisition target. Just over 40 percent of the responding CEOs specifically check this physical feature as important. This is not surprising in view of the heavy emphasis placed on household (retail) banking services by many interstate firms. The location and condition of branch offices, ATMs, and other customer-convenient facilities are vital elements in a retail-oriented interstate expansion strategy. Then, too, the age and value of branch offices and other physical facilities significantly influence the amount of depreciation expense that can be written off annually, helping the bank to shelter its earnings from taxation.

STATES VIEWED AS MOST PROMISING
FOR FUTURE ENTRY

What states are viewed as most desirable for future bank entry by the CEOs of interstate banking organizations? Not surprisingly, the most frequently mentioned states are those with the largest populations and usually are among the leaders in business and personal income growth as well. The leading states include California, Florida, Illinois, Michigan, Missouri, New York, Texas, and Virginia, with Illinois mentioned most often by responding bankers (as indicated in Table 9–4).

California has captured considerable attention recently because it has announced it will open its borders to nationwide banking in 1991 and be-

Table 9-4

States Viewed as Most Promising for Future Entry by Interstate Acquiring Banks

Most Promising States for Future Entry	Precentage of Respondents Indicating the State As Most Promising for Future Entry
Illinois	28%
California	14
Florida	14
Michigan	14
Missouri	14
New York	14
Pennsylvania	14
Virginia	14
Texas	7

Note: Other states mentioned less frequently, but still viewed as desirable by some interstate banking organizations for future entry included Delaware, Hawaii, Idaho, Indiana, Kansas, Minnesota, Nevada, New Mexico, and Tennessee.

cause it is, in and of itself, a large market for retail and business banking services and a possible stepping stone to the nations of the Pacific Rim. Illinois, Michigan, Pennsylvania, and Virginia are viewed as attractive for similar reasons, also having huge retail banking markets that are not as heavily penetrated by financial-service competitors as California and New York. New York is heavily favored due to its position at the heart of the domestic and international money markets. Texas is viewed as a potentially huge retail market, and while the timing of its future recovery from declining oil prices is uncertain, the banking community general regards this recovery as inevitable. Finally, Florida is viewed as an affluent market likely to continue to grow rapidly in the future with increasing numbers of affluent elderly and retired citizens.

What is particularly remarkable about the information summarized in Table 9-4 is the relative *homogeneity* of bankers' rankings of the leading states for future bank entry. No single state commanded a dominating position in the opinion of those individuals who, most likely, must make the ultimate "go" or "no go" decision about future expansion across state lines. Illinois comes the closest, chosen by nearly one in three responding CEOs, while California, Florida, Michigan, Missouri, New York, Pennsylvania, and Virginia were chosen by about one in eight of all survey respondents. One possible explanation lies in the asymmetrical pattern of state banking laws where a few states have opened their borders to entry from any state in the nation, while most have limited entry to only selected states, usually within the same region of the nation. This is understandable, but it also suggests a potential problem with *planning* in the banking industry. Few bank presidents were willing to look beyond the current matrix of banking laws to that distant era when entry may be possible from virtually anywhere in the nation. Such a short-sighted view suggests that many U.S. banks have not fully prepared themselves for long-run changes in laws and regulations that could have a profound impact on their strategic position and future profitability.

Another equally plausible explanation rests on the different environments — economic and financial — faced by interstate acquiring companies. To the extent that geographic and cash-flow diversification is an important consideration in planning future acquisitions, different banking organizations will require a different combination of markets and target institutions. Moreover, as we discussed in the preceding chapter, interstate acquirers tend to prefer states closer to home rather than far away.

Several states are viewed as *not* particularly promising for future bank entry. These less-well-regarded states appear to fall into two groups: (1) those with weak economies where the prospects for future bank growth and profitability seem unlikely or, at least, highly questionable; and (2) those states likely to have continuing legal barriers to unrestricted interstate banking operations. Alaska, Wyoming, and Colorado lead the list of states regarded as having weakened economies and many troubled loans that would be unlikely to attract significant interstate banking activity. On the other hand, the New England states — Connecticut, Maine, Massachusetts, New Hampshire, Rhode Island, and Vermont — are viewed as unattractive by many outsiders to that region predominantly because of their restrictive regional banking laws. However, this negative image may well change as several New England states (e.g., Maine and Massachusetts) have recently passed nationwide banking legislation allowing more outside entrants into their territories. There may also be concern that some portions of the heretofore strong New England economy are weakening.

BANKING SERVICES EMPHASIZED BY INTERSTATE ACQUIRING INSTITUTIONS

Recent research suggests that full-service interstate banking firms have tended to be heavily retail-banking oriented, stressing service menus designed mainly to appeal to household customers (particularly installment credit, savings, and checkable deposits). Consistent with this notion, interstate acquirers have tended to pursue banks with above-average numbers of branch offices or holding companies with large numbers of affiliated banks in order to acquire a ready-made system for retail service delivery. Further reflecting this bias among interstate firms toward retail service production and delivery, interstate acquirers have also tended to stress insurance sales, credit cards, trust accounts, investment advisory services, community development, travel agency operations, and property appraisals. Moreover, bankers interviewed in all parts of the nation have expressed a preference for high-volume services and those that can most easily be computerized and automated.

ADVANTAGES INTERSTATE BANKS WILL HAVE OVER OTHER BANKING INSTITUTIONS

While the expansion of banks across state boundaries into new regions and even nationwide brings its own unique management challenges and problems, many bankers who have launched full-service interstate acquisition programs believe there are offsetting benefits, some of which have great strategic significance for the future. As Table 9–5 suggests, one of these is the acquiring of a broader loan base. This may provide greater stability in customer demand for bank services and improved earnings stability as fluctuations in loan demand in one state or region may be counterbalanced by offsetting changes in loan demand in another state or region. Moreover, to the extent that banking services can be mass produced, a broader market base will tend to result in lower unit production costs (especially lowering the fixed cost of large-scale branch-office systems) due to economies of scale and scope. The achievement of lower service production costs would represent a definite competitive edge for interstate banks relative to their intrastate rivals, some of whom may ultimately be driven from the market. With the prospect of selling larger volumes of services across state lines, interstate banks may reap the advantage of being able to make more complete use of the computer for the automated production and delivery of banking services. Computerized systems tend to deliver services faster and with greater accuracy, giving interstate bankers an edge with customers valuing those same features.

An even more important advantage of interstate banking, as seen by bank CEOs, is the potential reduction of risk through diversification. This is the number-one advantage cited by these CEOs of full-service interstate banking organizations. Some bankers see diversification as primarily geographic in nature as their organizations are able to penetrate different regions with differing economic characteristics. Other respondents see more risk-reducing diversification in their ability to offer different services across state lines because some new markets prefer a somewhat different service mix than do

Table 9-5
The Most Important Advantages Interstate Banking Firms Have
over Noninterstate Banks

Advantages Cited by Interstate Banking Organizations	Percentage of Respondents Mentioning the Advantage
Greater Geographic and Service Diversification	36%
Broader Marketing Opportunities	21
Economies of Scale Due to Larger Production and Sales Volumes (lowering production cost per unit)	14
Access to New Markets	7
Broader Lending Base in Order to Provide Greater Stability in Revenues and Net Earnings	7

Note: Other advantages mentioned by a few bankers included the avoidance of some competition, new growth opportunities, the spreading of fixed costs, increased ability to offer computer-based specialized services, and reduced vulnerability to a takeover.

the old markets served in the past. Still a third group simply sees interstate expansion as broadening the types of markets they already occupy, allowing more sales of traditional banking services.

CHANGES MADE IN OPERATING POLICIES AND PRACTICES AT ACQUIRED BANKS

One of the most controversial issues in interstate banking is the question of whether buying out a bank results in changes in its prices, services, and operations that benefit the public and perhaps bank employees as well. Alternatively, are changes set in motion that ultimately prove damaging to the public or result in a loss of banking jobs?

The evidence from the responses supplied by CEOs of acquiring interstate banks is mixed. Some beneficial changes have occurred, but most banks change very little. As shown in Table 9-6, only about one-quarter of the responding interstate bankers report raising loan rates or other service fees,

Table 9-6
Changes Made in Policies and Practices at Banks Acquired Across State Lines

Possible Changes in Policies and/or Practices Made in the Banks and Bank Holding Companies Acquired Across State Lines	Percentage of Respondents Reporting the Change Was Made
Offered New Services Not Previously Offered by the Acquired Institution	86%
Raised Fees on Some Miscellaneous Services (other than on loans and deposits)	64
Built Some New Service Facilities	57
Raised Interest Rates Offered on at Least Some Deposits	36
Closed Some New Service Facilities	29
Opened Facilities for Longer Hours for Greater Customer Convenience	29
Raised Interest Rates and Service Fees on At Least Some Loans	29
Other Changes Made (including instituting marketing on a consolidated basis, improving management practices, installing new management information systems, implementing better loan-review procedures, and improving internal auditing practices)	14

and only a slightly greater proportion (36 percent) have altered deposit interest rates in the upward direction. While more banks have raised miscellaneous service fees than have not (about two-thirds have adjusted these nondeposit and noncredit fees upward), slightly more than one-quarter of the banks responding now open their facilities for longer hours to provide greater convenience for their customers. Offering new services is the most frequent change, with about 86 percent claiming new services are now being offered through their newly acquired banking institutions. However, the drive for lower operating costs has resulted in the frequent closing of some bank facilities (reported by 29 percent of bankers replying). Yet more bankers (57 percent) report building some new facilities. And there have been potentially beneficial internal changes: improved management practices, new management information systems, and improved internal audits and loan review procedures are mentioned by a few of the participating interstate bankers.

THE TRACK RECORD OF GOAL ACHIEVEMENT
FOR INTERSTATE BANKS

Interstate acquirers enter new markets for a wide variety of reasons and often are armed with many different goals. As yet, few have achieved spectacular or even exceptional performance in the pursuit of their goals. As Table 9-7 indicates, most acquisitions appear to generate results that are about in line with management's expectations. For example, when the surveyed interstate bankers were asked if the profitability of their acquiring institutions had improved following their most recent acquisition, about three-quarters reported that their profits had been no more than expected following these takeovers, while only 14 percent reported achieving profits *beyond* their original expectations. Those who sought a foothold position in a new market generally achieved that result, with about 20 percent believing they had done better than expected in this regard.

Banks seeking new sources of core deposits generally meet their expectations for these more stable deposit accounts which carry greater reliability for the banker. However, there is greater variability in the survey results for the goal of generating new loan demand. About two-fifths of the responding bankers have achieved more loan demand than expected, but about one-fifth of the respondents have either attracted *less* new loan demand from their acquisitions than they had planned or have completely failed to achieve this goal. Only 7 percent of interstate acquisitions have resulted in exceptional additions to capital for the acquirer, and nearly 36 percent have scored below their expectations for improving overall capital strength. A small proportion — about 7 percent — of these bank CEOs report making acquisitions that have increased their stock price, improved asset quality, and achieved better name recognition in the markets they serve.

Table 9-7
Goals Achieved in Banking Acquisitions Across State Lines

Goals Associated with Making Interstate Acquisitions	The Goals Sought Were				
	Achieved Beyond Expectations	Achieved About as Expected	Achieved Less than Expected	Not Achieved at All	No Opinion
Improved Profitability of the Acquiring Institution	14%	79%	0%	0%	7%
Gave the Acquirer a Firm Foothold in a New Market Area	21	64	0	7	8
Opened Up New Sources of Core Deposits	7	71	7	7	8
Generated New Loan Demand Not Seen Before	21	43	14	7	15
Brought in Additional Capital to Strengthen the Acquiring Organization	7	36	7	29	21

Note: Other goals pursued by acquiring banking firms included increasing stock prices, improving the quality of assets held, and developing greater name recognition.

IMPLICATIONS OF THE NATIONAL SURVEY

The unfolding drama of interstate banking has been greeted warmly in many states because of the greater economic stability, improved service availability, and increased availability of jobs it was hoped might be ushered in with it. Moreover, as the national survey results discussed in this chapter suggest, the majority of interstate bankers themselves believe that the interstate banking movement has indeed delivered on its promises, reducing the risk of bank failure, making more services available, improving service quality, and promoting more rapid economic growth. The evidence suggests, however, that these positive outcomes arise from only *some* interstate combinations and certainly not all.

Few interstate banking transactions achieve all or even a majority of the internal and external goals set for them. Many of the reasons for this are self-evident. No merger is completely under a banker's control; competition, regulation, and the economy all play decisive roles in the unfolding drama of an interstate acquisition. In addition, the meshing together of two different banking organizations that arise out of different management philosophies, objectives, and geographic backgrounds always presents serious challenges to goal achievement. Moreover, it is often the banks themselves, not the banking industry or the public in a given state, that benefits the most from interstate expansion.

Perhaps we should be satisfied as citizens and as consumers of banking services that, if there are no appreciable public benefits from interstate banking, there is also no convincing evidence yet of significant damage to the public welfare. Interstate banking may not shower us with economic benefits, such as lower service fees, improved service quality, and abundant new jobs, but at the least it does not appear to engulf us in a tumult of failing banks, lost jobs, and economic collapse in city, county, state, and regional markets. And there is always the hope that better outcomes for the public may lie just beyond the horizon. To paraphase the nineteenth century French economist St. Simon, perhaps the real long-run benefits of interstate banking still lie before us, not behind us.

10

Guideposts for Public Policy and the Management of Interstate Banking Firms

American banking today is passing through a revolution in services, regulation, and organizational structure unprecedented in at least half a century. Not since the Great Depression of the 1930s have U.S. banks been so severely buffeted by the combined forces of economic turbulence, competition from within the industry and from without, rapid technological innovation, and a constantly changing set of federal and state government rules. Together, those forces of economics, competition, technology, and regulation have combined to produce consolidation in the banking industry on an unprecedented scale. Small banks and bank holding companies that have been numerically dominant in the industry for generations are disappearing in many local markets, absorbed by large, geographically diversified, and product-diversified financial-service firms.

In many ways the American banking system is groping, in its own unique style, along the path toward the large-bank-dominated financial systems that have operated in other industrialized nations of the Western world for centuries. Today, the most visible aspect of that movement is the spread of interstate banking across the nation's diverse landscape. More than four-fifths of the states passed new banking laws in the 1980s, permitting banking organizations from other states to enter their domain with a full menu of services and compete against local banks for financial-service customers in hundreds of local communities. The number of full-service interstate banks quadrupled between 1983 and 1988 alone and in 1989 accounted for over half of all interstate offices operated by U.S. banking organizations. As we have seen in the pages of this book, the interstate revolution in American banking has multiple causes, not the least of which is pressure from foreign banks (especially the largest institutions headquartered in Canada, France,

Japan, and the United Kingdom) that have recently captured a growing share of U.S. domestic customers, particularly in the market for corporate banking services.

THE RISKS OF INTERSTATE BANKING

The interstate revolution in American banking, like most revolutions, will not leave the people and the institutions that it touches unscarred. A new financial landscape is emerging in which both bankers and their customers will have to adjust, comfortably if possible, to *new* circumstances: intense competition for all customers in all markets, service prices and terms of trade determined by market dynamics and not by government fiat, service proliferation and innovation as a daily fact of life, and an ever-present vulnerability to failure in a volatile and treacherous marketplace. The availability and price of banking services will change in yet unknown ways, benefitting some consumers and burdening others.

Few institutions will remain unaffected by interstate banking because banking services are such a vital ingredient in the personal and professional lives of Americans. The high standard of living that most Americans enjoy today is crucially dependent on the continuing capacity and willingness of U.S. banks to release a massive flow of credit to support household consumption, business investment, and government spending. Commercial banks are the number-one supplier in the United States of loans to individuals and families, the number-two supplier of credit to the business community, and, in most years, the front-ranked purchaser of federal, state, and local government bonds and notes for themselves and for their customers. If that credit flow is ever reduced or diverted, the economy's growth will slow, the availability of jobs will decline, and the high standard of living enjoyed by thousands of American families will be imperiled.

In many ways interstate banking in the United States is on trial. American public policy has a history of commitment, dating at least as far back as the Employment Act of 1946, to preserving jobs; maintaining stable, noninflationary growth; and protecting the public's savings. If interstate banking threatens that commitment now or at any time in the future, it is clear from the legislative record that the federal government and the states will not hesitate to step in and "re-regulate" the geographic and service powers of American banks.

Interstate banking is truly an American "social experiment"—something new to a nation that is suspicious of large corporations, especially large banking institutions, and the power over people's lives they often seem to possess. That experiment *may* fail; partial deregulation and a volatile economy *may* ultimately bring American banks to the same disastrous fate as American savings and loan associations. Free markets issue *no* guarantees concerning the future. And there are scores of foreign competitors—including British, Canadian, French, and Japanese banks, as well as leading European and Asian securities houses and insurance firms — ready to fill in the financial-services vacuum, should the nation's leading banks and the regulatory milieu that surrounds them falter and decline.

In financial affairs at least, American public policy and the American consumer face a race against time and circumstances. The core issue is this: can we safely and quickly free American banking from the restraints of geographic and product regulation built up over generations and still preserve the integrity of the American financial system? We have failed miserably with savings and loan associations. What makes us believe that we will succeed with the nation's banks? The real danger for U.S. banks and bankers is that any sign of systemic failure, such as the collapse of several large money-center banks — however misleading that signal might be — will set in motion powerful political constituencies that can force American banking back into a working environment where *more*, rather than less, regulation holds sway. Nor can we be sure that other nations will follow us with new regulations of their own, should we elect to "re-regulate" this industry. Foreign banking institutions may remain much as they are today — largely deregulated, multi-faceted financial-service firms that have the capability of wresting still more of the American banking market away.

THE PUBLIC POLICY ISSUES THAT REMAIN

The future of interstate banking today *is* in doubt. Several large question marks surround this American financial revolution, with few safe answers yet to be found. There are, for example, some critical issues of public policy about which we have only limited clues on how to proceed.

One of these issues centers on the potential benefits and costs of full-service nationwide banking for the economic growth and development of states and local communities. As we saw in Chapters 2 and 3, the majority of states willingly passed interstate banking laws because they believed (or, at least, hoped) that legal milestone would add to their prospects for attracting new industry, strengthening local economies, and increasing the availability of jobs. The research evidence amassed to date suggests most of those states are likely to be sadly disappointed on the economic front. There is little supporting evidence, thus far, that changes in the ownership and organization of local banks or shifts in the control of local banks from residents to nonresidents will result in more rapid growth in new industries, new jobs, an expanded output of goods and services, greater personal savings, or higher standards of living. Other nonbanking factors — such as the availability of natural resources, the adequacy of transportation and communications links, the thrift habits of local businesses and households, the quality of local schools, and the geographic features of the local landscape — appear to have a far more important impact on local community living standards and the availability of jobs and new industry than does the ownership configuration of local banks. The best that most states and local communities can count on is that interstate bank expansion probably will have *no adverse impact* on local and regional economic conditions.

There may be other significant effects, however, from the spread of U.S. full-service banks across state borders that will have a profound impact on some cities, towns, and rural communities for years to come. For example, there will be some loss of *local* control over each community's banks. Many customers fear that this means bank managers will no longer really care about local customers, especially small businesses and families. Loans may go only to those customers willing to pay the highest interest rates and service fees or to those customers with the soundest balance sheets. Other considerations — such as the welfare of the local community, issues of social justice, and customer loyalty through good times and bad — may be regarded as unimportant by the new type of American banking organization that is emerging.

The research evidence to date on this issue is *not* particularly persuasive, however. While local control over banking *may* be impaired, the influence of local customers on their banks need not be reduced. Larger banking organizations tend to be more aggressively managed and often are highly responsive to customer requests and complaints, largely because their staffs tend to be better trained in marketing techniques and because they are surrounded on all sides by intense competition from equally large domestic and foreign financial-service firms. Then, too, recent decisions of the Federal Reserve Board and the Comptroller of the Currency (the Administrator of National Banks) suggest much greater regulatory concern over the quality of banking service the public is receiving and over whether banking services are being offered fairly and without discrimination to *all* segments of a local community. In February of 1989, for example, the proposed acquisition of Grand Canyon State Bank of Scottsdale, Arizona, by Illinois' Continental Bank was disapproved by federal regulators on grounds that the acquirer did not have an acceptable record of affirmative action in serving all segments of the customer community as required by the Community Reinvestment Act of 1977. It was the first denial in U.S. history of a bank merger under the terms of a law that requires affirmative action in the banking industry.

The 1980s have ushered in deep-seated fears about the soundness of hundreds of American banks, particularly those headquartered in the agriculture-dominated Midwest and the energy-dominated Rocky Mountains and Southwest. In this area interstate banking organizations may offer real hope in reducing the rate of bank failures, especially for the large metropolitan banks and bank holding companies they prefer to acquire. Failure rates generally decline with bank size, probably because larger banks enjoy the benefits of both greater geographic diversification (with branch offices and affiliated firms spread across the landscape) and greater product-line diversification (with more services on the menu and more new services under development). Diversification of either the geographic or the product-line variety tends to reduce the variability of cash flows through the consolidated banking firm, contributing to a more stable flow of dividends to the firm's stockholders and the greater availability of low-cost capital to strengthen the individual banking firm.

Will full-service interstate banking improve the availability of banking services to the public? Certainly research over the last two decades suggests that larger branch banking organizations tend to provide greater public convenience by establishing more offices relative to the population size of the counties and cities they serve. Depending on the geographic distribution of those additional offices, the public may have to travel shorter distances to access banking facilities, and the cost of banking transactions generally would be reduced for the typical bank customer. However, this is not necessarily the end of the story on public convenience because in the 1980s large branching organizations moved aggressively to close down local branch offices that appeared to be unprofitable or unproductive in fund raising. In 1987, for example, according to the *Annual Report* of the FDIC, more than 1,300 U.S. bank branch offices were closed, though across the entire nation there was a net gain in this measure of public convenience because more than 1,600 new branch offices were opened in the same year. On the critical issue of public convenience and interstate bank expansion, therefore, we must await more research evidence before pronouncing a verdict.

Many legislators, local government officials, and businesses have expressed fear that local funds will be channeled to distant markets once a community's banks are owned by large interstate organizations. In one sense, especially from the perspective of the economist who focuses on the *global* impact of individual business decisions, resources in the U.S. economy would be more efficiently allocated if banks directed their credit funds to those customers whose projects were expected to yield the highest returns, regardless of where and how those funds are to be used. Frequently this does require a bank to take deposits supplied by smaller outlying communities and use them to make loans to large corporations in major metropolitan areas or even overseas. However, in a global context such a lending strategy merely reflects profit-maximizing behavior by bankers and their customers and, in the long run, should lead to a more efficient distribution of scarce resources throughout the U.S. economy.

Nevertheless, as a practical matter, there is little convincing evidence to support the claim that interstate banking organizations drain scarce loanable funds out of their local communities and channel these funds to distant projects, leaving local cities and neighborhoods devoid of sufficient capital to grow. As we saw in Chapter 4, recent research at the Federal Reserve Bank of Boston suggests the opposite—that larger branch banks in New England, for example, have returned about as large a volume of credit funds to their local communities as they have collected there in deposits. In contrast, smaller banks without branches or with only a few branch offices tended to send *more* loanable funds out of their local communities relative to the volume of local funds collected, presumably to diversify their assets and reduce their dependence on the revenues generated from a relatively small local area.

Thus far the only shred of evidence we have that large regional banking organizations can damage their local communities by draining away local credit resources comes from the Southwest. In that region a slumping economy, plagued by persistent problems in the agricultural and energy sectors, generated massive loan losses – centered principally in loans made to energy producers, to developers of large real estate projects, and to farmers and ranchers in the region. In order to shore up their lead money-center banks, some holding companies in the Southwest found themselves borrowing huge amounts from their smaller affiliated banks in satellite communities, resulting in credit scarcity and increased business bankruptcies in some of those local areas. In these instances many leading banking firms appear to have changed their central strategy from directing new loans toward their highest-return uses in favor of a defensive posture designed to salvage any remaining value locked up in troubled loans.

It seems likely, then, that under normal circumstances most local deposits will stay close to home, and local loans will roughly counterbalance local sources of funding, even in a large branch banking organization. However, when the economy turns down into a deep recession and resource scarcity becomes a particularly acute problem, funds may well flow out of smaller cities and suburban communities, creating greater credit stringency for local businesses and household borrowers. We should not conclude that this pattern of bank behavior in periods of economic decline is either new or unique to interstate banking. It is not even unique to our own time, but was evident even before the turn of the century. In fact, the tendency of large correspondent banks in the central cities to drain funds from local communities was evident in the late nineteenth century and was one of the principal reasons why the Federal Reserve Act was passed in 1913 to create the nation's central bank, the Federal Reserve System. The Federal Reserve was designed to be a "lender of last resort" to local banks when their communities were in need of liquidity and unable to find it from traditional sources.

There is little question that the concentration of industry resources in the banks at the top will increase as interstate banking organizations grow and expand. Indeed, such a trend has been underway for more than a decade. As Federal Reserve economists Amel and Jacowski (1989) have noted, the number of insured U.S.–chartered commercial banks declined 4 percent between 1976 and 1987, while the total number of U.S. banking organizations (including all holding companies and independent banks) declined 17 percent over the same period. The share of the industry's total assets controlled by the largest 1 percent of all American banks rose from 53 percent in 1976 to 62 percent in 1987.

Potentially at least, interstate banking *may* lead to reduced service quality and quantity, as well as higher prices for banking services, if a handful of multiple-office, multi-market organizations come to dominate American banking. Canada, France, the United Kingdom, West Germany, and most other industrialized economies have highly concentrated banking systems in which the top five banks control 50 percent or more of the total resources in the domestic banking system. Interstate banking will move the United States *closer* to that kind of banking concentration. We must bear firmly in mind, however, that this does not necessarily imply that competition in the thousands of local banking markets that serve individuals, families, and local businesses will be diminished. For one thing, competition is a matter of individual firm behavior, not a function of the numbers of potential competitors. A community served by only two banks may have access to services that are as ample in quantity and quality as those in communities served by dozens of banks, provided only that the managements of local banking institutions resolve to compete rather than to collude on prices and market shares.

PRESSING POLICY ISSUES FOR THE FUTURE

There are today a large number of public policy issues about which little is known and on which almost nothing has been resolved. Indeed, some of these issues have yet to be taken seriously by the regulatory community and by the Congress. But serious issues they are, nevertheless.

First, it is incumbent on each of the federal banking agencies — the Federal Reserve System, the Comptroller of the Currency, and the Federal Deposit Insurance Corporation — as well as the Department of Justice, to evaluate each bank merger or acquisition in terms of its probable impact on competition. If a proposed acquisition is judged to have a "substantially adverse" impact on competition in the "potentially most damaged market" each bank serves, the federal banking agencies must reject the application, and the Justice Department must sue to block the acquisition, if necessary. In the past that "potentially most damaged market" has been defined to include households — individuals and families — and the smallest business firms, most of which have limited options for accessing financial services if the local banks turn them down.

As we suggested earlier in Chapter 5, almost certainly there will be in the future the need for a broader definition of the "potentially most damaged market" in reviewing the competitive implications of interstate mergers and acquisitions. Unfortunately, the historical standard for judging competitive damage from a proposed acquisition — the impact on households and the smallest firms—will no longer tell the whole story when interstate bank mergers are involved. Instead, a significantly broader market for credit and other banking services directed at middle-size businesses will demand a closer look from the regulatory agencies in the future. Such firms may be serviced by any number of banks from a whole region. Acquisitions of banks located in different cities in the same region can eliminate significant competitors and deal a lethal blow to competition in serving the growing middle-size business customer segment. The potential for significant damage to the public interest in this service area is very great; new policies and procedures must be developed to deal with the problem.

Second, the advent of interstate banking in the 1980s heralded the re-emergence of the *states* as a significant regulatory force in American banking. In the 1950s, 1960s, and 1970s the federal government dominated banking regulation in the United States, principally because of the passage of the Bank Holding Company Act in 1956, the Bank Merger Act of 1960, and subsequent amendments to these path-breaking laws. Federal regulation under the holding-company and merger laws potentially could reach into local communities anywhere in the nation, reshaping banking competition and, therefore, the terms under which financial services could be sold in thousands of cities and towns serving millions of business and household customers. In some states the structural changes in banking okayed by federal regulators profoundly altered local service markets. In Florida and Texas, for example, federal approval of holding-company acquisitions in less than a decade raised these multiple-office banking organizations to a dominant position, controlling half or more of banking resources in those two states. The 1980s reversed the trend toward "federalization" of the nation's banking industry; many of the states took control of their own banking industry, deciding what kinds of banking organizations could enter and what traditional and unique services they could offer. The continued malaise in Congress over what the future American banking structure and banking service menu should look like has only strengthened the hand of the states in shaping bank behavior and services within their borders.

The future, however, is likely to usher in a totally different scenario—one in which the states will have literally "worked themselves out of a job." The ongoing consolidation of U.S. banking points to an era, probably within the next two decades, in which no more than three dozen dominant holding companies will have a presence in the majority of states and will have the financial striking power to enter *any* local market judged to be economically rewarding. In this future scenario the individual states will have little power—legal or otherwise—to reshape the structure and organization of these dominant bank holding companies or the services they offer.

Still, there is a real danger with the current arrangement of bank regulatory powers in the United States. The danger is that either the federal government, or the states, or both will *compete* in enacting the most permissive banking legislation and in fashioning the most lenient regulations. This "competition in laxity" is motivated by the common desire of most state and federal regulatory agencies to expand their control, to broaden their constituency within the industry, and to increase their budget. Thus, more permissive banking rules are born and soon begin to multiply, adding to the risk of failure for those banking organizations that move aggressively to take advantage of increasingly liberalized rules. We are already seeing competition in laxity among the states, particularly in those states such as Alaska, Arizona, California, and South Dakota that have granted their banks new service powers to offer insurance or real estate development services that Congress, thus far, has refused to approve for federally supervised banks. Yet some of these new services — particularly in the real estate field — have been shown to increase the risk exposure of individual banking firms, especially for those banks that have weak internal restraints and management judgment and that look to the regulatory authorities to guide them into new service fields, often at their peril.

Almost certainly there will be a need for greater supervisory resources as the deregulation of U.S. banking proceeds. As we noted in the foregoing paragraphs, even as banks in the United States receive broader service powers (product-line deregulation) and broader territorial powers (geographic deregulation), the potential for abuse of those powers has increased. The clear lesson brought to us from the record of banking regulation in the 1980s is simply this: deregulation of an industry that has a tradition of close regulation may necessitate more regulatory supervisors, not less. Indeed, the successful pursuit of interstate banking may require a whole *new* generation of bankers in the future who are more sensitized to market forces in a new environment of unregulated and intense competition. Those bankers who honed their professional skills in the older environment of heavy regulation may be ill-suited to deal with the problems posed by a more permissive and open environment where the potential rewards are greater, but the risk of failure also has risen. New banking skills may be needed before the supervisory role of federal and state governments can safely be pushed back and the regulatory structure gradually dismantled. Otherwise, more banks will fail and public confidence can be severely shaken, causing a contraction of deposits and assets and reducing the level of efficiency of the American financial system.

There are many professionals inside and outside banking today who believe that bank mergers, particularly full-service interstate mergers, should be more tightly controlled or even halted. The only exception that generally receives popular approval is the use of interstate mergers to deal with failing banks that because of their large size threaten the integrity of the federal insurance fund. In contrast, most interstate acquisitions, it is argued, reduce competition, create unemployment, and add nothing of value to investors and to consumers of banking services.

The problem here is that both empirical evidence and theory tend to contradict the foregoing assertions. Interstate mergers and acquisitions arise essentially because management and shareholders of the acquiring banking firms believe they can manage an acquired bank more productively and profitability than the present owners and management can do. For this reason interstate bank acquisitions command premium prices that, typically, will substantially exceed the book values of acquired banking organizations. The vast majority of research studies show that the shareholders of *acquired* banking firms nearly always gain from these transactions as the stock market increases the value of the stock issued by the acquired companies. Much smaller gains normally are reaped by the stockholders of *acquiring* companies, but those gains, nevertheless, are usually *positive*.

Thus, interstate bank acquisitions probably do create value for most bank shareholders. If this were not the case, an efficient market would soon bring an end to the bank merger and acquisition process. No one would bid to acquire a banking firm without those expected gains in stockholder wealth. Therefore, if there are no significantly damaging effects on the nation's social goals of the efficient allocation of resources, the promotion of competition, and the preservation of public confidence in the banking system — and there is, to date, no convincing evidence of significant damage to any of these broad social objectives by interstate bank acquisitions — then, in conscience, the interstate banking movement should not be impeded by arbitrary regulations based on untested conclusions.

MANAGEMENT CHALLENGES IN THE INTERSTATE FINANCIAL-SERVICES MARKET

Not only public policymakers, but also bank managers will be required to make critical adjustments in this new era of global competition for financial services. The most important steps that bank managers must consider for the future are discussed in the paragraphs that follow.

First, the managers of interstate banking firms must find better ways to monitor and manage the performance of acquired banking firms in order to achieve their organizational goals. The key to success here is an improved planning system that encourages coordination among all units, both new and old, of the consolidated banking firm. Local managers must be given sufficient flexibility to develop their own plans for the bank or branch they manage and to make quick decisions on larger loan requests where speed in decision making would salvage a good bank-customer relationship. At the same time, frequent meetings between senior bank management and local branch office managers, coupled with detailed reporting requirements for all units within the consolidated banking firm, can help nurture individual initiative, while giving department heads and local branch managers a sense of "belonging" to a unified organization that shares with them a common sense of purpose.

Bank management must find new sources of capital for interstate banks in a world of stiffening international capital requirements — perhaps by tapping foreign sources of capital and using innovative new financing instruments, such as perpetual or limited-life preferred stock, mandatory convertible debentures, and equity commitment notes. The era when a bank could escape heavy capital requirements by fleeing to another jurisdiction and, thus, avoid asking their stockholders to make a more substantial investment in the firm is rapidly disappearing. A new system of common capital standards for banks in twelve of the leading industrialized nations (including Canada, the United States, and the United Kingdom) began on March 15, 1989, and is scheduled to be fully in place by December 31, 1992. These tougher capital standards not only impose minimum capital requirements on *all* banks, but also levy higher required capital-to-asset ratios on those banking organizations that have chosen to accept more risk in their lending programs. It is a regulatory step long overdue and will, partially at least, shore up sagging public confidence in major banks around the globe.

Bank managers must develop improved methods for identifying all the prospective costs that the interstate acquiring bank will be forced to address once an acquisition is made. These costs, which the new owners cannot run away from but usually must tackle head on, include the condition of the acquired banking organization's branches and other public-service facilities, data processing and management information systems, unprofitable office locations, and aging or poorly trained management who ultimately will need to be replaced or retrained. In short, acquiring interstate organizations must sharpen their skills in evaluating the targets of their strategic plans, so that long-run benefits become more attainable.

Management of interstate banks must seek out community and regional acceptance, in both public and private sectors, as each merger or acquisition is completed in order to reassure the public and bank employees that the proposed acquisition will benefit them. This step usually will require establishing a "hot line" to handle customer and employee questions and holding focus group meetings between management and staff members of both the acquiring and the acquired banking organizations *before* the merger is consummated. This gives all staff members a sense of "belonging" to the newly combined organization and "sharing" in its successes and failures.

Management must work to preserve employee morale in any acquisition, but especially in an acquisition that crosses state lines. In a "long-distance" interstate merger, the likelihood of regional discrepancies in salary schedules, promotion policies, and managerial styles is very great. Employees of both interstate acquiring and acquired institutions need to be aware that their concerns over the stability of future employment and income are addressed at the highest levels of management with sensitivity and care. Otherwise, the uncertainties that normally accompany any merger will spread and may even be telegraphed to the customers themselves.

The most critical questions facing interstate bank managers in the future, however, will center on the marketing of banking services. There are no guarantees that interstate-controlled banking firms will be able to succeed at the expense of their smaller rivals. Indeed, as we saw in Chapter 4, the limited research evidence that we have concerning the performance of interstate banking organizations that were grandfathered by federal anti-branching statutes suggests that these early forerunners of today's interstate banking companies actually lost market share, on average, compared to competing noninterstate banking organizations. Interstate banks must find new and better ways for opening up retail and small business markets in the new communities they choose to enter. The critical steps that will be required on a long-term basis include developing interpersonal relationships between senior officers and branch managers and between the branch managers and staff and the households and business customers that reside and operate within their local market areas. Branch managers must feel that they are an important part of the decision-making loop within an interstate banking organization, particularly in areas that impinge on personnel policies, services offered, and prices charged customers. Interstate banking institutions must grant more decision-making authority to local branch managers and loan officers who know their own customers best and know what service-pricing schedules are reasonable and competitive in the local area.

One of the most challenging steps in any interstate merger or acquisition is to maintain as much stability as possible in customer-contact positions in order to preserve long-standing working relationships that may exist between bank personnel and their local customers. This will help reassure those customers that, even if ownership has changed as a result of a full-service interstate merger, the customer will still find "familiar faces" at the local bank office. Moreover, the interstate banking organization can court households and local business customers successfully by setting up centers for retail, small business, and middle-market customers, staffed by experienced bank personnel. Such a step would demonstrate the bank's continuing commitment to those important customer segments.

For example, Seattle First National Bank recently set up 15 special business banking centers with trained loan officers to help both new and old business clients. The development of personal computers and advanced software for small computers has brought about a dramatic increase in the growth of small and medium-size businesses all over the United States. Many of these new firms tend to bypass interstate banking organizations, often because they have received an unsympathetic bank response to their special problems and needs in the past. The development of specialized business banking centers like those at Seattle First National is a promising idea to deal with a developing problem area for interstate banks: how to concentrate banking expertise near the location of the customers the bank most wishes to serve.

Serving small business customers can be one of the most important sources of revenue and profits for interstate banks in the future. Recent research studies show that while small business loans generally are costlier to make and more risky for the bank than are large corporate loans, they also tend to be more profitable due to higher average interest charges, and especially because they often generate more profitable deposits per dollar loaned than do large firms (as found by Churchill and Lewis [1985], for example, in a study of bank earnings from small business lending). There may be less competition for loans to small and medium-size domestic firms, particularly in cities where foreign banks and banking agencies operate and have aggressively stolen away a larger share of the corporate banking services market in the United States. Moreover, smaller businesses are a major, if not *the* most important, source of new jobs and business innovation in the U.S. economy. For example, Birch and McCracken (1984) found recently in a study of selected American neighborhoods that small businesses with 100 or fewer workers accounted for about a third of all jobs in existence in the United States, but represented about 70 percent of all newly created jobs.

Interstate banks can strengthen their image in local communities by offering training programs that both bank employees and small business owners can attend. These programs can be slanted toward how to prepare and present the most important pieces of information that banks need to know about their business customers before a loan request can be granted, such as credit histories, personal finances of the owners, management profiles, market analyses, aging of payables and receivables, credit policies and inventory controls, assessment of fixed assets, and evaluation of capital requirements. This type of customer-oriented program both upgrades the knowledge of bank employees and makes the submission of credit applications from smaller business customers smoother and easier. Videotape programs can be developed that explain the bank's services to households and expand each customer's horizon of knowledge on how to access new sources of funding, as well as educational information on household budgeting, record keeping, and planning for large purchases.

Another important marketing strategy for interstate banks involves inviting representatives from the household, small business, and middle-market customer segments in the local communities where the bank sells its services to serve on the bank's board of directors (perhaps as nonvoting members), demonstrating a commitment to these important customer segments and opening up new channels for marketing services. A related step is to appoint customer panels or advisory committees that meet periodically to review the bank's policies, pricing schedules, and service performance, as well as to assess changing customer needs. Interstate banks, like it or not, are often viewed as "outsiders" in local communities and need to work to dispel the negative connotation that often becomes attached to a business takeover by individuals and organizations not part of the local area.

Finally, bankers, public policymakers, and the public they serve ultimately must answer the most important question of all: can the deregulated private market for financial services work effectively and efficiently under interstate banking? Based on the research evidence amassed so far and the opinions of bankers themselves, the answer appears to be "yes," provided there are adequate resources allocated to supervisory authorities in order to ensure that all laws and regulations designed to protect the customers' deposits and maintain public confidence are enforced. The record-breaking bank failures of the 1980s painfully remind us that deregulation does *not* always imply that we need less vigilance, either as individuals or as a society. Indeed, where the public safety is at risk and there is reason to believe that deregulation will lead to frequent abuses against the public interest, the need for frequent bank examinations and close supervision may increase.

Moreover, there is more at risk here than just avoiding bank failures in the future. The American banking system lies at the core of a vast financial network of security brokers and dealers, pension funds, insurance firms, and thousands of other financial institutions — more than 70,000 American financial-service firms in total — that channel scarce public savings into capital investment in new plants and equipment. The savings-investment process is the heartbeat of a market-driven capitalist economy, without which the whole economic system would falter and run down, creating massive unemployment and crippling losses of those funds set aside for family and business savings. For the economy to work well, the financial system and its savings-investment channels must also work well. But the essential ingredient for that to happen is public confidence — a sense of well-being among bank customers that their savings and future investment income are secure. Once that public confidence is lost, regaining it can be the highest mountain of all for bank managers and for governments to climb.

Bank examinations must be more frequent and more thorough than has generally been the case in recent years. (Indeed, a start has already been made in this direction: in the spring of 1989 the FDIC announced it would conduct nearly 5,000 safety and soundness examinations during the year — substantially more than in the past.) Moreover, we must, in the long run, move forward toward a banking system in which both the capital pledged by banks to help protect their depositors and the fees banks pay for federal deposit insurance are scaled to reflect the amount of risk their boards of directors and managers have chosen to take on. Banks that elect to accept greater risk exposure must pay higher insurance fees to receive the benefits from government backing of their deposits. Banking organizations that reach for riskier loans must be prepared to have a greater portion of their assets funded by their owners, not by their depositors or other creditors of the bank. Only by ensuring that bank stockholders fully shoulder the normal risks of business ownership can we be reasonably certain that banks will discipline themselves, so that their future exposure to risk is reduced.

Ultimately, we must move closer to a banking system where the public is armed with more information about the real condition of banks. In this way, decisions about which bank to use for vitally needed financial services can be both more rational and more solidly based. Government-provided deposit insurance has snapped the link between the failure of one bank and depositor runs on neighboring banks. There is no longer any real excuse for failing to disclose to the public how well its banks are performing and how prudently they are managing and safeguarding the public's money.

Appendixes

APPENDIX A

Important Interstate Banking Mergers and Acquisitions in Recent Years

Acquiring Bank or Bank Holding Company		Acquired Bank or Banking Company	
Name of Acquirer	Location of Acquirer	Name of Acquired Firm	Location of Acquired Firm
1989			
Banc One Corp.	Columbus, OH	MCorp (Deposit Insurance Bridge Bank)	Dallas, TX
Old National Bancorp.	Evansville, IN	First National Bank of Harrisburg	Harrisburg, IL
Union Planters Corp.	Memphis, TN	United Southern Corp./United Southern Bank	Clarksdale, MS
Equimark Corp./Equimanagement, Inc.	Pittsburgh, PA	Treasure Valley Bancorp, Inc.	Fruitland, ID
CNB Bancshares, Inc.	Evansville, IN	Bank of St. Helens	Shively, KY
First of America Bank Corp./ First of Amer. Bancorp.--Illinois	Kalamazoo, MI Libertyville, IL	Whiteside County Bank	Morrison, IL
First Wisconsin Corp./ F.W.S.B. Corp.	Milwaukee, WI	Stillwater Holding Company/ First National Bank in Stillwater Hugo Bancorporation, Inc./First State of Hugo	Stillwater, MN Stillwater, MN Hugo, MN
1988			
First Wisconsin Corp.	Milwaukee, WI	Metro Bancorp., Inc./Metropolitan Bank	Phoenix, AZ
Fifth Third Bancorp	Cincinnati, OH	New Palestine Bancorp	New Palestine, IN
First Banc Securities, Inc.	Morgantown, WV	First Bank, N.A.	Uniontown, PA

APPENDIX A (continued)

Acquiring Bank or Bank Holding Company		Acquired Bank or Banking Company	
Name of Acquirer	Location of Acquirer	Name of Acquired Firm	Location of Acquired Firm
Old National Bancorp	Evansville, IA	First Service Bancshares, Inc. First State Bank of Greenville	Greenville, KY Greenville, KY
Barnett Banks, Inc.	Jacksonville, FL	ANB Bankshares, Inc.	Brunswick, GA
Sovran Financial Corp.	Norfolk, VA	First Bank of Marion County	South Pittsburg, TN
Sovran Financial Corp.	Norfolk, VA	First National Bank of Collierville	Collierville, TN
Citicorp/Citicorp Holdings, Inc.	New York, NY New Castle, DE	Citibank (Florida) and National Association	Dania, FL Dania, FL
NBD Bancorp, Inc.	Detroit, MI	NBD New Castle Bank	Newark, DE
Security Pacific Corp.	Los Angeles, CA	Nevada National Bancorporation	Reno, NV
Comerica Inc.	Detroit, MI	Grand Bancshares, Inc.	Dallas, TX
Chemical Banking Corp.	New York, NY	Horizon Bancorp	Morristown, NJ
National City Corp./ NC Acquisition Corp.	Cleveland, OH	First Kentucky National Corp.	Louisville, KY
NCNB Corp.	Charlotte, NC	USBancorp., Inc.	St. Petersburg, FL
Norwest Corp.	Minneapolis, MN	Ranch National Bank, N.A.	Scottsdale, AZ
Norwest Corp.	Minneapolis, MN	PB Bancorp/Peoples Bank & Trust Company	Cedar Rapids, IA
Lincoln Financial Corp.	Lincoln, IL	Rush County National Corp./ Rush County National Bank of Rushville	Rushville, IN Rushville, IN
Old National Bancorp	Evansville, IN	Peoples National Bank in Lawrenceville	Lawrenceville, IL

APPENDIX A (continued)

Acquiring Bank or Bank Holding Company		Acquired Bank or Banking Company	
Name of Acquirer	Location of Acquirer	Name of Acquired Firm	Location of Acquired Firm
Bank of Boston Corp.	Boston, MA	BankVermont Corp.	Burlington, VT
First Interstate Corp. of WI	Kohler, WI	First Interstate Bank of Northern Indiana, NA	South Bend, IN
Commerce Bancshares, Inc.	Kansas City, MO	Midwest Financial Group, Inc.	Peoria, IL
Key Corp	Albany, NY	First Wyoming Bancorporation	Cheyenne, WY
Southwest MO Bancorporation, Inc.	Carthage, MO	Bank of Miami	Miami, OK
PNC Financial Corp.	Pittsburgh, PA	Clayton Bank & Trust Company	Clayton, DE
U.S. Bancorp	Portland, OR	Bank of Loleta	Eureka, CA
U.S. Bancorp	Portland, OR	Western Independent Bancshares, Inc.	Auburn, WA
U.S. Bancorp	Portland, OR	Auburn Valley Bank	Auburn, WA
First Wisconsin Corp.	Milwaukee, WI	Anthony Bancorporation, Inc.	Omaha, NE
F.W.S.B. Corp.	Milwaukee, WI	St. Anthony National Bank	Omaha, NE
State Bancshares, Inc.	Haverford, PA	Jefferson Bank of New Jersey	Mount Laurel, NJ
Commerce Bancorp, Inc.	Cherry Hill, NJ	Commerce Bank/Harrisburg	Camp Hill, PA
Kentucky Bancorporation, Inc.	Covington, KY	First National Bank of Georgetown	Georgetown, OH
RHNB Corp.	Rock Hill, SC	Metrobank, NA	Charlotte, NC
Dahlonega Bancorp, Inc.	Dahlonega, GA	First National Bank of Polk County	Copperhill, TN
First Fidelity Bancorporation	Newark, NJ	First Executive Bancorp, Inc.	Philadelphia, PA
First Wisconsin Corp.	Milwaukee, WI	Metropolitan Bank Group, Inc.	Bloomington, MN

198

APPENDIX A (continued)

	Acquiring Bank or Bank Holding Company		Acquired Bank or Banking Company	
Name of Acquirer	Location of Acquirer	Name of Acquired Firm	Location of Acquired Firm	
F.W.S.B. Corp.	Milwaukee, WI	Metropolitan Bank Group, Inc.	Bloomington, MN	
F & M National Corp.	Winchester, VA	Blakely Bank & Trust Company	Ranson, WV	
First Interstate Bancorp	Los Angeles, CA	Alaska Continental Bank	Anchorage, AK	
First Virginia Banks, Inc.	Falls Church, VA	Monroe Bancshares, Inc.	Madisonville, TN	
First Virginia Banks, Inc.	Falls Church, VA	Bank of Madisonville	Madisonville, TN	
CB&T Bancshares, Inc.	Columbus, GA	Fort Rucker Bancshares, Inc.	Chillicothe, MO	
CB&T Bancshares, Inc.	Columbus, GA	Fort Rucker National Bank	Fort Rucker, AL	
First Wisconsin Corp.	Milwaukee, WI	Rose Holding Co.	Roseville, MN	
First Wisconsin Corp.	Milwaukee, WI	The Roseville Bank	Roseville, MN	
NBD Bancorp/NBD Midwest Corp.	Detroit, MI	Charter Bank Group, Inc.	Northfield, IL	
NBD Bancorp/NBD Midwest Corp.	Detroit, MI	Bank of Glennbrook	Glenview, IL	
NBD Bancorp/NBD Midwest Corp.	Detroit, MI	Bank of Northfield	Northfield, IL	
NBD Bancorp/NBD Midwest Corp.	Detroit, MI	Bank of Wheaton	Wheaton, IL	
NBD Bancorp/NBD Midwest Corp.	Detroit, MI	Bank of Winfield	Winfield, IL	
NBD Bancorp/NBD Midwest Corp.	Detroit, MI	Charter Group Life Insurance Company	Northfield, IL	
NBD Bancorp/NBD Midwest Corp.	Detroit, MI	Charter Agency Inc.	Northfield, IL	

APPENDIX A (continued)

Acquiring Bank or Bank Holding Company		Acquired Bank or Banking Company	
Name of Acquirer	Location of Acquirer	Name of Acquired Firm	Location of Acquired Firm
NCNB Corp.	Charlotte, NC	First RepublicBank Corp.	Dallas, TX

1987

Citizens Banking Corp.	Flint, MI	Commercial National Bank of Berwyn	Berwyn, IL
First Interstate Bancorp	Los Angeles, CA	Heritage Bank & Trust	Salt Lake County, UT
First Union Corp.	Charlotte, NC	City Commercial Bank	Sarasota, FL
First Union Corp.	Charlotte, NC	Commercial National Bank	Naples, FL
First Wachovia Corp.	Winston-Salem, NC	First American Bank of Walton	Monroe, GA
First Wisconsin Corp.	Milwaukee, WI	Dupage Bancshares, Inc.	Glen Ellyn, IL
Southern National Corp.	Lumberton, NC	Liberty National Bank	Charleston, SC
UST Corp.	Boston, MA	Valley Bank & Trust Company	Bridgeport, CT
BancOne Corp.	Columbus, OH	Northwest National Bank	Rensselaer, IN
First Chicago Corp.	Chicago, IL	Beneficial National Bank	Wilmington, DE
Key Corp.	Albany, NY	Seattle Trust & Savings Bank	Seattle, WA
Marine Corp	Milwaukee, WI	Banco Di Roma of Chicago	Chicago, IL
Mercantile Bancshares Corp.	Baltimore, MD	Eastville Bank	Eastville, VA
NCNB Corp.	Charlotte, NC	Central Bank Inc.	Baltimore, MD

APPENDIX A (continued)

Acquiring Bank or Bank Holding Company		Acquired Bank or Banking Company	
Name of Acquirer	Location of Acquirer	Name of Acquired Firm	Location of Acquired Firm
Primerica Corp.	Greenwich, CT	First National Bank of Navasota	Navasota, TX
U.S. Bancorp	Portland, OR	Old National Bancorporation	Spokane, WA
Ameritrust Corp.	Cleveland, OH	Midwest National Bank of Indianapolis	Indianapolis, IN
Bancorp Hawaii, Inc.	Honolulu, HI	First National Bank of Arizona	Phoenix, AZ
Citizens & Southern Corp.	Atlanta, GA	Southern Bank of Tallahassee	Tallahassee, FL
Fifth Third Bancorp.	Cincinnati, OH	First Bancorporation of Batesville	Batesville, IN
First Union Corp.	Charlotte, NC	Community Banking Corp.	Bradenton, FL
Huntington Bancshares, Inc.	Columbus, OH	United Midwest Bancorp Ltd.	Troy, MI
Key Corp	Albany, NY	Lewis & Clark State Bank	Lake Oswego, OR
Manufacturers National Corp.	Detroit, MI	Affiliated Banc Group, Inc.	Morton Grove, IL
Mountain Parks Financial Corp.	Minneapolis, MN	Middle Park Bank	Granby, CO
Norwest Corp.	Minneapolis, MN	Toy National Bank	Sioux City, IA
Riggs National Corp.	Washington, DC	First Fidelity Bank of Rockville	Rockville, MD
Trustcorp, Inc.	Toledo, OH	Ypsilanti Savings Bank	Ypsilanti, MI
BancOne Corp.	Columbus, OH	American Fletcher Corp.	Indianapolis, IN
Union Bancorp	San Francisco, CA	United Bancorp of Arizona	Phoenix, AZ
Security Pacific Corp.	Los Angeles, CA	Arizona Bancwest Corp.	Phoenix, AZ
Chemical New York Corp.	New York City, NY	Texas Commerce Bancshares, Inc.	Houston, TX

APPENDIX A (continued)

	Acquiring Bank or Bank Holding Company		Acquired Bank or Banking Company	
Name of Acquirer	Location of Acquirer		Name of Acquired Firm	Location of Acquired Firm
Associated Banc Corp.	Green Bay, WI		Chicago Commerce Bancorporation	Chicago, IL
Fleet Financial Group, Inc.	Providence, RI		Norstar	Albany, NY
Key Corp	Albany, NY		Commercial Security Bancorp.	Ogden, UT
PNC Financial Corp.	Pittsburgh, PA		Bank of Delaware Corp.	Wilmington, DE
Sovran Financial Corp.	Norfolk, VA		Commerce Union Corp.	Wilmington, DE
Old Kent Financial Corp.	Grand Rapids, MI		Illinois Regional Bancorp	Elmhurst, IL
NBD Bancorp	Detroit, MI		State National Corp.	Evanston, IL
NBD Bancorp	Detroit, MI		Americabancs, Inc.	Highland Park, IL
First Illinois Bancorp., Inc.	East St. Louis, IL		Lindell Trust Company	St. Louis, MO
First Wisconsin Corp.	Milwaukee, WI		North Shore Bancorp., Inc.	Northbrook, IL
First of America Bank Corp.	Kalamazoo, MI		BancServe Group, Inc.	Rockford, IL
First Banks, Inc.	Manchester, MO		First National Bank of Pittsfield	Pittsfield, IL
First of America Corp.	Milwaukee, WI		Keystone Bancshares, Inc.	Kankakee, IL
Mark Twain Bancshares, Inc.	St. Louis, MO		Bankers Trust Company	Belleville, IL
Citizens Banking Corp.	Flint, MI		Commercial National Bank of Berwyn	Berwyn, IL
First Wisconsin Corp.	Milwaukee, WI		Naper Financial Corp.	Naperville, IL
NBD Bancorp	Detroit, MI		U.S. American-Banca	Highland Park, IL
Mercantile Bancorp	St. Louis, MO		First Bancshares Corp.	Alton, IL
United Missouri Bancshares, Inc.	Kansas City, MO		FCB Corp.	Collinsville, IL

APPENDIX A (continued)

Acquiring Bank or Bank Holding Company		Acquired Bank or Banking Company	
Name of Acquirer	Location of Acquirer	Name of Acquired Firm	Location of Acquired Firm
First of America Bank Corp.	Kalamazoo, MI	Premier Bancorp, Inc.	Libertyville, IL
Landmark Bancshares Corp.	St. Louis, MO	MidAmerican BancShares Inc.	Fairview Heights, IL
		1986	
Ameritrust Corp.	Cleveland, OH	First National Bank & Trust Co.	Sturgis, MI
BancOne Corp.	Columbus, OH	First National Bank in Marion	Marion, IN
Citicorp	New York, NY	Great Western Bank & Trust	Phoenix, AZ
Citizens & Southern Corp.	Atlanta, GA	Farmers & Merchants of Walterboro	Walterboro, SC
Citizens Fidelity Corp.	Louisville, KY	Indiana Southern Bank	Sellersburg, IN
Citizens Fidelity Corp.	Louisville, KY	United Bank of Indiana	Clarksville, IN
First Interstate Bancorp	Los Angeles, CA	Norman Bank of Commerce	Norman, OK
First Wachovia Corp.	Winston-Salem, NC	Forsyth County Bank	Cummings, GA
Hartford National Corp.	Hartford, CT	People's Bank of Rhode Island	Providence, RI
Key Corp	Albany, NY	Northwest Bancorp	Albany, OR
Principal Financial Corp.	Des Moines, IA	Delaware Charter Guarantee & Trust Co.	Wilmington, DE
Rainier Bancorporation	Seattle, WA	Security National Bank	Anchorage, AK
Security Pacific Corp.	Los Angeles, CA	Harbor Security Bank	McCleary, WA
Shawmut Corp.	Boston, MA	Fidelity Trust Co. of Stamford	Stamford, CT
Southern National Bank	Lumberton, NC	Capital Bank & Trust Co.	Belton, SC

203

APPENDIX A (continued)

	Acquiring Bank or Bank Holding Company		Acquired Bank or Banking Company	
Name of Acquirer	Location of Acquirer	Name of Acquired Firm	Location of Acquired Firm
Union of Arkansas Corp.	Little Rock, AR	First National Bank of Temple	Temple, OK
United Carolina Bancshares	Whiteville, NC	Bank of Greer	Greer, SC
Chemical New York Corp.	New York, NY	Bank of North America	Houston, TX
Imperial Bancorp	Los Angeles, CA	National Bank of America	Scottsdale, AZ
Mountain Parks Financial Corp.	Minneapolis, MN	Mountain Valley Bank	Conifer, CO
First Interstate Bancorp.	Los Angeles, CA	New Mexico National Bank	Albuquerque, NM
First Fidelity Bancorporation, Inc.	Fairmont, WV	National Bank of Glouster County	Woodburg, NJ
Hartford National Corp.	Hartford, CT	Arltru Bancorporation	Lawrence, MA
Bancorp Hawaii, Inc.	Honolulu, HI	Bank of America Trusts & Savings Assoc.	San Francisco, CA
United Virginia Bankshares	Richmond, VA	Bethesda Bancorporation	Bethesda, MD
Ameritrust Corp.	Cleveland, OH	Franklin Bank & Trust	Franklin, IN
Central Bancorporation	Cincinnati, OH	Citizens National Bank of Benton County	Fort Wright, KY
First Bank Systems, Inc.	Minneapolis, MN	Mid-Valley Bank	Omak, VA
Hartford National Corp.	Hartford, CT	First Bank of Chelmsford	Chelmsford, MA
Chase Manhattan Corp.	New York, NY	Park Bank of Florida	St. Petersburg, FL
Citicorp	New York, NY	Utah First Bank	Salt Lake City, UT
Commercial Federal Corp.	Omaha, NE	Sierra Federal S&L Association	Denver, CO
First American Corp.	Nashville, TN	First Ashland Corp.	Ashland, KY

APPENDIX A (continued)

Acquiring Bank or Bank Holding Company		Acquired Bank or Banking Company	
Name of Acquirer	Location of Acquirer	Name of Acquired Firm	Location of Acquired Firm
First Union Corp.	Charlotte, NC	Citizens Dekalb Bank	Clarkston, GA
Hartford National Corp.	Hartford, CT	Provident Institution for Savings in the Town of Boston	Boston, MA
NCNB Corp.	Charlotte, NC	Bankers Trust of South Carolina	Columbia, SC
Great Western Financial Corp.	Beverly Hills, CA	Intercapital Savings Bank	Jacksonville Beach, FL
Metropolitan Holding Co.	Washington, DC	Metropolitan Federal Savings Bank	Bethesda, MD
First Interstate	Los Angeles, CA	Olympic Bank of Everett	Everett, WA
		1985	
First Fidelity Bancorp.	Fairmont, WV	Century Bank	Phoenix, AZ
NCNB Corp.	Charlotte, NC	Centrabank of Baltimore	Baltimore, MD
First Interstate Bancorp	Los Angeles, CA	Olympic Bank of Everett	Everett, WA
		1984	
NCNB Corp.	Charlotte, NC	Ellis Banking Corp.	Brandenton, FL
Norwest Corp.	Minneapolis, MN	Bankshares of Nebraska, Inc.	Grand Island, NE
Atlantic Financial Federal	Philadelphia, PA	San Francisco Bancorp	San Francisco, CA
General Bancshares Corp.	St. Louis, MO	First National Bank of Savannah	Savannah, TN
Bank of Boston Corp.	Boston, MA	Casco-Northern Corp.	Portland, ME

APPENDIX A (continued)

Acquiring Bank or Bank Holding Company		Acquired Bank or Banking Company	
Name of Acquirer	Location of Acquirer	Name of Acquired Firm	Location of Acquired Firm
First Atlanta Corp.	Atlanta, GA	Southeast Banking Corp.	Miami, FL
General Bancshares Corp.	St. Louis, MO	Mid-Central Bancshares Corp.	Charleston, IL
Key Banks, Inc.	Albany, NY	Depositors Corp.	Augusta, ME
Zions Utah Bancorp	Salt Lake City, UT	Nevada State Bank	Las Vegas, NV
Bank of Boston Corp.	Boston, MA	Chittenden Corp.	Burlington, VT

1983

General Bancshares Corp.	St. Louis, MO	First National Bank of Benld	Benld, IL
General Bancshares Corp.	St. Louis, MO	First National Bank of Savannah	Savannah, TN
Rainier Bancorporation	Seattle, WA	Peoples Bank & Trust	Anchorage, AK
Norstar Bancorp., Inc.	Albany, NY	Northeast Bankshares Association	Portland, ME
Mellon National Corp.	Pittsburgh, PA	Globe Industrial Bank / Centaur Industrial Bank	Boulder, CO / Lafayette, CO
Bank America Corp.	San Francisco, CA	Seafirst Corp.	Seattle, WA
General Bancshares Corp.	St. Louis, MO	Security Bank & Trust	Mount Vernon, IL

1982

AmSouth Bancorporation	Birmingham, AL	South Carolina National Corp.	Columbia, SC

206

APPENDIX A (continued)

	Acquiring Bank or Bank Holding Company		Acquired Bank or Banking Company	
Name of Acquirer	Location of Acquirer	Name of Acquired Firm	Location of Acquired Firm	
First National Boston Corp.	Boston, MA	Casco-Northern Corp.	Portland, ME
Girard Co.	Philadelphia, PA	Guarantee Bancorp, Inc.	Atlantic City, NJ
South Carolina National Corp.	Columbia, SC	AmSouth Bancorporation	Birmingham, AL
Chase Manhattan Corp.	New York, NY	Equimark Corp.	Pittsburgh, PA
Chemical New York Corp.	New York, NY	Florida National Banks of Florida, Inc.	Jacksonville, FL
Chemical New York Corp.	New York, NY	Northeast Bancorp	Stamford, CT
First Bank System	Minneapolis, MN	Banks of Iowa	Des Moines, IA
General Bancshares Corp.	St. Louis, MO	Mid-Continent Bancshares, Inc.	Belleville, IL
NCNB Corp.	Charlotte, NC	Gulfstream Banks, Inc.	Boca Raton, FL
NCNB Corp.	Charlotte, NC	Downtown National Bank	Miami, FL
U.S. Bancorp	Portland, OR	Beneficial Corp.	Wilmington, DE
CBT Corp.	Hartford, CT	Hospital Trust Corp.	Providence, RI
First National Boston Corp.	Boston, MA	Colonial Bancorp Inc.	Waterbury, CT
NCNB Corp.	Charlotte, NC	Exchange Bancorporation Inc.	Charlotte, NC
First Interstate Bancorp	Los Angeles, CA	Fidelity Mutual Savings Bank	Spokane, WA
NCNB Corp.	Charlotte, NC	First National Bank of Lake City	Lake City, FL
City Federal S&L	Elizabeth, CA	Boca Raton Federal S&L Mohawk S&L	Boca Raton, FL Newark, NJ
Glendale Federal S&L	Glendale, CA	First Federal S&L of Broward County	Broward County, FL

APPENDIX A (continued)

Acquiring Bank or Bank Holding Company		Acquired Bank or Banking Company	
Name of Acquirer	Location of Acquirer	Name of Acquired Firm	Location of Acquired Firm
First National Boston Corp.	Boston, MA	Casco-Northern Corp.	Portland, ME
Marine Midland Banks, Inc.	New York, NY	Industrial Valley Banks & Trust Co.	Philadelphia, PA

1981

First National Bank of Minneapolis	Minneapolis, MN	Rainier International Bank	New York, NY
Key Banks of Albany	Albany, NY	Depositors Corp.	Augusta, ME
Crown Bancshares, Inc.	Kansas City, MO	Merchants National Bank of Topeka	Topeka, KS
Provident National Corp.	Philadelphia, PA	Harris Bancorp., Inc.	Chicago, IL
Girard Co.	Philadelphia, PA	Farmers Bank	Wilmington, DE

1980

Northwest Bancorp	Minneapolis, MN	Atlantic State Bank	Atlantic, IA
Central Bancorp	Miami, FL	Peoples Bank	Nelsonville, OH

Sources: The Wall Street Journal Index, press releases of the Federal Reserve Board, and merger decisions of the Comptroller of the Currency and Federal Deposit Insurance Corporation.

APPENDIX B
Key State Banking Laws Applying to Branching, Holding-Company Activity, and Interstate Banking

The New England Region

Connecticut —   Branch banking and holding—company activity are
                     permitted across the state without geographic
                     restrictions; however, there is a home—office
                     protection rule that limits branching into the
                     home—office community of a bank by branching systems
                     in other parts of the state. Banks from other New
                     England states may enter with a full line of services,
                     and banks from other regions of the nation may add up
                     to two nondeposit office facilities in each 12—month
                     period. No formal restrictions apply to holding
                     companies.

Maine —   Statewide branching was legalized in the 1970s and
                     bank holding—company activity is not regulated.
                     Interstate bank entry is now permitted from any other
                     state in the nation.

Massachusetts —   In the mid—1980s a statewide branching law was
                     enacted, and holding—company activity is not currently
                     regulated. In addition, by the end of 1982 interstate
                     bank entry became legal for banking companies from any
                     other state in New England. An anti—leapfrogging
                     provision prohibits banks outside New England from
                     entering Massachusetts if they already have an
                     affiliate in another New England state. A nationwide
                     bank entry bill was being debated by the state
                     legislature in 1989.

New Hampshire —   New branch offices were permitted to expand statewide
                     beginning in 1979, subject to certain restrictions on
                     the size of local communities entered in order to
                     protect banks already headquartered in the communities
                     involved. A cap has been placed on statewide
                     holding—company growth in which these companies cannot
                     hold more than 15 percent of total New Hampshire
                     deposits or control more than 12 affiliated
                     institutions. Interstate entry is allowed from any
                     other New England state.

Rhode Island —   Branch banking is permitted across the whole state
                     without significant restrictions, but holding—company
                     acquisitions are restricted in terms of the size of
                     their deposits relative to the size of the holding
                     company. In the mid—1980s interstate entry was
                     legalized, provided that entry came from the New
                     England region; however, in 1986 entry from any other
                     state in the nation became legal, provided Rhode
                     Island banks were also granted entry privileges.

Vermont —   Vermont permits branching across the entire state.
                     Moreover, holding—company activity is not constrained
                     by significant regulations. The legislature has
                     sanctioned interstate entry on a reciprocal basis from

any other state in the nation beginning in February 1990, provided Vermont banks are granted the same liberties. The nationwide law will supersede an earlier interstate banking bill that allowed entry only from other New England states.

The Middle Atlantic Region

New Jersey –

Branching can take place statewide subject to certain restrictions in the form of home–office protection requirements and required population sizes of the communities to be entered. While bank holding–company activity was not permitted earlier in the state's history, holding companies are now allowed to operate as long as any one company controls no more than 20 percent of all deposits in New Jersey. Interstate entry is permitted nationwide with reciprocity.

New York –

In 1976 after a long period of gradually widening branch banking powers, New York banks were allowed to branch statewide without significant barriers. However, in the smallest New York communities branching may be restricted if another bank is headquartered there. Holding–company activity is permitted without major regulatory barriers in the largest metropolitan areas. In 1982 the state legislature voted to permit entry from any other state in the nation under the proviso that New York banks were granted reciprocal treatment.

Pennsylvania –

A complicated branching law amended in 1982 limits branching to home–office and adjacent counties. However, branching in the two largest cities – Philadelphia and Pittsburgh – was permitted without significant restrictions. By 1990 Pennsylvania will move into the statewide branching arena. Multibank holding–company activity will not be restricted beginning in 1990. Nationwide interstate banking with reciprocal privileges for Pennsylvania banks is scheduled to become law in March of 1990. Prior to that date outside entry is allowed only from Washington, D.C., and from the states of Delaware, Kentucky, Maryland, New Jersey, Ohio, Virginia, and West Virginia.

The Pacific Coast Region

Alaska –

Nationwide entry is allowed without reciprocity. Alaska permits statewide branch banking and does not generally restrict holding–company operations.

California –

Beginning in July of 1987 entry from banking firms in selected other states in the region (including Alaska, Arizona, Colorado, Hawaii, Idaho, Nevada, New Mexico, Oregon, Texas, Utah, and Washington) was permitted, provided California banks were granted parallel privileges. Effective at the beginning of 1991 California will permit entry from any other state in the nation that also lets California banks enter.

California has been a statewide branch banking state for many years and the activities of bank holding companies are not generally restricted.

Hawaii —
Statewide banking has been permitted without restrictions since the first day of 1986. No significant regulations limit bank holding—company activity, and banks from selected other Pacific islands may enter Hawaii, but entry from another state has not yet been aproved.

Oregon —
In July of 1989 Oregon became a nationwide entry state. Previously entry into the state without the need for reciprocal treatment of Oregon banks was permitted from the states of Alaska, Arizona, California, Hawaii, Idaho, Nevada, Utah, and Washington, but under the proviso that the banking firms acquired by out—of—state companies had to operate for at least three years before their acquisition. Oregon generally allows branch banking statewide. Bank holding companies do not appear subject to restrictive regulations in Oregon.

Washington —
In 1985 Washington became a statewide branching state, replacing a much older regime of countywide branching. Before the decade of the 1980s began, multi—bank holding—company activity was not allowed; however, subsequently these restrictions were removed. In July of 1987 Washington voted to permit entry by banking firms from any other state in the nation as long as reciprocal treatment was given to Washington banks interested in interstate expansion. Failing banks may be acquired by banking firms from any other state.

The Rocky Mountain Region

Arizona —
Statewide branching without significant restriction and holding—company activity have been permissible for many years. Arizona was one of the first states to sanction nationwide interstate banking without a reciprocity requirement. Its interstate banking law became effective on October 1, 1986. In 1992 out—of—state banking companies will also be allowed to charter new banks in the state.

Colorado —
Branch banking has been prohibited in Colorado for many years, but bank holding—company activity is permissible without significant regulation. Beginning in July 1988, Colorado allowed outside entry by acquisition from the surrounding states of Arizona, Kansas, New Mexico, Nebraska, Oklahoma, Utah, and Wyoming if Colorado banks were granted reciprocal entry privileges. However, leapfrogging into the region from other states was not allowed. Beginning in January 1991 entry from any other state in the union extending reciprocal entry privileges to Colorado banks will become permissible, subject to a maximum of 25 percent of the state's deposits being acquired by any one out—of—state banking firm and a minimum capital adequacy ratio (i.e., capital to assets) of at least 6 percent. Newer Colorado banks

in operation less than five years are protected from acquisition by outsiders until July 1993.

Idaho —

Statewide branch banking and bank holding—company activity are permitted, and at the beginning of 1988 nationwide bank entry was allowed without significant restrictions. Previously Idaho had limited entry to banks from Montana, Nevada, Oregon, Utah, Washington, and Wyoming.

Montana —

Branch banking is prohibited, though holding—company operations are legal. Montana had not yet approved interstate banking as of the date of publication of this book.

Nevada —

Beginning in 1989 Nevada opened its borders to nationwide banking through acquisition or to de novo branches without requiring reciprocity. Previously entry with reciprocity was permitted only from other states in or bordering the Rocky Mountain region. Bank holding companies and statewide branching have been sanctioned for many years.

New Mexico —

Bank holding—company activity has been permitted statewide for many years, while branch banking has been limited primarily to home—office counties. Also, New Mexico banks can establish branches in contiguous counties or within a radius of 100 miles from the bank's headquarters if another bank does not serve the targeted county already. Interstate banking will be approved from any other state in the nation beginning in January 1990 without a reciprocity requirement.

Utah —

Bank holding—company activity is not restricted and, as the 1980s began Utah allowed statewide branch banking following revisions of its earlier laws that had restricted branching to cities and counties. Beginning in 1988 Utah sanctioned nationwide entry. Earlier, interstate entry had been restricted to banking firms from other states in the Rocky Mountain region plus Alaska, Hawaii, and Washington with reciprocity for Utah banks and excluding de novo charterings.

Wyoming —

Interstate banking from any other state in the nation is permissible without reciprocity, but branching is prohibited within the state as a matter of practice.

The South Atlantic Region

Delaware —

Interstate entry from any other state in the nation, provided Delaware banks have reciprocal entry privileges, will be permitted beginning in June 1990. Earlier entry with reciprocity was allowed only for banking firms in Maryland, New Jersey, Ohio, Pennsylvania, and Virginia. Delaware allows special-purpose banks to be set up even by banking organizations outside its region. Holding companies face no significant regulatory barriers, and statewide branching has been sanctioned for many years.

Florida –   During the 1970s branching via merger and through the
establishment of de novo branches was permitted so
long as these new facilities were confined to the
home–office county and were limited in number.
Beginning in 1980 branching via merger throughout
Florida was sanctioned. Bank holding companies face
no significant regulatory barriers. Beginning in
July, 1985, Florida allowed out–of–state banks to come
in from states in the surrounding region and purchase
Florida banking firms that had been open for at least
24 months. The states granted entry privileges with
reciprocity included Alabama, Arkansas, Georgia,
Louisiana, Maryland, Mississippi, North Carolina,
South Carolina, Tennessee, Virginia, and West
Virginia, as well as Washington, D.C. Two banking
companies (NCNB and Northern Trust Company) were
grandfathered from earlier restrictions against entry
and these firms can acquire additional Florida banks
even if there were no interstate entry law.

Georgia -   Countywide branching was allowed in the 1970s and
later expanded to allow branching into neighboring
counties. Statewide branching by merger now prevails.
Holding companies were given branching powers in 1980
subject to state approval and allowed to acquire banks
that had been in operation for at least five years.
Beginning in 1985 interstate banking with reciprocity
was allowed from the neighboring states of Alabama,
Florida, Kentucky, Louisiana, Maryland, Mississippi,
North Carolina, South Carolina, Tennessee, and
Virginia.

Maryland -   Currently the state permits entry from a total of 14
other states, including Alabama, Arkansas, Delaware,
Florida, Georgia, Kentucky, Louisiana, Mississippi,
North Carolina, Pennsylvania, South Carolina,
Tennessee, Virginia, and West Virginia provided
parallel privileges are granted Maryland's banking
firms. Outside entrants may also set up special-
purpose banks. Maryland currently permits statewide
branch banking and does not formally restrict holding-
company activities.

North Carolina -   Both branch banks and holding companies face few
significant barriers to statewide expansion.
Beginning in 1985 entry into the state was allowed
from Alabama, Arkansas, Florida, Georgia, Kentucky,
Louisiana, Maryland, Mississippi, South Carolina,
Tennessee, Virginia, West Virginia, and Washington,
D.C., provided these areas extended comparable
privileges to North Carolina banks.

South Carolina -   Branch banking and holding-company activity are
permitted statewide in South Carolina. Entry from out
of state is also permitted with reciprocity from
Alabama, Arkansas, Florida, Georgia, Kentucky,
Louisiana, Maryland, Mississippi, North Carolina,
Tennessee, Virginia, West Virginia, and Washington,
D.C., beginning in 1986. However, new banking firms

                            cannot be purchased before they have operated for at
                            least five years.

Virginia -   The state's current interstate statute permits entry
                            from states in the surrounding region and from banks
                            headquartered in Washington, D.C. if Virginia's banks
                            are given the same entry privileges. The states
                            approved for entry include Alabama, Arkansas, Florida,
                            Georgia, Kentucky, Louisiana, Maryland, Mississippi,
                            North Carolina, South Carolina, Tennessee, and West
                            Virginia. Virginia allows statewide branching via
                            merger with a five-year protection rule, and limited
                            branching in city, community, or countywide areas
                            otherwise. Bank holding-company activity does not
                            face formal restrictions.

West Virginia -   Provided reciprocal privileges are extended to West
                            Virginia banks, the state permits entry by banking
                            companies from any other state in the nation,
                            including states where entry via the buy-out of
                            failing banks is permissible. Currently the state
                            limits branch banking to contiguous counties but is
                            scheduled to convert to statewide branch banking the
                            first day of 1991. Bank holding-company activity is
                            now allowed as long as the deposits in all in-state
                            affiliates of the same company do not add up to more
                            than 20 percent of statewide deposits.

The East North Central Region

Illinois -   Branching activity has been prohibited through most of
                            Illinois' history, but the law was slightly modified
                            in 1982 to allow limited-service facilities in the
                            home-office county. Beginning in 1982 multi-bank
                            holding-company operations were legalized, provided
                            they were constrained to designated regions within the
                            state. Nationwide reciprocal interstate banking
                            becomes legal in December 1990, whereas earlier entry
                            was only permitted with reciprocity from Indiana,
                            Iowa, Kentucky, Michigan, Missouri, and Wisconsin,
                            though acquisition of large failed banking
                            organizations (over $1 billion in assets) by banks
                            from any state is allowed.

Indiana -   Entry through branching into neighboring counties was
                            approved in 1985, after years of confining branching
                            to home-office cities and counties and statewide
                            branching by merger is now permitted. Holding
                            companies can hold no more than 12 percent of
                            statewide deposits. Entry from selected states in the
                            region (including Illinois, Iowa, Kentucky, Michigan,
                            Missouri, Ohio, Pennsylvania, Tennessee, Virginia,
                            West Virginia, and Wisconsin) was allowed with
                            reciprocity after 1985. Beginning in July 1992
                            nationwide entry with reciprocity is scheduled to
                            become effective.

Michigan -   Beginning in October 1988 Michigan voted to allow
                            nationwide bank entry if Michigan banks were also

granted entry privileges from other states.
Countywide branching was the rule for much of
Michigan's history, but the state eventually converted
to statewide branch banking. Bank holding-company
activity faces no significant barriers.

Ohio -   Beginning in October 1988 Ohio allowed banks to enter
                 from any portion of the country, provided other states
                 did not restrict the entry of Ohio banks and provided
                 any one outside entrant does not control more than 10
                 percent of total banking and thrift institution
                 deposits. In January 1989 Ohio became a statewide
                 branching state after years as a countywide branching
                 state. There are no significant limitations on bank
                 holding-company activity.

Wisconsin -   The state does not restrict bank holding-company
                 operations, but branching activities are generally
                 limited to counties with home-office protection and
                 mileage limits. Interstate entry is allowed, provided
                 reciprocity is granted from Illinois, Indiana, Iowa,
                 Kentucky, Michigan, Minnesota, Missouri, and Ohio.

The West North Central Region
Iowa -   Interstate banking currently is not approved by the
                 state legislature, but Norwest Corporation has been
                 grandfathered and authorized to acquire Iowa banking
                 institutions since the 1970s. However, multi-bank
                 holding companies may operate as long as their deposit
                 totals do not climb above 10 percent of total Iowa
                 deposits. For most of Iowa's history, branch banking
                 was not allowed, but more liberal rules were set up in
                 the 1970s and 1980s, permitting branching in home-
                 office cities and counties and in neighboring counties
                 under special conditions.

Kansas -   Interstate bank entry has not yet been approved as of
                 the date of publication of this book. Full-service
                 branching was outlawed in Kansas for many years, but
                 limited-service facilities (which recently have been
                 granted lending powers) have been allowed for about
                 four decades in localized areas. Statewide branching
                 by merger is now permitted. After being
                 prohibited for many years multi-bank holding companies
                 were permitted beginning in 1985, but any one holding
                 company cannot gain control of more than 9 percent of
                 statewide deposit holdings.

Minnesota -   The state's current interstate banking statute allows
                 entry with reciprocity from eleven other states in the
                 surrounding regions, including the states of Colorado,
                 Idaho, Illinois, Iowa, Kansas, Missouri, Montana,
                 North and South Dakota, Washington, and Wyoming.
                 Minnesota limits branch banking to home-office cities
                 and towns and to adjacent communities lying within a
                 25-mile radius of the home office. Holding-company
                 activities are not currently regulated.

Missouri -   Current interstate law allows entry from eight other
                 states in surrounding areas (including Arkansas,

Illinois, Iowa, Kansas, Kentucky, Nebraska, Oklahoma, and Tennessee) provided parallel opportunities are extended by these states to Missouri banks. Inside the state, branching is restricted by city and community boundaries unless special geographic circumstances apply. Holding-company activity is permitted if banks acquired by the same company do not hold more than 13 percent of statewide deposits.

Nebraska -

Branching has been either prohibited or severely restricted for most of Nebraska's history, though in the 1980s a failing bank could be turned into a branch. Later up to five branches were allowed in the home-office city. More recently Nebraska banks have been allowed to branch throughout the state via acquisition. Bank holding companies are limited to no more than 11 percent of statewide deposits. Nebraska is scheduled to allow nationwide bank entry with reciprocity in 1991, but currently permits entry (if its own banks are equally treated) from the states of Colorado, Iowa, Kansas, Minnesota, Missouri, Montana, North and South Dakota, Wisconsin, and Wyoming and also permits the entry of special-purpose banks.

North Dakota -

Bank holding companies face no significant limitation on their growth across the state. Branching has been prohibited for many years, though banks can operate limited-service facilities apart from the home office. Interstate entry was not authorized at the time this book was going to press, but a grandfathered banking company that had already purchased an ownership interest in North Dakota banks could sell its interest to other out-of-state firms.

South Dakota -

Branch banking is permitted across the state without significant restrictions. The same is true for bank holding-company activities. Out-of-state banking companies may enter from any other state nationwide provided reciprocal privileges are extended to South Dakota banks. Moreover, special-service banks can establish a single office to offer wholesale services (such as managing credit card accounts).

The East South Central Region

Alabama -

Bank holding companies do not face significant restrictions under state law and regulation. Beginning in the 1980s branch banking could expand statewide through bank mergers or to rescue banks about to fail. Alabama has a regional reciprocity interstate banking law allowing in banks from the surrounding region (including banks from Arkansas, Florida, Georgia, Kentucky, Louisiana, Maryland, Mississippi, North Carolina, South Carolina, Tennessee, Virginia, West Virginia, and Washington, D.C.).

Kentucky -

Beginning in July of 1986 Kentucky agreed to let in banking firms from any other state in the nation,

provided Kentucky banks were given reciprocal
privileges and subject to a limit of no more than 15
percent of the state's total deposits. Branching is
generally limited to home-office territories where
competing banks would not be damaged. Multi-bank
holding companies were given greater latitude
beginning in 1982, provided they do not exceed limits
on the percentage of statewide deposits controlled,
and new banks are protected from holding-company
takeover for at least five years.

Mississippi —   In July of 1988 Mississippi was opened to bank entry
(as long as reciprocal privileges were extended to
Mississippi's banks) by banking organizations from
Alabama, Arkansas, Louisiana, and Tennessee; however,
by July of 1990 the list of states allowed to enter
will be extended to include Florida, Georgia,
Kentucky, Missouri, North Carolina, South Carolina,
Tennessee, Texas, Virginia, and West Virginia. The
state does not permit holding-company activities.
Branch offices are allowed within a radius of 100
miles of each bank's home office and in adjacent
counties, provided no more than 15 branches are
opened. Statewide branching by merger was changed to
statewide branching via establishing new offices in
1989.

Tennessee —   This state has a long history of allowing banks to
branch throughout their home-office counties. In 1985
approval was granted to convert the banks affiliated
with a holding company into branch offices. Tennessee
allowed entry from a selected group of states
(including Alabama, Arkansas, Florida, Georgia,
Indiana, Kentucky, Louisiana, Mississippi, Missouri,
North Carolina, South Carolina, Virginia, and West
Virginia) beginning in July 1985 if reciprocity is
granted to Tennessee banks. However, out-of-state
acquirers were not given permission to charter new
banks and those banks operating for less than five
years were not eligible for out-of-state acquisition.

The West South Central Region

Arkansas -   A complicated branching statute is in force that
severely limits branch banking unless the state
banking commission approves. Commission approval may
be granted for branching, for example, in
unincorporated areas, if a bank is failing, or in
home-office counties where another bank is not already
headquartered. In 1999 Arkansas is scheduled to
convert to statewide branching. Bank holding
companies are limited in their bank acquisitions to no
more than 15 percent of Arkansas' total deposits.
Interstate banking is limited to the surrounding
region encompassing 16 states (including Alabama,
Florida, Georgia, Kansas, Louisiana, Maryland,
Mississippi, Missouri, Nebraska, North Carolina,
Oklahoma, South Carolina, Tennessee, Texas, Virginia,
and West Virginia) as well as Washington, D.C., with
reciprocity.

Louisiana –   Countywide (parish) branching has been the rule in
                  Louisiana with limited entry into other counties if
                  other state–chartered banks are not operating there.
                  While Louisiana was closed to multi–bank holding
                  companies for many years, they were allowed to expand
                  across county (parish) boundaries under certain
                  conditions beginning in the mid–1980s. Entry of
                  banking firms from any other state in the nation was
                  legalized beginning in January of 1989, provided
                  Louisiana banks were granted similar entry privileges.

Oklahoma –   In July 1987 Oklahoma first permitted out–of–state
                  banking companies to enter, provided Oklahoma banks
                  were extended similar entry privileges. If Oklahoma
                  banks are denied entry, then a banking company from
                  the state involved that acquires an Oklahoma bank must
                  wait four years before it can make additional
                  acquisitions in the state. Oklahoma through most of
                  its history prohibited full–service branching, but
                  over time these rules were liberalized to allow
                  branching near the home office. Today, statewide
                  branching by merger is permitted. In 1983 holding
                  companies were allowed to control up to 11 percent of
                  statewide insured deposits, and new banks were
                  shielded from acquisitions for five years unless the
                  bank to be acquired was about to fail.

Texas –   Beginning with an amendment to the state's
                  constitution in 1904 Texas prohibited full–service
                  branch offices, and limited–service facilities (such
                  as drive–ins) could only be placed near a bank's home
                  office. In 1986 limited branching was permitted
                  within the same community as the home office, and ATMs
                  were permitted over wider geographic areas. Multi–
                  bank holding companies were discouraged until the late
                  1960s and early 1970s when the first of these
                  organizations, launched by leading money–center banks,
                  were allowed to make bank acquisitions. Faced with
                  serious economic problems in the mid–1980s, Texas
                  passed an interstate banking law in the fall of 1986
                  that allowed banking company entry from anywhere in
                  the nation without a reciprocity requirement.

Bibliography

Adams, Jerry. "Making All Systems Go For 'Day One' of a Merger." *American Banker*, May 13, 1986: 28–29.

Alberts, William W. "Have Interstate Acquisitions Been Profitable?" *American Banker*, September 18, 1986: 2–3.

Alhadeff, David A. and Charlotte P. Alhadeff. "Growth and Survival Patterns of New Banks, 1948–70." *Journal of Money, Credit, and Banking* 8 (1976): 199–208.

Amel, Dean F., and Michael J. Jacowski. "Trends in Banking Structure Since the Mid-1970s." *Federal Reserve Bulletin*, March 1989: 120–33.

American Bankers Association. "Location Poses Dilemma in Southeast Mergers." *American Banker*, February 18, 1987: 3, 63.

Apcar, Leonard M. "No Hero's Welcome Awaited NCNB on Arrival in Texas." *The Wall Street Journal*, October 12, 1988, Southwest Edition.

Baer, Herbert, and Larry R. Mote. "The Effects of Nationwide Banking on Concentration: Evidence from Abroad." *Economic Perspectives* (Federal Reserve Bank of Chicago), January-February 1985: 3–17.

Baer, Herbert, and Christie A. Pavel. "Does Deregulation Drive Innovation?" *Economic Perspectives* (Federal Reserve Bank of Chicago), March-April 1988: 3–16.

Baer, Herbert, and Elizabeth Pongracic. 1984. "The Development of Banking Structure Histories in Five Countries." Typescript.

Bain, Joe. 1957. *Barriers to New Competition*. Cambridge, Mass.: Harvard University Press.

Baumol, William J., John C. Panzar, and Robert D. Willig. 1982. *Contestable Markets and the Theory of Industry Structure*. New York: Harcourt, Brace, Jovanovich, Inc.

Beatty, Randolph P., John F. Reim, and Robert F. Schapperle. "The Effects of Barriers to Entry on Shareholder Wealth: Implications for Interstate Banking." *Journal of Bank Research*, Spring 1985: 8–15.

Beidleman, Carl R. 1985. *Financial SWAPS: New Strategies in Currency and Coupon Risk Management*. Homewood, Ill.: Dow-Jones Irwin.

Bennett, Andrea. "Huntington Bancshares Looking to Buy More Banks in Midwest." *American Banker*, February 2, 1987: 251.

Benston, George J., Allen N. Berger, Gerald A. Hanweck, and David Humphrey. 1983. "Economies of Scale and Scope." In *Proceedings of a Conference on Bank Structure and Competition*. Chicago: Federal Reserve Bank of Chicago.

Benston, George J., Gerald A. Hanweck, and David B. Humphrey. "Scale Economies in Banking: A Restructuring and Reassessment." *Journal of Money, Credit, and Banking* 14 (1982): 435–56.

Birch, David L., and Susan J. McCracken. 1984. *The Role Played by High Technology in Job Creation*. Cambridge: Massachusetts Institute of Technology, Program on Neighborhood and Regional Change.

Boczar, Gregory E. "An Empirical Study of Multibank Holding Company Activity in Local Markets." *Atlantic Economic Journal* 3 (1975): 325–41.

──────. "Market Characteristics and Multibank Holding Company Acquisitions." *Journal of Finance* 23 (1977): 131–46.

Brickley, James A., and Leonard D. Van Drunen. 1988. "Why Firms Restructure: An Empirical Analysis." Rochester, N.Y.: Department of Finance, University of Rochester. Photocopy.

Brown, O. M. "Bank Holding Company Performance and the Public Interest: Normative Uses for Positive Analysis?" *Review* (Federal Reserve Bank of St. Louis), March 1986: 26–34.

Bryan, Lowell, and Paul Allen. "Geographic Strategies for the 1990s: Preparing for a Smart Endgame." In *The Bankers' Handbook* (Dow-Jones Irwin, 1988), Chapter 3.

Budzeika, George. 1986. "A Model of Financial Constraints in Interstate Bank Expansion." Research Paper No. 8802. New York: Federal Reserve Bank of New York.

Burck, Arthur. "Banking Will Be Dominated by a Handful of Giants." *Vital Speeches of the Day*, 1984: 656–60.

Calem, Paul. "Interstate Bank Mergers and Competition in Banking." *Business Review* (Federal Reserve Bank of Philadelphia), January-February 1987: 3–14.

Calem, Paul, and Janice Moulton. 1987. "Competitive Effects of Interstate Bank Mergers and Acquisitions." Working Paper No. 87-6. Philadelphia: Federal Reserve Bank of Philadelphia.

──────. "Competitive Issues in Bank Merger Analysis Under Interstate Banking." *Issues in Bank Regulation*, Winter 1988: 23–29.

Carlson, Eugene. "More Trials Expected for Great Lakes States." *The Wall Street Journal*, September 13, 1988, Southwest edition.

Cates, David C. "Banks Are Paying Too Much to Merge." *Fortune*, December 23, 1985: 151–54.

Cherin, Antony C., and Ronald W. Melichen. "Branch Banking and Loan Portfolio Risk Relationships." *Review of Business and Economic Research* 22 (1987): 1–13.

Christie, Rick, and John Helyan. "NCNB Wages Battle on Two Fronts." *The Wall Street Journal*, October 12, 1988, Southwest edition.

Clark, Jeffrey A. "Economies of Scale and Scope at Depository Financial Institutions: A Review of the Literature." *Economic Review* (Federal Reserve Bank of Kansas City), September-October 1988: 15-33.

Connor, Michael C. "The Redirection of Power in American Banking." *Mergers and Acquisitions*, Winter 1985: 48-53.

Coughlin, Cletus C., and Thomas B. Mandelbaum. "Why Have State Per Capita Incomes Diverged Recently?" *Review* (Federal Reserve Bank of St. Louis), September-October 1988: 24-36.

Cox, Raymond A.K., and Alan E. Grunewald. "Bank Acquisitions and Stockholder Wealth." *Review of Research in Banking and Finance*, Fall 1988: 1-16.

Curry, Timothy J., and John T. Rose. "Diversification and Barriers to Entry: Some Evidence from Banking." *Antitrust Bulletin* 24 (1984): 759-73.

Darnell, Jerome C. "Banking Structure and Economic Growth." In *Changing Pennsylvania's Branching Laws: An Economic Analysis*. Philadelphia: Federal Reserve Bank of Philadelphia, 1973.

Day, Kathleen. "Regulatory Cutbacks Proved To Be Costly at Banks, S&Ls." *The Washington Post*, October 2, 1988.

De, Sankar, and Marcia H. Millon. 1988. "An Examination of Stock Market Reactions to Interstate Bank Mergers." Dallas: Edwin L. Cox School of Business, Southern Methodist University. Photocopy.

Dennis, Debra K., and John J. McConnell. "Corporate Mergers and Security Returns." *Journal of Financial Economics* 16 (1986): 143-87.

Di Clemente, John J., and Diane Fortier Alemprese. "Justice's Merger Guidelines: Implications for the District Banking." *Economic Perspectives* (Federal Reserve Bank of Chicago), September-October 1983: 14-23.

Duncan, F. H. "Intermarket Bank Expansions: Implications for Interstate Banking." *Journal of Bank Research* 15 (1985): 16-21.

Dunham, Constance R. "Interstate Banking and the Outflow of Local Funds." *New England Economic Review* (Federal Reserve Bank of Boston), March-April 1986: 7-19.

Dunham, Constance R., and Richard F. Syron. "Interstate Banking: The Drive To Consolidate." *New England Economic Review* (Federal Reserve Bank of Boston), May-June 1984: 11-28.

Dunkelberg, William C., and Jonathan A. Scott. "Small Business Evaluates Its Banking Relationships." *Bankers Magazine*, November-December 1983: 40-46.

Easton, Nina. "Bankers in California and Nation Jockey for Position as State Prepares to Open Gates to Interstate Banking." *American Banker*, January 27, 1987: 14, 16.

Edwards, Franklin R. "The Banking Competition Controversy." *National Banking Review* 3 (1965): 1-34.

Eisemann, Peter. "Diversification and the Congeneric Bank Holding Company." *Journal of Bank Research* 7 (1976): 68-77.

Eisenbeis, Robert A., Robert S. Harris, and Josef Lakonishok. "Benefits of Bank Diversification: The Evidence from Shareholder Returns." *Journal of Finance* 39 (1984): 881-92.

Erdevig, Eleanor H. "New Directions for Economic Development—The Banking Industry." *Economic Perspectives* (Federal Reserve Bank of Chicago), September-October 1988: 17-24.

Evanoff, Douglas D., and Diana Fortier. 1986. "The Impact of Geographic Expansion in Banking: Some Axions to Grind." In *Toward Nationwide Banking*. Chicago: Federal Reserve Bank of Chicago.

Federal Reserve Bank of Dallas. "Bank Structure—Market for Bank Services Changes in Texas." *Review*, April 1971: 1–22.

Federal Reserve Bank of New York. 1987. *International Integration of Financial Markets and U.S. Monetary Policy*. New York: Federal Reserve Bank of New York. 57–59.

Forman, Craig. "Republic New York Restructures Units in Europe, Returning Safra to Spotlight." *The Wall Street Journal*, September 20, 1988, Southwest edition.

Fortier, Diana L. "Hostile Takeovers and the Market for Corporate Control." *Economic Perspectives* (Federal Reserve Bank of Chicago), January-February 1989: 2–16.

Frieder, Larry A. "Interstate Banking: Landscape, Policy, and Misconceptions." *Review of Research in Banking and Finance*, Fall 1987: 1–17.

Frodin, Joanna H. "Electronics: The Key to Breaking the Interstate Banking Barrier." *Business Review* (Federal Reserve Bank of Philadelphia), September-October 1982: 3–11.

Gilbert, R. Alton. "Bank Market Structure and Competition: A Survey." *Journal of Money, Credit, and Banking* 16 (1984): 617–45.

Goldberg, Lawrence G., and Gerald A. Hanweck. "What Can We Expect from Interstate Banking?" *Journal of Banking and Finance* 12 (1988): 51–67.

Guenther, Robert. "Chemical Bank's Texas Commerce Unit to Post an Unexpected Profit for 1988." *The Wall Street Journal*, January 4, 1989, Southwest edition.

Hamilton, Alexander. [December 13, 1790] 1984. "Report on a National Bank." Reprinted in *Papers on Public Credit, Commerce and Funding*, ed. Samuel McKee, Jr. New York: Columbia University Press.

Hannan, Greg. "Mutual Awareness Among Potential Entrants: An Empirical Investigation." *Southern Economic Journal* 47 (1981): 805–8.

———. "Prices, Capacity and the Entry Decision: A Conditional Logit Analysis." *Southern Economic Journal* 44 (1983): 539–50.

Hanweck, Gerald A. 1971. "Bank Entry into Local Markets: An Empirical Assessment of the Degree of Potential Competition via New Bank Formation." In *Proceedings of a Conference on Bank Structure and Competition*, 161–73. Chicago: Federal Reserve Bank of Chicago.

Hanweck, Gerald A., and Stephen A. Rhoades. "Dominant Firms and Local Market Competition in Banking." *Journal of Economics and Business* 36 (1984): 391–402.

Heggestad, Arnold A., and Stephen A. Rhoades. "Concentration and Firm Stability in Commercial Banking." *Review of Economics and Statistics* 58 (1976): 443–52.

Hess, Dan W. "How Bankers Can Develop the Small Business Market." *Journal of Commercial Bank Lending*, September 1985: 11–17.

Hill, G. Christian. "First Interstate Will Spin Off Troubled Assets." *The Wall Street Journal*, September 23, 1988, Southwest edition.

Horvitz, Paul M., and Bernard Shull. "The Impact of Branch Banking on Bank Performance." *National Banking Review* 2 (1964): 143–88.

Humphrey, David B. and Allen N. Berger. "The Check-Processing Market After Interstate Banking." *Bankers Magazine*, September-October 1988: 34–39.

Humphrey, O. B. 1985. "Costs and Scale Economies in Bank Intermediation." In *Handbook for Banking Strategy*, ed. Richard C. Aspinwall and Robert C. Eisenbeis, 617–45. New York: Wiley.

Hunter, William C., and Stephen G. Timme. "Technical Change, Organizational Form and the Structure of Bank Production." *Journal of Money, Credit, and Banking* 43 (1986): 152–66.

———. "Concentration and Innovation: Striking a Balance in Deregulation." *Economic Review* (Federal Reserve Bank of Atlanta), January-February 1987: 11–20.

———. 1988. "Technological Change in Large U.S. Commercial Banks." Working Paper No. 88-6. Atlanta: Federal Reserve Bank of Atlanta.

James, Christopher, and Peggy Wier. "An Analysis of FDIC Failed Bank Auctions." *Journal of Monetary Economics* 20 (1987): 141–253.

Jones, Steven. "Asia's Success-Story: Nation's Learning How to Consume," *The Wall Street Journal*, November 1, 1988, A26. Southwest edition.

Kaufman, George, Larry R. Mote, and Harvey Rosenblum. "Implications of Deregulation for Product Lines and Geographic Markets of Financial Institutions." *Journal of Bank Research* 14 (1983): 8–21.

King, B. Frank, Sheila L. Tschinkel, and David D. Whitehead. "Interstate Banking Developments in the 1980s." *Economic Review* (Federal Reserve Bank of Atlanta), May-June 1989: 32–51.

Korobow, Leon, and George Budzeika. "Financial Limits on Interstate Bank Expansion." *Quarterly Review* (Federal Reserve Bank of New York), Summer 1985: 13–27.

Kutschen, Ronald E. "Projection 2000: Overview and Implications of the Projection to 2000." *Monthly Labor Review*, September 1987: 3–9.

Labrecque, Thomas G. "Who Cares About Interstate Banking? You Should!" *Vital Speeches of the Day*, 1984: 670–72.

Levy, Haim, and Marshall Sarnat. "Diversification, Portfolio Analysis and the Uneasy Case for Conglomerate Mergers." *Journal of Finance* 28 (1970): 795–802.

Lewellen, W. "A Pure Financial Rationale for the Conglomerate Merger." *Journal of Finance* 26 (1971): 521–37.

Liang, Nellie, and Stephen A. Rhoades. "Geographic Diversification and Risk in Banking." *Journal of Economic and Business* 40 (1988): 271–84.

Lister, Roger C. "The Expansion of Banking in the Metropolitan Areas of the Southwest." *Voice* (Federal Reserve Bank of Dallas), June 1979: 1–9.

Lowenstein, Roger. "Chase Plans Partial Pull-Out from New York." *The Wall Street Journal*, September 14, 1988, Southwest edition.

McCall, Alan S., and John T. Lane. "Multi-Office Banking and the Safety and Soundness of Commercial Banks." *Journal of Bank Research* 11 (1980): 87–94.

Mason, Edward A., and P. Goudzaard. "Performance of Conglomerate Firms: A Portfolio Approach." *Journal of Finance* 31 (1976): 39–48.

Matthews, Gordon. "Fleet-Norstar Pact May Spur Regional Mergers." *American Banker*, April 20, 1987a: 14.

_____. "Lower Prices for Midwest Banks Prompt Flurry of Acquisitions." *American Banker*, July 16, 1987b: 1, 11.

_____. "Interstate Mergers Dwindle as Superregionals Become Selective." *American Banker*, July 12, 1988: 4.

Mester, Loretta J. "Efficient Production of Financial Services: Scale and Scope Economies." *Business Review* (Federal Reserve Bank of Philadelphia), January-February 1987a: 15-25.

_____. "Multiple Market Contact Between Savings and Loans." *Journal of Money, Credit, and Banking* 19 (1987b): 538-49.

Miller, Stephen M. "Counterfactual Experiments of Deregulation on Banking Structure." *Quarterly Review of Economics and Business* 28 (Winter 1988): 38-49.

Morrissey, William J. "The Case for Merging." *Journal of Commercial Bank Lending*, March 1986: 15-21.

Moynihan, Jon. "The Strategy Factor: How Some Banks Have Made Their Acquisitions Pay Off." *American Banker*, May 29, 1984: 4, 6, 8, 21-23.

Petersen, William M. "Competitive Strategies at Regional Banks." *Bankers Magazine*, November-December 1987: 36-39.

Pettway, Richard, and J. W. Trifts. "Do Banks Overbid When Acquiring Failed Banks?" *Financial Management*, Summer 1985: 5-15.

Phillis, Dave and Christine Pavel. "Interstate Banking Game Plans: Implications for the Midwest." *Economic Perspectives* (Federal Reserve Bank of Chicago), (March-April 1986): 23-39.

Rhoades, Stephen A. "A Reevaluation of the Effect of Diversification on Industry Profit Performance." *Review of Economics and Statistics* 55 (1974): 557-59.

_____. "Characteristics of Banking Markets Entered by Foothold Acquisition." *Journal of Monetary Economics* 2 (1976): 399-408.

_____. "Aggregate Concentration: An Emerging Issue in Bank Merger Policy." *Antitrust Bulletin*, Spring 1979: 1-16.

_____. 1982. *Structure-Performance Studies in Banking: An Updated Summary and Evaluation*. Staff Economic Study No. 119. Washington, D.C.: Board of Governors of the Federal Reserve System.

_____. "National and Local Market Banking Concentration in an Era of Interstate Banking." *Issues in Bank Regulation*, Spring 1985: 29-36.

Rhoades, Stephen A., and Arnold A. Heggestad. "Multimarket Interdependence and Performance in Banking: Two Tests." *Antitrust Bulletin*, Winter 1985: 975-95.

Rhoades, Stephen A., and Roger D. Rutz. "The Impact of Bank Holding Companies on Local Market Rivalry and Performance." *Journal of Economics and Business* 34 (1982): 335-65.

Ricks, Thomas E. "Branching Out—Attentive to Service, Barnett Banks Grows Fast, Keeps Profit Up." *The Wall Street Journal*, April 3, 1987, Southwest edition.

Rogowski, Robert J., and Donald G. Simonson. 1987. "Bank Merger Pricing Premiums and Interstate Bidding." Paper presented at the annual meeting of the Financial Management Association, Las Vegas.

Rose, John T. "The Attractiveness of Banking Markets for *De Novo* Entry: The Evidence from Texas." *Journal of Bank Research* 7 (1977): 284-93.

_____. "Buying a County Bank: *De Novo* Entry and Market Attractiveness." *Banking Law Journal* 96 (1979): 242–43.

_____. "Interstate Banking, Potential Competition, and the Attractiveness of Banking Markets for New Entry." *Antitrust Bulletin* 30 (1985): 729–43.

_____. "Interstate Banking and Small Business Finance: Implications from Available Evidence." *American Journal of Small Business*, Fall 1986: 23–39.

_____. "New Independent Bank Entry in an Era of Financial Deregulation: Motivations, Available Evidence, and Outlook." *Review of Research in Banking and Finance*, Fall 1988: 45–59.

Rose, Peter S. "The Pattern of Bank Holding Company Acquisitions." *Journal of Bank Research*, Autumn 1976: 236–40.

_____. "Entry into U.S. Banking Markets: Dimensions and Implications of the Charter Process." *Antitrust Bulletin* 25 (1980): 195–215.

_____. "Improving Regulatory Policy for Mergers: An Assessment of Bank Merger Motivations and Performance Effects." *Issues in Bank Regulation*, Winter 1987: 32–39.

_____. 1988a. "The Firms Acquired by Interstate Banks: Testable Hypotheses and Consistent Evidence." College Station: Finance Department, Texas A&M University. Photocopy.

_____. 1988b. "The Banking Firms Making Interstate Acquisitions: Theory and Observable Motives." College Station: Finance Department, Texas A&M University. Photocopy.

_____. 1988c. "Bidding Theory and Bank Merger Premiums: The Impact of Structural and Regulatory Factors." Paper presented to the Industrial Organization Society, San Antonio.

Rose, Peter S., and William L. Scott. "The Performance of Banks Acquired by Holding Companies." *Review of Business and Economic Research*, 14, no. 3 (1979): 18–37.

_____. "Heterogeneity in Performance Within the Bank Holding Company Sector: Evidence and Implications." *Journal of Economics and Business* 36 (1984): 1–14.

Savage, Donald T. "Interstate Banking Developments," *Federal Reserve Bulletin*, February 1987: 79–92.

Savage, Donald T., and Stephen A. Rhoades. 1979. "The Effect of Branch Banking on Pricing, Profits, and Efficiency of Unit Banks." In *Proceedings of a Conference on Bank Structure and Competition*, 187–96. Chicago: Federal Reserve Bank of Chicago.

Schlesinger, Jacob M. "First of America to Buy Midwest Financial Group." *The Wall Street Journal*, Southwest edition, January 24, 1989.

Shaffer, Sherrill, and David Edmond. 1986. "Economies of Superscale and Interstate Expansion." Research Paper No. 8612. New York: Federal Reserve Bank of New York.

Shull, Bernand. 1972. "Multiple-Office Banking and the Structure of Banking Markets: The New York and Virginia Experience." In *Proceedings of a Conference on Bank Structure and Competition*, 30–43. Chicago: Federal Reserve Bank of Chicago.

Smye, Marti D., and Anthony Grant. "The Personnel Challenges of Mergers and Acquisitions." *Canadian Banker* 96 (January-February 1989): 44–49.

Solomon, Elinor H. "Banking Merger Policy and Problems: A Linkage Theory of Oligopoly." *Journal of Money, Credit, and Banking* 2 (1970): 323–36.

Stover, Roger D. "A Reexamination of Bank Holding Company Acquisitions." *Journal of Bank Research* 13 (1982): 101–8.

Sullivan, Michael P. "Understanding of Cultures Is Critical in Managing Acquisitions." *American Banker*, November 26, 1986: 4, 7, 10.

Swartz, Steve, and Beatrice E. Garcia. "Urge To Merge Raises Some Eyebrows." *The Wall Street Journal*, August 31, 1988, Southwest Edition.

Syron, Richard F. "The 'New England Experiment' in Interstate Banking." *New England Economic Review* (Federal Reserve Bank of Boston), March-April 1984: 5–17.

Talley, Samuel H. 1974. "The Impact of Holding-Company Acquisitions on Aggregate Concentration in Banking." Staff Study No. 80. Washington, D.C.: Board of Governors of the Federal Reserve System.

Taylor, Robert E. "Powers of Banks Expand Little in Latest Bill." *The Wall Street Journal*, September 23, 1988, Southwest edition.

Trescott, Paul B. 1963. *Financing American Enterprise: The Story of Commercial Banking*. New York: Harper & Row Publishers.

Trewatha, Robert L., Ronald Hampton, Bobby C. Vaught, and Stephen Parker. "A Multiple Branch Location Model: A Method to Analyze Site Selection Factors." *Akron Business and Economic Review* 19 (Fall 1988): 66–75.

Trifts, Jack W., and Kevin P. Scanlon. "Interstate Bank Mergers: The Early Evidence." *Journal of Financial Research* 10 (Winter 1987): 305–11.

U.S. Congress. Senate. Committee on Banking, Housing and Urban Affairs. Subcommittee on Financial Institutions. *Compendium of Issues Relating to Branching by Financial Institutions.* 94th Cong., 2d sess., 1976.

Weintraub, Robert and Paul F. Jessup. 1964. *A Study of Selected Banking Services by Bank Size, Structure, and Location*. Report prepared for the House Committee on Banking and Currency. Committee Print. Washington, D.C.: Government Printing Office.

Welles, Chris. 1975. *The Last Days of the Club*. New York: E.P. Dutton & Co., Inc.

Whitehead, David, and J. Luytjees. "Can Interstate Banking Increase Competitive Market Performance? An Empirical Test." *Economic Review* (Federal Reserve Bank of Atlanta), January 1984: 4–10.

Woodard, George J. "Analyzing Multi-Bank Holding Company Acquisitions Through Economic Research." *Magazine of Bank Administration* 52 (1976): 46–49.

Woodard, George J., and James E. Goldsberry. "Economic Research as an Aid to Regional Bank Holding Company Expansion." *Journal of Bank Research* 14 (1984): 302–4.

Wriston, Walter B. 1981. *You Can't Tell the Players with a Scorecard*. New York: Citicorp, Inc.

Index

Age of residents, as factor in selecting new markets to enter, 121, 124

Antitrust enforcement, changes during Reagan administration, 42

Arizona: factors stimulating interstate legislation, 73–74; interstate banking legislation, 72–73

Automated systems, 150

Bank failures: acquired by interstate banks, 182, 187; causes, 1–2, 4; effects of interstate banking on, 162; recent statistics, 1

Bank holding companies: advantages of, 51; history of, 6–7, 50–51; laws regulating, 6–8, 53–55; nonbank businesses, 11–13; regulation of nonbank business activities, 55

Bank Holding Company Act: the Douglas Amendment, 53–55; 1956 provisions of, 53; provisions of nonbank business acquisitions, 54–55; response of the states, 53–54

Banking Act of 1933. *See* Glass-Steagall Act, provisions of

Bank Merger Act of 1960, provisions dealing with competition, 102

Bank profitability and risk, as factors in motivating interstate banking activity, 128–30; methods for improving, 151–52, 175

Barnett Banks, managerial strategies, 35, 44 n.5

Basel Group: agreement regarding bank capital requirements, 148, 189; bankers' opinions regarding, 168–69; nations included, 148

Branch banking, opposition to, 51–53

Branch banking laws, in American history, 48–50

Branch offices: and prospective costs, 156; changing roles of, 151–52

California, interstate legislation, 74–75, 146

Canada: concentration of banking resources, 105; regulations applying to foreign banks, 41

Chemical Bank of New York, strategy for acquisition of Texas Commerce Bancshares, 142

Citicorp, penetration of California markets, 117, 146

Colorado, interstate legislation, 69, 72–73

Commercial paper market, competition with bank lending programs, 35–36

Community Reinvestment Act, 182

Competitive Equality in Banking Act, imposed moratorium on new bank services, 38

Comptroller of the Currency: assessing competition in mergers, 185; effect of interstate banking on future role, 109; and history of branch banking regulation, 48–50

Consolidation, nature of, in the U.S., 186

Continental Illinois Bank, interstate acquisition denied on affirmative action grounds, 182

Core deposits, importance in choosing new markets to enter, 165–66, 169, 175

Delaware, economic development legislation, 60–61, 64

Department of Justice, and assessing competition in mergers, 185

Depository Institutions Deregulation and Monetary Control Act: provisions of, 3; role in lifting deposit interest-rate ceilings, 39–40

Depository Institutions Deregulation Committee (DIDC): composition of, 40; role of, 48

Deregulation: causes of, 2; definition of, 2; effects of lifting deposit-rate ceilings, 39–40; potential losses from, 2; problems caused for interstate expansion, 145–46; of product lines, 3

Dilution of earnings, problems raised by mergers, 137–38, 142–43

Diversification: effects of, 172–73, 182–83; geographic, 3–4, 12; product-line, 4, 12–13

Earnings per share: formula for, 136; role in evaluating merger targets, 136–38

Economic cycles, as a factor in choosing states to enter, 127–28

Economic growth, and interstate banking, 177, 181

Economies of scale: consequences for industry structure, 42; nature of, 44; research evidence on, 83–84, 96

Economies of scope, nature of, 41–42

Edge Act and Agreement Corporations, 31, 44 n.2

Efficient markets theory: nature of, 42–43; role in antitrust policy, 42–43

Energy loans: cause of interstate legislation in the Southwest, 66, 68; causes of deterioration, 4, 28; effects on banks in Texas and Oklahoma, 28, 30

Eurodollar market, competitive challenge for U.S. banks, 36

Examination and supervision, effects of interstate banking on, 109–12

Excess profits: definition of, 78; entry barriers, 78–79; research evidence concerning, 79–81

Expedited Funds Availability Act (1987), provisions of, 107

Federal Deposit Insurance Corporation, and assessing competition in mergers, 185

Federal deposit rate ceilings: explicit and implicit returns, 44; impact on growth of bank offices, 44–45 n.6

Federal Reserve Board: control over holding companies, 4; role in expanding bank security underwriting powers, 38–39

Federal Reserve System: and assessing competition in mergers, 185; impact of industry concentration on role and services, 107

Financial Center Development Act, 60

Financial synergy, 33

First and Second Banks of the United States, 48

First Interstate Bancorp, Los Angeles, merger with Allied Bancshares of Houston, 17–18

France: concentration of banking resources, 105; regulations on outside bank entry, 41

Franchise banking: nature of, 36–37; networks, 37; requirements for participating banks, 37; services offered, 37

Garn-St Germain Depository Institutions Act, provisions of, 3, 44 n.1
Geographic diversification: as a factor in selecting acquisition targets, 118–19; nature of, 82; research evidence for, 82–83
Geographic intermediation: benefits for the public, 183; impact of interstate banking on, 94; nature of, 94; possible costs, 183–84
Glass-Steagall Act, provisions of, 5, 52–53
Gross State Product (GSP): as a factor in targeting state for entry, 127; nature of, 126

Herfindahl-Hirschmann Index: definition of, 103–4; role in regulatory evaluation of bank mergers, 104

Insurance services, authorized in selected states, 39
International Lending and Supervision Act (1983), provisions of, 147–48
Interstate banking laws, types of laws, 7, 9–10
Interstate expansion strategies: expand retail markets, 85–97; innovation to reduce production costs, 86; search for deposits, 86, 88, 97
Investment banking, and the Glass-Steagall Act, 53

Japanese banking, regulations on entry from outside, 41

Loan production offices (LPOs), 31, 44 n.4
Local control, and interstate banking, 182

Louisiana, reciprocal interstate banking law, 67–69

McFadden-Pepper Act: provisions of, 5, 52; response of the states, 53
Maine, interstate legislation, 55–56, 58
Management training programs, 34
Market concentration: effect on competition, 185; effect on cost and efficiency of the payments system, 106–7; effects on structure of the Federal Reserve System, 107; and the growth of interstate banking, 184–85; in local and national markets, 94–95, 105–6; in most damaged market, 103
Massachusetts, interstate legislation, 56, 58
Merger hotlines: contributions of, 152–53; nature of, 152
Merger premiums: danger of excess, 134–35, 143; definition of, 133; effect of interstate banking on, 134; sizes of, 134
"Middle Market": importance in U.S. banking, 36; nature of, 36; possible impact of interstate banking on, 102, 141–42
Most damaged market, changes needed in definition of, 185–86

National Bank Act of 1863: limitations on bank lending, 49, 76 n.1; provisions on bank branching, 49
National banking system, origins, 49
NCNB Corp.: First RepublicBank acquisition, 17, 21; initial community acceptance problem in Texas, 155; premium paid for First Republic, 138
New England, summary of interstate laws, 55–59
New York, interstate legislation, 56, 65
Nonbank banks, nature of, 13
Nonbank businesses: affiliated with holding companies, 54–55; regulation of acquisitions of, 55; risks to banking firms, 55; types of, 54
Nonreciprocity statute, 30

Northeast Bancorp case, 57, 59
NOW accounts, development in the
New England states, 32

Oklahoma, nonreciprocity interstate
law, 67–68
One-bank holding companies, causes of
growth, 54–55
Operating synergy, 33

Performance: of acquired banks, 86–87;
of acquiring banks, 85–86
Personal income, as a factor in entering
new states, 120, 126
Population density, as a factor in
market entry decisions, 121
Population size, as a factor in interstate
acquisitions, 113–14, 121, 124
Primary capital, current regulatory
requirements, 148; definition of, 148
Problem areas for interstate banks:
dealing with unexpected and
prospective costs, 149–52; finding
adequate capital, 147–49; overcoming
managerial conflicts between
acquiring and acquired banks, 156–
58; preparing for legislative changes,
146–47; winning acceptance by new
communities entered, 152–56
Production economies, and bank size,
41–42
Prospective costs, improved evaluation
needed, 189; nature of, 149

Quiet life hypothesis; nature of, 83;
research evidence of, 83

Regional acquisition strategies, nature
of, 130–31
Retail banking: interstate acquisition
strategies, 141–43; nature of, 36
Rocky Mountain region: economic
problems, 146; problems in attracting
interstate banks, 146–47
Rural banks, as targets for interstate
acquisition, 118

Savings and loan associations, failures,
2
Service availability, and interstate
banking, 162–63, 174, 177
Service pricing, and interstate banking,
164, 173–75
Service quality, and interstate banking,
163–64
Signaling effect, nature of, 82
Smaller banks, impact of interstate
banking on, 92–93
South Dakota: center of credit-card
services, 59, 64; role in new bank
service powers, 38, 59–60
Spread compression, 36
State regulation, effect of interstate
banking on, 108
Statewide branching, state laws
permitting, 5–6
Stock market crash, and bank capital
requirements, 148
Structure of a banking market: impact
on choice of target markets to enter,
114–15; nature of, 114; static versus
dynamic, 114
Supervision and examination, need for
staffing with deregulation, 192
Switzerland, regulation of foreign
banks, 41
Synergistic effects: benefits from, 134;
nature of, 134

Technological change, impact on branch
banking, 50
Texas: economic problems, 66, 68;
unique interstate law, 67–68
Thrift institutions: acquisitions of, 13–
14; types of, 13

United Kingdom: concentration of
banking resources, 105; regulation of
foreign banks, 41

Wholesale banking, importance for
interstate acquisition strategies,
143

About the Author

PETER S. ROSE holds the Jeanne and John Blocker Chair of Business Administration in the Department of Finance at Texas A&M University.